Editor's Preface

Christopher Stephen Lutz

Alasdair MacIntyre has spent his career seeking and demanding rational justification for social and philosophical theories. Unlike some of his contemporaries who were content to be initiated into one tradition or another and to work within the canons of their own traditions, MacIntyre has continually pursued questions that have shown him the limits of traditions. In the early 1950s he began his career in Great Britain as a Marxist and as a fideist Barthian philosopher of religion. In the 1960s he passed through a period of atheism and participated in the New Left. Coming to the United States in 1970, he spent a decade reassessing his approach to philosophy before adopting a revolutionary form of Aristotelianism which would inform his landmark book *After Virtue* (1981) and all the work that has followed it. MacIntyre's Aristotelianism became Thomistic in the mid 1980s.

MacIntyre came to Aristotle and Thomas Aquinas as theorists who offered justifiable solutions to real questions he was asking about human agency and rational justification. MacIntyre did not approach Aristotle or Thomas Aquinas because they were presented to him as the right answers by his tradition; he accepted Aristotle's and Thomas Aquinas's theories of human action because he found that their accounts of the human person enabled him to recast the narrative of modern philosophical history in a way that made sense of its failures and that opened a way to philosophical progress.

MacIntyre's work draws upon and contributes to a variety of fields within and beyond the conventional borders of philosophy, thus it is helpful to approach it with the assistance of specialists who represent a broad spectrum of those specializations. This special issue of the *American Catholic Philosophical Quarterly* presents a variety of perspectives on MacIntyre's work, its sources, and its application to contemporary issues.

Six essays serve to interpret MacIntyre's philosophical perspective. My own contribution, "Tradition as a Fragile Practice" and Stanley Hauerwas's "How I Think I Learned to Think Theologically" consider some the problems of rational justification at the heart of MacIntyre's theories of tradition and rationality.

©2014, *American Catholic Philosophical Quarterly*, Vol. 88, No. 4   pp. 615–617
doi: 10.5840/acpq201492232

Christophe Rouard provides an outstanding treatment of MacIntyre's Thomism. John Caiazza examines MacIntyre's debts to Thomas Kuhn's philosophy of science and compares those debts to the influence of Imre Lakatos; Caiazza's article should be an important source for any new work on MacIntyre's use of the philosophy of science. Paul Blackledge illuminates MacIntyre's Marxist past as well as the continuing influence of Marx in MacIntyre's ethics and politics. Kelvin Knight investigates modern notions of history and progress, particularly those of Collingwood's *Autobiography*, that have shaped MacIntyre's approaches to historicism and to truth.

Three essays apply MacIntyre's ethics and politics to contemporary issues. Bryan Cross examines university education from a MacIntyrean perspective. Sante Meletta takes a MacIntyrean approach to issues of religion in public life. Geoff Moore, Ron Beadle, and Anna Rowlands team up to apply Moore and Beadle's work on the ethics of organizations to Rowlands's work on Catholic Social Teaching.

Alasdair MacIntyre provides a suitable conclusion to the issue with "Ends and Endings," a revised version of a lecture originally delivered in the School of Philosophy of the Catholic University of America in honor of Msgr. Robert Sokolowski on September 25, 2009. MacIntyre's lecture takes as its starting point Msgr. Sokolowski's article, "What is Natural Law? Human Purposes and Natural Ends."[1] MacIntyre develops Sokolowski's distinction between natural ends and chosen purposes, contrasting Sokolowski's account with that of Harry Frankfurt, who draws no distinction between ends and purposes. The critique of Frankfurt that follows highlights the importance of natural ends to the intelligibility of human action, of human development, and of human success and failure. MacIntyre then draws on the work of Francis Slade to argue that it is impossible to tell a story without presupposing the reality of ends prior to any character's choice of purposes. To demonstrate the truth of this relationship, MacIntyre's essay ends with endings; it ends by considering Irish author Máirtín Ó'Cadhain's novel *Cré na Cille*, a pointless tale in which dead souls interact in a cemetery. Those characters are trapped forever in the habits of judgment they formed in life; they have no ends, thus their actions lead nowhere. Their story is nonetheless intelligible, not in terms of the ends and purposes of its characters, but as the work of its author, whose ends as an author give intelligibility to the story as a work that pursues its author's purpose.

"Ends and Endings" leaves little doubt about MacIntyre's convictions concerning the pursuit of truth, even if his historicist account of rationality tends to highlight the difficulties of reaching the truth. The essay confirms a remark in

---

[1]Msgr. Robert Sokolowski, "What is Natural Law? Human Purposes and Natural Ends," *The Thomist* 68, no. 4 (October 2004): 507–29, at 511.

American Catholic Philosophical Quarterly

(Formerly *The New Scholasticism*)

Volume 88   Issue No. 4   Fall 2014

Table of Contents

Articles

Kelvin Knight's essay, "What MacIntyre has . . . added to Peirce is that enquiries as to the truth of an object are plural and rival, so that even science may advance through revolutions. What he adds to Collingwood is that truth is singular." The video of the original lecture has been available online for some time, but this is its first appearance in print; we are indebted to Alasdair MacIntyre for contributing it to this special issue of the *ACPQ*.

I wish to thank all those who made this special MacIntyre issue of the *American Catholic Philosophical Quarterly* possible, particularly the contributors for their excellent work and editorial staff of the *American Catholic Philosophical Quarterly* who have guided us through the editorial process with professionalism and grace. Here as elsewhere, we owe a great debt of gratitude to Alasdair MacIntyre for struggling with the big questions and doing the hard work that has yielded a body of literature that rewards those who study it.

Tradition as a Fragile Practice: Some Implications of Alasdair MacIntyre's Theory of Rationality for the Study of Philosophy

Christopher Stephen Lutz

Abstract. This paper has four parts. The first part gives an overview of Alasdair MacIntyre's theory of rationality; the remaining three parts examine the theory's implications through the consideration of three examples. Two examples, the reception of MacIntyre's mature work and the study of Thomas Aquinas's Five Ways, illustrate the implications of MacIntyre's theory for reading and interpreting contemporary literature and historical texts. A third example, the investigation of late medieval nominalism, shows how the more straightforward problems of reading and interpreting can be exacerbated during periods of transition within traditions. Traditions, it turns out, can be fragile, yet once broken they are capable of concealing their incoherence and inconsistency from their current and future scholars. If MacIntyre's theory that rationality is both tradition-constituted and tradition-constitutive is truthful, it follows that the work of contemporary reading, traditional interpretation, and historical scholarship always requires careful attention to differences in rationalities, lest readers misinterpret by filling gaps in their readings with their own presuppositions.

I.

Introduction. The year 1988 marked two important achievements for Alasdair MacIntyre: the publication of *Whose Justice? Which Rationality?*[1] and the presentation of *Three Rival Versions of Moral Enquiry* as the Gifford Lectures at the University of Edinburgh.[2] These twin works present a theory of rationality that affirms Thomas Aquinas's metaphysical account of truth as the goal of human enquiry even as it acknowledges the insights of historicism

---

[1]Alasdair MacIntyre, *Whose Justice? Which Rationality?* (Notre Dame, IN: University of Notre Dame Press, 1988).

[2]See Alasdair MacIntyre, *Three Rival Versions of Moral Enquiry: Encyclopaedia, Genealogy, and Tradition* (Notre Dame, IN: University of Notre Dame Press, 1990).

©2014, *American Catholic Philosophical Quarterly*, Vol. 88, No. 4   pp. 619–640
doi: 10.5840/acpq201492234

concerning the difficulties of human enquiry.[3] This essay focuses on the latter issue. In the first article of the *Summa Theologiae*, Thomas Aquinas points out the human need for divine revelation, explaining that without it, "the truth about God, such as reason could discover, would only be known by a few, and that after a long time, and with the admixture of many errors."[4] MacIntyre's theory of rationality reminds us that human reason faces similar difficulties in many areas of study besides theology. This essay begins with an overview of MacIntyre's theory of rationality, and then explores three examples that illustrate the implications of MacIntyre's theory at three different levels: First, differences in rationalities can burden our readings of contemporary authors. Second, differences in rationalities present a constant challenge in the reading of historical texts. Third, recognizing differences in the rationalities of historical authors, their historical interpreters, and their historical critics introduces a humbling complexity to the study of the history of philosophy.

II.

MacIntyre's Theory of Rationality. First, what does it mean to make progress in philosophy? MacIntyre offered an answer to this question in his 1977 essay, "Epistemological Crises, Dramatic Narrative, and the Philosophy of Science."[5] In that essay, MacIntyre began by considering the kind of events from which serious philosophical questions arise. Changes in the ways that we view our world come about in response to "epistemological crises;" such changes attempt to resolve periods of doubt and confusion when teachings and theories that make up the narratives we trust to interpret our world are undermined by their failure to make sense of some new experience. To make philosophical progress is to resolve an epistemological crisis.

Epistemological crises cannot be conjured up. Descartes's decision to employ radical doubt as a philosophical method makes more sense as a rhetorical ploy in an argument against skepticism[6] than it does as a fruitful approach to discovering anything.[7] MacIntyre calls the project of radical doubt "an invitation not to philosophy, but to mental breakdown, or rather to philosophy as a means of

---

[3]MacIntyre refers to *After Virtue* as "an historicist defense of Aristotle" in Alasdair MacIntyre, "Postscript to the Second Edition," in *After Virtue*, 3rd ed. (Notre Dame, IN: University of Notre Dame Press, 2007), 277.

[4]Aquinas, *ST* I, q. 1, a. 1.

[5]Alasdair MacIntyre, "Epistemological Crises, Dramatic Narrative and the Philosophy of Science," *The Monist* 60, no. 4 (October 1977): 453–72; reprinted in *The Tasks of Philosophy* (Cambridge, UK: Cambridge University Press, 2006), 3–23.

[6]Alasdair MacIntyre, *God, Philosophy, Universities: A Selective History of the Catholic Philosophical Tradition* (Lanham, MD: Rowman and Littlefield, 2009), 114.

[7]MacIntyre, "Epistemological Crises," 8–9.

mental breakdown,"[8] and he offers Hume's description of his own radical doubt as an example of the approach to mental breakdown.[9] Real epistemological crises arise through the experience of specific inadequacies in our tradition-informed understanding of the world.[10]

Epistemological crises are not resolved simply by replacing a false theory with a true one. An epistemological crisis involves a loss rational self-confidence; thus, the resolution of an epistemological crisis demands that the enquirer recover self-confidence by coming to understand the origins of her or his mistakes. MacIntyre writes:

> When an epistemological crisis is resolved, it is by the construction of a new narrative which enables the agent to understand *both* how he or she could intelligibly have held his or her original beliefs *and* how he or she could have been so drastically misled by them.[11]

To make rational progress we need to understand one thing about the world and three things about ourselves. First, we need better theories to explain the phenomena that caused our crises in the first place; but in addition, we need to regain confidence in our ability to interpret the world, and this requires that we understand (1) where we stood prior to our epistemological crises, (2) why our positions made sense to us then, and (3) how those positions prevented us from seeing and understanding the issues that led us into our crises.

What is it, then, that makes one theory better than another? In this same essay, MacIntyre compares the approaches to the philosophy of science taken by Thomas Kuhn and Imre Lakatos. Kuhn, in *The Structure of Scientific Revolutions*, had concluded that large bodies of scientific theory called "paradigms" are incommensurable, and that the choice to move from one paradigm to another is not so much a rational judgment as it is a kind of conversion,[12] so that those who are not moved to convert cannot be faulted rationally by those who are.

Lakatos, in *The Methodology of Scientific Research Programmes*, took a different position; he concluded that large bodies of theory called "scientific research programmes"[13] differ by their core theories, and that they can demonstrate their own superiority to their rivals by their predictive power—by their ability to turn anomalous data into clues leading to dramatic and unexpected discoveries. The

---

[8]Ibid., 12.

[9]Ibid., 13–4.

[10]Ibid., 10–2.

[11]Ibid., 5.

[12]Thomas Kuhn, *The Structure of Scientific Revolutions*, 2nd ed. (Chicago: University of Chicago Press, 1970), 150–8.

[13]Imre Lakatos, *The Methodology of Scientific Research Programmes*, Philosophical Papers, vol. 1, ed. John Worral and Gregory Curie (Cambridge, UK: Cambridge University Press, 1978).

classic example the predictive power of a theory is the discovery of Neptune, which was found after its size had been determined and its position plotted as an explanation of the irregular movement of Uranus; this discovery proved the Newtonian theory of gravitation.

MacIntyre's position draws from both Kuhn and Lakatos. MacIntyre views traditions in some ways as analogous to Kuhn's paradigms: a tradition may appear to be rationally adequate to its own adherents even though rivals claim to have strong evidence that that tradition's narratives are false. Nevertheless, MacIntyre concludes, along the lines of Lakatos, that careful engagement with anomalous data can break down one's convictions and lead the enquirer, through rational progress, to better theories.

The theory of rationality set down in "Epistemological Crises" bears certain similarities to the treatment of ideology that MacIntyre had presented in the first chapter of *Against the Self-Images of the Age* (1971). There MacIntyre had argued that ideological commitment and philosophical inquiry tended to oppose each other, so that philosophical inquiry could serve as "a solvent of ideological conviction," while "the dominance of a particular ideology may limit or inhibit philosophical inquiry."[14] In "Epistemological Crises," however, MacIntyre's examination of the problems of Kuhn's paradigms and Lakatos's research programmes led him to take a closer look at the roles that philosophical traditions play in determining the ways that we judge truth and falsity, reasonableness and unreasonableness. Reflecting on "Epistemological Crises" in the preface to *The Tasks of Philosophy*, MacIntyre explains:

> What I learned from Kuhn, or rather from Kuhn and Lakatos read together, was the need first to identify and then to break free from ["the larger conceptual framework within which and by reference to which I and others formulated" "a number of issues . . . as separate and distinct"] and to enquire whether the various problems on which I had made so little progress had baffled me not or not only because of their difficulty, but because they were bound to remain intractable so long as they were understood in the terms dictated by those larger assumptions that I shared with many of my contemporaries.[15]

MacIntyre had discovered that he was working within an unworkable paradigm, a degenerating research program, an exhausted tradition.

---

[14]Alasdair MacIntyre, "The End of Ideology and the End of the End of Ideology," in *Against the Self-Images of the Age* (London: Duckworth, 1971/Notre Dame, IN: University of Notre Dame Press, 1978), 6.

[15]MacIntyre, *The Tasks of Philosophy*, viii.

The major project that MacIntyre took up in the 1970s would lead to a kind of Kuhnian paradigm shift—but it would be a shift justified rationally after the fashion of Lakatos's research programmes. MacIntyre described this change in an interview published the journal *Cogito* in 1991:

> I set out to rethink the problems of ethics in a systematic way, taking seriously for the first time the possibility that the history both of modern morality and of modern moral philosophy could only be written adequately from an Aristotelian point of view. In the same period, after 1971, I had occasion to rethink the problems of rational theology, taking seriously the possibility that the history of modern secularization can only be written adequately from the standpoint of Christian theism, rather than vice versa.[16]

MacIntyre began to realize, as early as 1971, that the framework in which he conducted his enquiries might be an obstacle to his work.

After Virtue (1981) presented MacIntyre's new Aristotelian research program to the public. In MacIntyre's Aristotelianism, moral philosophy builds on a tradition that examines excellence in human action and studies the development of practical rationality in human agents in order to discover what it takes to build a society of people who have transformed their desires to pursue the good life for man. The book was widely celebrated, yet MacIntyre acknowledged in the "Postscript to the Second Edition" that the work remained incomplete without "the sequel" that presents the account of rationality that justifies his Aristotelian project.[17] *Whose Justice? Which Rationality?* is that sequel:

> I . . . recognized that these conclusions required support from an account of what rationality is, in the light of which rival and incompatible evaluations of the arguments of *After Virtue* could be adequately accounted for. I promised a book in which I should attempt to say both what makes it rational to act in one way rather than another and what makes it rational to advance and defend one conception of practical rationality rather than another. Here it is.[18]

Whose Justice? Which Rationality? and its companion text, *Three Rival Versions of Moral Enquiry* stand together as the main sources for MacIntyre's theory of rationality.

---

[16]Alasdair MacIntyre, "An Interview for Cogito," in *The MacIntyre Reader*, ed. Kelvin Knight (Notre Dame, IN: University of Notre Dame Press, 1998), 267–75, at 268.

[17]MacIntyre, *After Virtue*, 264.

[18]MacIntyre, *Whose Justice? Which Rationality?*, ix.

As the title of the book suggests, *Whose Justice? Which Rationality?* rejects the notion of universal reason. For MacIntyre, rationality names the criteria by which we judge truth and falsity, good and evil. Rationality must be trained; thus, it is intimately connected to traditions, and hence varies from one tradition to another:

> Rationality itself, whether theoretical or practical, is a concept with a history: indeed, since there are a diversity of traditions of enquiry, with histories, there are, so it will turn out, rationalities rather than rationality, just as it will turn out that there are justices rather than justice.[19]

Each tradition has its own rational standards and its own conception of justice. *Whose Justice? Which Rationality?* presents rationality as "tradition-constituted" and "tradition-constitutive."[20] It argues that rationality is always social, and that it is always embodied within traditions, even within traditions that professedly eschew any notion of tradition. *Three Rival Versions of Moral Enquiry*, MacIntyre applies his theory of rationality to the conflicts between modern, post-modern, and traditional approaches to the study of philosophy. *Three Rival Versions* compares rationality to a "craft"[21] and argues that only a tradition that acknowledges its traditional nature and structure can recognize that its greatest successes offer nothing better than the best theory "so far,"[22] and that only a community that grasps its tradition informed limitations can reflect adequately upon its past successes and failures in order to move forward constructively towards a more adequate account of the truth.

To say that rationality is "tradition-constituted" is to affirm that as human agents we learn to judge the world using terms and criteria provided by the traditions that have formed us. We learn what counts as a good reason, what counts as a bad reason, which sources are authoritative, and which are spurious within a perspective shaped by a particular tradition. Our rationality, the set of intellectual tools that we use to make substantive judgments of truth and falsity, good and evil,[23] is in this sense constituted in us by the tradition that trains us.

To say that rationality is "tradition-constitutive" is to say that rationality is not static. Members of a tradition can discover or establish new ways of judging, and when this happens their rationality changes their tradition and

---

[19]Ibid., 9.

[20]See MacIntyre, *Whose Justice? Which Rationality?*, 7–10, 354–68. See also Christopher Stephen Lutz, *Tradition in the Ethics of Alasdair MacIntyre: Relativism, Thomism, and Philosophy* (Lanham, MD: Lexington Books, 2004), 33–60.

[21]MacIntyre, *Three Rival Versions of Moral Enquiry*, 61, 66, 127.

[22]MacIntyre, *Whose Justice? Which Rationality?*, 358, 362, 364; MacIntyre, *Three Rival Versions of Moral Enquiry*, 65, 89, 107, 124; MacIntyre, *After Virtue*, 277.

[23]See Lutz, *Tradition in the Ethics of Alasdair MacIntyre*, 9–10.

becomes "tradition-constitutive." Ordinarily, the limitations and shortcomings of our own traditions remain invisible to us, because those limitations shape the lenses through which we see the world. Yet, sometimes a significant challenge[24] may cause an epistemological crisis that leads us to reevaluate conventional beliefs, practices, or attitudes. Sometimes these challenges and reevaluations may lead to successes, and these successes may be recognized as such; but it is also possible that our successes may be rejected as failures. Likewise, these challenges and reevaluations may sometimes end in failure, and these failures may be recognized as such, or they may be celebrated as successes. This is what it means to speak of "the situatedness of all enquiry:"[25] Philosophy is difficult; it demands sympathetic and attentive reading, honest examination and weighing of theories and ideas, and careful and precise writing, and even at its best it remains liable to error.

Intellectual humility has therefore played a central role in MacIntyre's theory of rationality since "Epistemological Crises." In that essay, MacIntyre compared common attitudes toward philosophical work to the title characters of Jane Austen's *Emma* and Shakespeare's *Hamlet*. Both stories present characters struggling through epistemological crises, but these crises are resolved very differently: Emma passes from a false worldview shaped by her own fantasies, illusions, and preconceptions through confusion to a complete understanding of herself and her community with the help of friends, particularly Mr. Knightly, whom she marries. "False interpretation has been replaced not by a more adequate interpretation, which itself in turn may one day be transcended, but simply by the truth."[26] Hamlet passes from one theory to another, trying to make sense of his circumstances, and dies before reaching a clear determination of the truth. "Philosophers," MacIntyre observes, "have customarily been Emmas and not Hamlets."[27] MacIntyre's treatment the role of tradition in human enquiry, in "Epistemological Crises," in *Whose Justice? Which Rationality?*, and in *Three Rival Versions of Moral Enquiry*, invites philosophers to become Hamlets, to reject the false comfort of Emma's unwarranted certitude, to take nothing for granted in the pursuit of truth.

III.

Problems of Rationality in Contemporary Reading. MacIntyre's theory of rationality has immediate implications for the reading of contemporary literature. Faithful reading of any author's work demands attentive openness to the

---

[24]See Lutz, *Tradition in the Ethics of Alasdair MacIntyre*, 85–7.
[25]MacIntyre, "Prologue: *After Virtue* after a Quarter of a Century," in *After Virtue*, 3rd ed., vii.
[26]MacIntyre, "Epistemological Crises," 6.
[27]Ibid., 6.

intentions of the author, sympathy for the author's circumstances, and knowledge of the events and ideas that make up the background of the work. This kind of sympathetic reading need not be favorable to the arguments and conclusions of the author, but it is essential to any real engagement with the author's concerns. Failing to read sympathetically nearly guarantees misinterpretation whether one responds approvingly or not; criticisms based on unsympathetic readings nearly always fail to engage the author's intentions. Scholars who approach the writings of unfamiliar contemporaries without due consideration of those author's peculiar backgrounds are likely to project their own ideas into unacknowledged lacunas.

The problems of reading and interpreting are well known to anyone who teaches. Nearly every pile of student essays offers at least one object lesson about the need for sympathetic reading. Yet, MacIntyre's theory of rationality implies that the challenge of reading a text on the author's terms is not just a problem for students; it implies that the professor who corrects a student's misreading is not Mr. Knightly setting Emma straight, but only one Hamlet offering guidance to another. A brief reflection on the reception of *After Virtue* among professional scholars bears this out.

The critical argument that makes up the first half of *After Virtue* ends with the ultimatum: "Nietzsche or Aristotle?" By 1981 MacIntyre had become convinced that Nietzsche and Aristotle represented the only ways forward for moral enquiry. The option of Nietzsche and his nihilism, taken by many of MacIntyre's contemporaries, recognizes that modern philosophy cannot make good on its promise to justify its objective moral claims and concludes that there is no moral truth. The nihilistic option accepts Nietzsche's critique of the unacknowledged arbitrariness and voluntarism of modern morality; it also accepts Nietzsche's notion of the nobility of the Übermensch, who stands against history and community and culture to follow his own lights.[28] MacIntyre rejects the Nietzschean option.

The second option also accepts Nietzsche's critique of modern moral philosophy, but then reconsiders Aristotle's account of the virtues that constitute human excellence; it looks to history and community and culture to discover how to live a truly human life. The second option finds an affirmation of Nietzsche's critique of modernity compatible with an affirmation of the tradition of the virtues rooted in Aristotle. Looking at contemporary culture from an Aristotelian point of view, MacIntyre argued that our culture is in a perilous condition, and that it cannot be fixed by political action or even by revolution; what is needed is virtue, which is best developed within local communities that are built for human development, rather than for political activism.

---

[28]MacIntyre, *After Virtue*, 256–9.

Critics received MacIntyre's choice of Aristotle over Nietzsche in a variety of ways, some of them revealing as much about the critics as about MacIntyre's text. MacIntyre catalogued some of the more notable critiques in the "Postscript to the Second Edition" (1984). William K. Frankena faulted MacIntyre for failing to distinguish philosophy from its history, "or giving the impression that a historical inquiry can establish a philosophical point."[29] Frankena, an analyst, would have preferred that MacIntyre make his philosophical points according to the canons of analytic philosophy. Abraham Edel, on the other hand, argued that MacIntyre remained enmeshed within the analytic tradition, and called MacIntyre "'a heretic analyst whose heresy remains bound by the cords of the analytic tradition."[30]

There were other critics. MacIntyre's friend Marx Wartofsky,[31] like many other Marxists and former Marxists, rejected *After Virtue* as an expression of political despair.[32] Martha Nussbaum leveled her critique of *After Virtue* in a review of *Whose Justice? Which Rationality?* Where she had taken *After Virtue* on its own to be open to a relativistic interpretation,[33] she concluded that taken together, the two books showed that "MacIntyre is in the grip of a worldview promulgated by authority rather than by reason."[34] Criticisms of *Whose Justice? Which Rationality?* engaged either MacIntyre's text or their authors' preconceptions over a broad spectrum, so that in a twist of poetic justice, some of the most strident condemnations of the book offered the best evidence in support of MacIntyre's theory.[35]

Some Thomists also faced challenges in reading MacIntyre's philosophy on its own terms. For some, MacIntyre's emphasis on human agency rather than metaphysics[36] has presented an obstacle. For others, MacIntyre's identification as a Thomist in *Whose Justice? Which Rationality?*[37] masked MacIntyre's differences with traditional Neo-Thomism—another mistake. Many of the terms that MacIntyre uses in his mature work—virtues, common goods, human action, teleology—seem familiar enough to a reader of Thomas Aquinas, even if

---

[29]William K. Frankena, *Ethics* 93 (1983): 500, quoted in *After Virtue*, 265.

[30]Abraham Edel, "Review of *After Virtue: A Study in Moral Theory*," *Zygon* 18 (1983): 343–9, at 344, quoted in *After Virtue*, 271.

[31]See MacIntyre, "Preface," in *After Virtue*, 2nd ed., x/3rd ed., xviii.

[32]Marx Wartofsky, "Virtue Lost or Understanding MacIntyre," *Inquiry* 27 (1984): 235–50.

[33]Martha Nussbaum, "Recoiling from Reason," *New York Review of Books* 36, no. 19 (December 7, 1989): 36–41, at 36.

[34]Ibid., 40.

[35]For a survey of the strengths and weaknesses of seven critiques of MacIntyre on the topic of relativism, see Lutz, *Tradition in the Ethics of Alasdair MacIntyre*, 73–106.

[36]Four essays in the *Tasks of Philosophy*, chapters 7 through 10 (chapter 8 is his Aquinas Lecture) provide the clearest statement of the role of metaphysics in MacIntyre's philosophy.

[37]MacIntyre, *Whose Justice? Which Rationality?*, 403.

MacIntyre's frequent use of the plural "common goods" raises an eyebrow. Yet MacIntyre's Thomism is contemporary, post-modern, and synthetic; it weaves into its fabric insights from a broad range of academic fields and schools of thought, and to fail to attend to that broader background is to overlook some things that are distinctive to MacIntyre's philosophy.

MacIntyre's theory of rationality helps to make sense of the misinterpretations of MacIntyre's philosophy in the secondary literature, and it turns misinterpretations by professional scholars into cautionary tales warning all of us of our own unacknowledged blind spots. Observing that a well-read and well-respected readers and interpreters can misread a contemporary's work can teach us to recognize our own liability to similar mistakes. It can teach us that even when we question those misreadings, we must assume the role of Hamlet helping another Hamlet, rather than that of Mr. Knightly setting Emma straight.

MacIntyre's turn to Aristotle and Thomas Aquinas misled some who read it, either critically or favorably, as an essentially arbitrary, conservative turn from the chaotic moral culture of the present toward some more orderly culture of the past. For them it appeared that MacIntyre's "embrace" of Aristotelianism and Thomism was an unjustifiable choice for a peculiar traditionalism, but nothing could be further from the truth. MacIntyre's option for Aristotle against Nietzsche is a choice between morality as manipulation and moral philosophy as enquiry into the truth about the natural demands of a society of human agents. The choice between Nietzsche and Aristotle is the choice between will and nature. It is the choice between Feuerbach and the early Marx of *The Theses on Feuerbach*.[38] It is the choice between the Marxism of Engels,[39] or Stalin,[40] or Gueverra,[41] and the same early Marx. It is the choice between William of Ockham and Thomas Aquinas.[42] It is the choice between the pseudoscientific

---

[38]MacIntyre, "*The Theses on Feuerbach*: A Road Not Taken" in *The MacIntyre Reader*, 223–34.

[39]Alasdair MacIntyre, *Marxism and Christianity* (New York: Schocken Books, 1968; reprinted Notre Dame: University of Notre Dame Press, 1984, revised edition with new preface 1995); Friedrich Engels, "Socialism: Utopian and Scientific," *Revue Socialiste* (March–May 1880), trans. Edward Aveling (1892 authorised by Engels), reprinted in *Marx/Engels Selected Works* (Progress Publishers, 1970), vol. 3, pp. 95–151, http://www.marxists.org/archive/marx/works/1880/soc-utop/index.htm.

[40]See MacIntyre, "Notes from the Moral Wilderness" in *The MacIntyre Reader*, 31–49; Emile Perreau-Saussine, "The Moral Critique of Stalinism," in *Virtue and Politics*, ed. Paul Blackledge and Kelvin Knight (Notre Dame: University of Notre Dame Press, 2011), 134–51; and Christopher Stephen Lutz, *Reading Alasdair MacIntyre's After Virtue* (New York: Continuum, 2012), 19–25.

[41]Alasdair MacIntyre, "Marxism of the Will," in MacIntyre, *Against the Self-Images of the Age*, 70–5.

[42]See Lutz, "Understanding the Disquieting Suggestion," in *Reading Alasdair MacIntyre's After Virtue*, 41–52.

abuse of the social sciences[43] and a patient acceptance of their limitations. MacIntyre's Aristotelian and Thomistic moral enquiry is not apologetic; it is not focused on the defense of traditional conventions. It is directed to the criticism of contemporary social structures in light of the natural demands of a society of human agents, for the purpose of renewing human agency and human society. It is oriented toward progress, not conservatism.[44]

IV.

Implications for the Study of the History of Philosophy: The Five Ways of Thomas Aquinas. The difficulty of reading even contemporary authors amplifies the implications of MacIntyre's theory of rationality for the study of historical authors and texts. If "there are rationalities rather than rationality,"[45] then interpreting historical texts faithfully, so that we can develop a truthful narrative of the history of ideas, demands that we recognize our own rationality, grasp the rationality of the past, and learn to negotiate the differences between them. MacIntyre's theory of rationality entails that rationality is not merely cumulative. The histories of traditions and their rationalities are not only histories of progress toward better ways of assessing truth and goodness, they are also histories of disagreements and errors. Thus the rationality of a culture may change in ways that exclude some of the rational resources of one period from the rationality of a later period.

The transformation of rationality over time is not any particular problem for a scientist. If a scientist wants to reject Thomas Aquinas's account of generation by putrefaction—spontaneous generation from decaying matter—that scientist is certainly not under any obligation to explain to us why Thomas believed that "it is from the power originally placed in the elements that they are able to produce animals . . . from . . . the influence of the stars."[46]

Historical changes in rationality do present a problem, however, for anyone engaged in a tradition that builds upon, develops, or is otherwise entangled with the teachings of Thomas Aquinas and his contemporaries. If a twenty-first-century Thomist wants to defend Thomas's account of the natural law in us, that Thomist must first be prepared to defend an Aristotelian account of nature and a Neo-Platonic account of truth, while simultaneously rejecting certain elements

---

[43]See Friedrich Engels, *Socialism: Utopian and Scientific*; Alasdair MacIntyre, *Marxism: An Interpretation*, 68–75; Karl Popper, "Science: Conjectures and Refutations," in *Conjectures and Refutations: The Growth of Scientific Knowledge* (New York: Harper and Row, 1963); and Imre Lakatos, "Science and Pseudoscience," online at http://www.lse.ac.uk/philosophy/About/lakatos/scienceAndPseudoscienceTranscript.aspx; and MacIntyre, *After Virtue*, 79–108.

[44]See MacIntyre, *After Virtue*, 222; and "Prologue: *After Virtue* after a Quarter of a Century," in *After Virtue*, 3rd ed., xiv–xv.

[45]MacIntyre, *Whose Justice? Which Rationality?*, 9.

[46]See, for example, Aquinas, *ST* I, q. 71, a. 1, ad 1.

of "Aristotle's metaphysical biology,"[47] and maintaining a view of creation that is amenable to the discoveries of modern science. This is a challenge that can be met in only two ways: either by the haphazard eclecticism of an unabashed ideologue or by the careful and attentive work of a philosopher.

Working philosophically in a tradition that builds upon ancient and medieval thought demands that we distinguish between the rational resources that we bring to our study of reality and the rationalities of the canonical authors we read. "Rationality . . . is a concept with a history."[48] Reasons, arguments, principles, and worldviews that scholars in one part of the history of a tradition accept as reasonable or even self-evident may be dismissed as irrational and absurd in the same tradition in another time. Thus, before we can adequately investigate the arguments of our predecessors, especially those of many centuries or even millennia ago, we must learn to approach them on their own terms, to understand those arguments, as much as possible, in terms of the substantive rationalities of their authors. Students who approach the history of philosophy without distinguishing their own substantive rationality from those of the texts they read are likely to project contemporary ideas into lacunas in their reading of the ancients and medievals.

Thomas Aquinas's five proofs for the existence of God offer an excellent example of the problem of rationality in the reading of historical texts. The Five Ways are well known and widely read, but they are easily misunderstood. The five ways respond, in part, to the objection that Aristotelian natural philosophy, understood as a closed causal system, makes the existence of God superfluous: "For all natural things can be reduced to one principle, which is nature; and all voluntary things can be reduced to one principle, which is human reason, or will. Therefore there is no need to suppose God's existence."[49] To refute this objection Thomas argues that far from being superfluous to natural philosophy, the existence of God is necessary to complete its accounts of causality, and he shows through five arguments drawn from the natural philosophy of his time that God must exist as first mover, as first efficient cause, as necessary being, as the cause of "being, goodness, and every perfection" to all other beings, and as the intelligent governor of the world.

Thomas's Five Ways have been widely used in college classrooms for generations. But how often are they accompanied by a course in Aristotelian physics adequate to their proper interpretation? It is not unusual for conservative Catholic undergraduate students with a taste for apologetics to decide defend

---

[47]See MacIntyre, *After Virtue*, 3rd ed., xi, 162–163, and Lutz, *Tradition in the Ethics of Alasdair MacIntyre*, 117–8, 119–20, 133.

[48]MacIntyre, *Whose Justice? Which Rationality?*, 9.

[49]Aquinas, *ST* I, q. 2, a. 3, arg. 2.

the Five Ways as a matter of principle even before reading them, but these students typically have difficulty distinguishing the first and second ways because they read both in terms of Newtonian physics. Secular students criticize the Five Ways, and read the fifth way as a design argument, although the fifth way has more to do with the activities of things than with their shapes. Both groups will treat the Five Ways straightforwardly as arguments that God exists. Thus the secular students may observe, and the Christian students may agree, that the *sed contra*, "It is said in the person of God: 'I am Who am.' (Ex. 3:14)"[50] is utterly circular. These contemporary students typically end their treatments of the Five Ways by arguing whether or not Thomas has successfully proved that God exists, when their time would be spent more profitably trying to discover what each argument actually means.

Twenty-first-century students misread Thomas Aquinas because the natural philosophy of our time shares very few of the presuppositions that Thomas and his contemporaries took for granted. Modern science does not define motion as Aristotle did in *Physics* II. In modern science there are no alterations, increases, decreases, or locomotions that are not explained by the laws of nature or by human will. In modern science there are only matter and energy interacting chemically and physically in the void. Moreover, change in momentum has displaced locomotion as an object of scientific study, thus modern science sees no need for—and cannot comprehend—the kind of first mover that Aristotle posited in *Physics* VIII. Three of the four causes of Aristotle's *Physics* and *Metaphysics* are absent from modern biology, chemistry, and physics; only material remains and it is radically transformed. There is no efficient causality of the Aristotelian kind in modern chemistry and biology, only evolutionary processes of matter and life, so modern science finds no reason to imagine a first efficient cause to explain natural efficient causality. Modern conservation laws see all matter as more or less necessary, and modern science treats material beings as arrangements of that matter. The materialist evolutionary view that rejects Aristotelian formal and efficient causality in nature has no place for the concept of "perfections" much less the notion that these perfections must have a source. Finally, modern science flatly rejects teleology in natural processes, so it has no interest in explaining teleology, even if scientists have found it impossible to extirpate teleological terms from their language.

The Five Ways confront most contemporary readers with a series of unintelligible puzzles, but that does not always stop students from making sense of the Five Ways by projecting contemporary causal notions into them. Here the temptation for the professor to play the role of Mr. Knightly setting the student Emmas straight may seem quite reasonable; but even in this case it is a temptation

---

[50]Ibid., I, q. 2, a. 3, s. c..

to complacency. Few of us approach the Five Ways except as moderns, and the recovery of Thomas Aquinas's thought remains an ongoing work. Teachers who would have students engage the Five Ways on Thomas Aquinas's own terms need to realize that unless we fully comprehend Thomas Aquinas's worldview, we remain liable to mistakes similar to our students'. Thus, we can only invite our students, as advanced Hamlets inviting novice Hamlets, to join the work of recovering Thomas's philosophy and theology, as a rationality distinct from our own, so that Thomas can challenge the preconceptions of our scientific age.

V.

Implications for the History of Ideas that We Study: Augustine, the Nominalists, and the Reformers. MacIntyre's theory that rationality, the criteria by which we judge truth and falsity, good and evil, is tradition-constituted and tradition-constitutive has demanding implications for the reading of contemporary and historical literature, and it follows that these implications play formative roles in the history of ideas that we study. For our history is made up of scholars reading texts, well or badly, recognizing problems raised in or by those texts, well or badly, and solving those problems, well or badly, in more or less authoritative texts that must be read and interpreted anew in succeeding generations of scholars and authors.

Late medieval and early modern interpretations of Saint Augustine's anti-Pelagian writings offer a remarkable example of the consequences of the tradition-constituted and tradition-constitutive nature of rationality for the history of ideas. Conflicting evaluations and interpretations of the content and authority of Augustine's theology played a central role in the doctrinal developments of the Protestant Reformation and the history of Jansenism. These historical movements were defined by complex doctrinal, ecclesial, economic, and political disputes and events, but there is no need to investigate all of that here. The purpose of this example is not to provide an exhaustive treatment of that history, but only to show how changes in rationalities have complicated the history of ideas and obscured the significance of those changes from modern scholars.

Heiko Oberman observed in the Introduction to his landmark study of the medieval sources of the Reformation, *The Harvest of Medieval Theology* (1963), "It is a curious—and dangerous—coincidence that the late medieval period is one of the least known in the history of Christian thought *and*, at the same time, a period in the interpretation of which there are a great many vested interests."[51]

---

[51]Heiko A. Oberman, *The Harvest of Medieval Theology* (Grand Rapids, MI: Eerdmans, 1963), 1.

Oberman found that modern research into the history of fourteenth-century scholastic thought was delayed through the middle of the twentieth century for two distinct but complementary reasons. For Protestants dedicated to defending the biblical origins and orthodoxy of Reformation theology, the origins of Reform theology in late medieval thought is an embarrassment: "There is a tendency in this school to stress contrasts between Luther and late medieval theologians and in general to assign Luther more to the tradition of St. Paul and St. Augustine than to that of William of Occam and Gabriel Biel."[52] For Catholic scholars defending Thomas Aquinas as the "apex" of medieval thought, late medieval philosophy and theology, "culminating in nominalism—the work of Occam, Biel, and their disciples—is characterized by the disintegration and rapid collapse of the Thomistic Synthesis."[53] Thus Catholics held the period to be less worthy of serious study than the more positive thirteenth century that had produced Thomas Aquinas. Consequently, even half a century after the publication of *The Harvest of Medieval Theology*, and in spite of the enormous contributions of Heiko Oberman, William Courtenay, and many others, fourteenth-century thought remains relatively unfamiliar outside of specialist fields.

In an article published in 1960, "Some Notes on the Theology of Nominalism: With Attention to its Relation to the Renaissance,"[54] Oberman uses a remarkable image, a dome, to explain the impact of nominalist theology on the Christian doctrines of grace and salvation.[55] According to Oberman, theologians of the nominalist movement committed themselves first and foremost to a defense of divine sovereignty. For Oberman, this theological commitment is the foundation of Nominalist theology and philosophy:

> Nominalistic philosophy is the reflection and echo of its theology and, in particular, of its concept of God's *potentia absoluta* . . . .[56]

> We do not look into the structure of [Ockham's] logic, but into that of his theology, for the real character of Nominalism; and, again, it is within the theological structure that the dialectics of God's *potentia absoluta* is the ruling principle.[57]

---

[52]Ibid.

[53]Ibid.

[54]Heiko A. Oberman, "Some Notes on the Theology of Nominalism: With Attention to its Relation to the Renaissance," *The Harvard Theological Review* 53, no. 1 (Jan. 1960): 47–76.

[55]This essay uses "Some Notes on the Theology of Nominalism" extensively, primarily to make use of the dome metaphor.

[56]Oberman, "Some Notes," 50.

[57]Ibid., 51.

The starting point for the Nominalist movement is not the wisdom of God as the principle of the intelligibility of the created world, as it had been in Thomism; rather, it is the sovereignty of God over creation.

The nominalist view of the sovereignty of God changes Christian anthropology and ethics.[58] In moral theology it makes the divine will the principle of justice, rather than the divine intellect.[59] Nominalist ethics is divine command ethics. Thomas Osborne explains that Ockham retained the notion of right reason in ethics, but understood it to be a consequence of God's divine command in the creation of the world.[60] In anthropology, Oberman found that the nominalist view of divine sovereignty jeopardizes human freedom: "The sovereignty of God, as understood by the Nominalist, would lead to an absolute determinism."[61] The nominalists, for their part, recognized this opposition between the principles of their theology and the Christian doctrine of free will.

Oberman reports that balancing doctrines of divine immanence with the freedom of the human will became an important project for theologians in the nominalist movement, and he catalogues several of the positions they adopted to address the problem. In the "left-wing" school of Robert Holcot and Adam Woodham, "the moral freedom of man is stressed; but, at the same time, God's government is so immediate that He has to take more than customary responsibility for man's sinful deeds."[62] "It is . . . in the left-wing of Nominalism that the Almighty God governs his creation so immediately that God is even made responsible for the evil deeds of men."[63] In the "right-wing" school of Gregory of Rimini, Henry of Oyta, and Thomas Bradwardine, God's sovereignty is made compatible with human freedom:[64] "The doctrine of coefficiency as formulated by Thomas Bradwardine indicates that the idea that no act is performed without God's creative and redeeming *concursus* is compatible with the freedom of the human will."[65]

[58]Servais Pinckaers, *The Sources of Christian Ethics*, trans. Sr. Mary Thomas Noble, OP (Washington, D.C.: Catholic University of America Press, 1995), 240–53.

[59]Cf. Aquinas, *ST* I, q. 21, a. 1, ad 2: "Since good as perceived by intellect is the object of the will, it is impossible for God to will anything but what His wisdom approves. This is, as it were, His law of justice, in accordance with which His will is right and just. Hence, what He does according to His will He does justly: as we do justly what we do according to law. But whereas law comes to us from some higher power, God is a law unto Himself."

[60]Thomas M. Osborne, "Ockham as a Divine Command Theorist," *Religious Studies* 41 (2005): 1–22. There is some contrast between Osborne's treatment of right reason in Ockham's created world and Pinckaers's emphasis on the potential capriciousness of Ockham's God in Pinckaers, 246–7.

[61]Oberman, "Some Notes," 64.
[62]Ibid., 54.
[63]Ibid., 62.
[64]Ibid., 55.
[65]Ibid., 62.

Thus, the right-wing school's "anthropology . . . sees in God not the opponent but the creator, preserver and cause of man's freedom,"[66] but in this, the "right-wing school finds itself deeply opposed to the main current of Nominalism."[67]

According to Servais Pinckaers, the doctrine that most clearly distinguishes William of Ockham and the nominalist movement from its predecessors is its definition of freedom.[68] The classical philosophy of Plato and Aristotle, the Neo-Platonism of Plotinus, the Christian theology of Augustine and Thomas Aquinas had defined freedom as the ability to recognize and do what is good and best, which Pinckaers calls "freedom for excellence."[69] For Ockham and his successors, by contrast, freedom cannot be tied to any particular outcome. Ockham writes:

> What I mean by freedom is the power I have to produce various effects, indifferently and in a contingent manner, in such a way that I can either cause an effect or not cause it without any change being produced outside of this power.[70]

In Osborne's words, "The will's freedom is an openness to opposites."[71] For most of the nominalists, this "freedom of indifference" would place God's sovereign freedom in opposition to human freedom.[72] If God's sovereignty implies that God rules absolutely everything in creation, then it seems that God must also rule human behavior; alternatively, if human beings act with freedom of indifference, it seems necessary to hold that God has no influence on human acts. This opposition between divine sovereignty and human freedom would have direct consequences for the nominalists' approach to the doctrine of grace, since it would make God's gift of grace, as understood in the traditional Augustinian doctrine, into a divine influence on human acts incompatible with human freedom of indifference.

In the traditional Augustinian thought of the Western Church, the human agent is not entirely free. Wounded by the effects of original sin and by the effects of our own sins, the human agent is enabled to meet the demands of the divine law only by accepting the assistance of divine grace.[73] Hence the Christian

---

[66]Ibid., 63.

[67]Ibid.

[68]Servais Pinckaers, *The Sources of Christian Ethics*, 327–53.

[69]Ibid., 354–78.

[70]William of Ockham, *Quodl.* I, q. 16, quoted in Pinckaers, *The Sources of Christian Ethics*, 242.

[71]Thomas M. Osborne, "William of Ockham on the Freedom of the Will and Happiness," *ACPQ* 86 (2012): 435–56.

[72]Pinckaers, *The Sources of Christian Ethics*, 246–7.

[73]Augustine, *Four Anti-Pelagian Writings*, trans. John A. Mourant and William J. Collinge (Washington, DC: Catholic University of America Press, 1992).

credits God's grace for any moral achievement in his or her life. On the other hand, God's grace is available to all who return to God in love[74] so that the human agent who refuses to seek God's assistance or rejects God's grace commits a sin of pride by asserting his or her self-sufficiency; thus, moral responsibility for willful sin always falls entirely upon the human agent.[75]

According to Oberman, the nominalists rejected this traditional anthropology because their doctrines of divine sovereignty and human freedom made it deterministic; in the context of Nominalism's underlying voluntarism, grace, understood as enabling right action, would take away the agent's freedom of indifference.

> Here not sin but grace appears to be the rival of freedom, and it is on this point that the Nominalist break with medieval tradition takes place. . . . Grace, always understood as the neutralizer of sin, does not liberate and heal the will; but it is only a status required of man by God, making grace a harmless competitor of free will.[76]

Ockham and Biel recognized that, in the context of their theology, if grace enables right action, the ability to act rightly would depend on God's sovereignty, not man's choice. Under freedom of indifference, if God is sovereign, and grace alone enables right action, man cannot be free; but if God is sovereign and man is free, grace cannot be necessary to enable right action.

William of Ockham and Gabriel Biel took the latter option: God is sovereign and man is free; thus, grace does not enable right action. For both, "man's freedom stems from man's position in the world,"[77] which Oberman describes as life under "a dome" that "shuts out the world of God's nonrealized possibilities and provides room on the inside for man's own realm, in which he, as the image of God, thinks and acts."[78] Western Christians since Augustine had held that grace enables human beings to act with true freedom, but the Nominalists saw Augustinian grace as a determining intrusion on human freedom; thus, they reduced it from a healing assistance from God that frees the human agent from bondage to the ignorance and weakness of sin, to a status bestowed freely by God, more or less in response to moral achievement.[79]

Ockham and Biel's solution to the problems of freedom and grace leaves the human agent both free and alone.[80] Oberman writes:

---

[74]Ibid., ch. 83.
[75]Ibid., ch. 25.
[76]Oberman, "Some Notes," 66.
[77]Ibid., 63, see also 68.
[78]Ibid., 63.
[79]For the relationship between merit and grace see Oberman, *Harvest*, 160–84.
[80]Oberman, "Some Notes," 68.

The Word, Sacraments, and clergy of the Church have undergone the metamorphosis from being vessels for growing participation in God's being through justification to mere requirements for graduation into eternal bliss. The supernatural world, instead of accompanying and nourishing the *viator*, has receded and become a hemisphere, a dome.[81]

"Man has complete autonomy within the dome,"[82] writes Oberman. This autonomy even extends to something that Augustine had rejected in Pelagianism;[83] Oberman writes:

> Man is *per se* able and free to fulfill the commandments and even—both Occam and Biel go this far—to love God not for our, but for His, sake, *ex puris naturalibus*, without the help of grace.[84]

Ockham and Biel avoided the key doctrine of Pelagianism—that one can achieve one's own salvation—by teaching that "God is no man's debtor,"[85] and that the grace of salvation must be freely granted by God; nonetheless, personal merit is ordinarily required for salvation, and God promises salvation to those who merit it.[86] The Nominalists had found a way to make human freedom coincide with voluntarism and nominalism, but in the process they had profoundly altered Christian anthropology and transformed the doctrine of grace.

Nominalist theology, Oberman observed, left to follow its own principles to their logical conclusions, "would lead to an absolute determinism."[87] So Oberman's dome represents an inconsistency, an artifice, by which that worldview is adjusted to make sense of our experience of freedom and the traditional concept of justice.[88] Yet, for the scholar who accepts freedom of indifference but views grace along Augustinian lines, Oberman's dome makes Ockham and Biel's theology effectively Pelagian. Correcting this apparent heresy within the nominalist worldview would require a determinist solution; for under the freedom of indifference, if God is sovereign and grace alone enables right action, man cannot be free.

Something very much like this kind of reassessment of sovereignty, grace, and freedom appears to have occurred in the theologies of Luther, Calvin, and Jansen.

---

[81]Ibid., 63.

[82]Ibid., 66.

[83]For a brief summary see Augustine, *On Nature and Grace*, ch. 23, paragraph 25.

[84]Oberman, "Some Notes," 66.

[85]Ibid., 65.

[86]See Oberman, *Harvest*, 185–90.

[87]Oberman, "Some Notes," 64.

[88]See Augustine, *On Free Choice of the Will*, trans. Anna S. Benjamin and L. H. Hackstaff (Englewood Cliffs, NJ: Prentice Hall, 1964), bk. 1, ch. 1; and Aquinas, *ST* I, q. 21, a. 4, and q. 83, a. 1.

In an honest attempt to return to the sources of Christian theology, it appears that they imported Augustine's doctrine of grace into the voluntaristic framework of Nominalism, collapsed Oberman's "dome," and in so doing, produced precisely that determinist doctrine that the dome was created to avoid. Yet the histories of these reassessments were rapidly masked from view by the polemics of the Reformation, the Counter-Reformation, and the struggle against Jansenism.

Oberman's 1960 essay suggests the outlines of a narrative of the pre-Reformation history of Western thought in the light of which affirmation of Catholic critiques of Reformation and Jansenist theologies can coincide with recognition that Luther, Calvin, Jansen and their followers may have been more consistent theologians than some of their critics. For Ockham and Biel's contrivance—Oberman's dome—appears to have relied upon experience and habits of orthodox conviction, rather than upon doctrinal consistency, for its support.[89] Freedom of indifference was widely held on both sides of the debates over the Reformation and Jansenism, indeed, John White notes that Ockham's tradition "dominated the Church's life for some 250 years and was . . . an important force at the Council of Trent."[90] Servais Pinckaers agrees:

> Even among Thomists, freedom of indifference was accepted. . . . The surest sign of the adoption of freedom of indifference . . . was concentration on the morality of obligation, which was admitted even by ethicists who, following St. Thomas, continued to use the order of the virtues, rather than that of the commandments.[91]

"Concentration on the morality of obligation" was a universal characteristic in the manuals that regulated the study of moral theology in Catholic seminaries from 1600 until the Second Vatican Council.[92]

More could be said, but this crude narrative sketch is sufficient for the example. Until the middle of the twentieth century, the history of the interpretation of late medieval Western Christian thought had been, for the most part, a history of polemics and apologetics for movements that preceded or followed it, polemics and apologetics that interpreted and assessed the nominalist movement by rationalities other than its own, or that imputed elements of its rationality to its predecessors as Thomism or as Pauline Augustinianism. The nominalist movement itself, in turn, appears to "embody a new concept of reason,"[93] a new form of rationality with novel notions of freedom and divine sovereignty, which

---

[89]Oberman, "Some Notes," 64.
[90]John White, "Ockham and Nominalism: Toward a New Paradigm," *Catholic Social Science Review* 6 (2001): 271–87, at 283.
[91]Pinckaers, *The Sources of Christian Ethics*, 352.
[92]Ibid., 260–79.
[93]MacIntyre, *After Virtue*, 53.

forced the early nominalists to recast the Augustinian narrative of grace and salvation in ways that later adherents of that same rational tradition would find unacceptable. Yet the polemical and apologetic interests of the sixteenth century would mask the details of that story from view for many generations to come.

Alasdair MacIntyre's account of rationality helps to highlight the difficulties of reading contemporary and historical texts. The faithful study of any text must include the work of recovering the rational resources that informed its author. When we fail to do this work, we risk misreading, with all of the dangers of error that come with the consequent misunderstandings of the texts. However, when interpretive errors are folded into those texts and into the practices of the traditions of interpreting those texts, the recovery of one author's tradition-informed rationality may not be sufficient to unlock the truth about that author's role in the history of ideas. The history of nominalism and its role in Western thought offers one example of history obscured by its own conventional interpretation; we can only wonder whether any similar historical movements lie similarly hidden behind other interpretive conventions.

The opening chapter of *After Virtue* proposes that a rational catastrophe lies hidden in the history of our culture.[94] MacIntyre foresees a challenge: "Yet our history lies open to view, so it will be said, and no record of any such catastrophe survives."[95] But one lesson of MacIntyre's theory of rationality is that history does not always lie open to view because the intelligibility of historical events is tied to traditions of interpretation, and those traditions consist not only of canonical books, but also of practices of interpreting those books, and those practices may be fragile. MacIntyre's philosophy implies that there is little reason for complacency in the study of the history of philosophy; standard interpretations need to be tested; overlooked periods and authors need to be investigated.

VI.

Conclusion. The greatest lesson to draw from MacIntyre's account of rationality concerns intellectual humility and openness to learning from everyone. In the conclusion of his interview for Alex Voorhoeve's 2009 book, *Conversations on Ethics*,[96] Alasdair MacIntyre flatly rejected the notion of writing off people "from whom we have nothing to learn or gain:"[97]

---

[94]For a short explanation of *After Virtue*'s hidden catastrophe, see Christopher Stephen Lutz, "Understanding the Disquieting Suggestion," in Lutz, *Reading Alasdair MacIntyre's After Virtue*, 41–51.

[95]MacIntyre, *After Virtue*, 3.

[96]Alex Voorhoeve, "The Illusion of Self-Sufficiency," in *Conversations on Ethics* (Oxford: Oxford University Press, 2009), 111–31.

[97]Ibid., 129 (from Voorhoeve's question).

Something that we badly need to learn is that that is false. We may start by writing off lots of people as those from whom we have nothing to learn, but then, if we are fortunate, we will discover that we were wrong. We are apt to find out that what we have to learn from and about others is unpredictable and surprising. And to act towards others in certain ways prevents us from learning this. So, for example, purely coercive relationships frustrate us and prevent us from learning what it is that we have to learn from those we coerce. And a great many people initially write off the disabled, not recognizing how much there is to be learnt only from them and with them. Only by learning from such others can we rid ourselves of illusions of self-sufficiency, illusions that stand in the way of our recognizing our need for some of the virtues that we need to flourish.[98]

Communities play a vital role in MacIntyre's account of rationality, because our friends and communities can challenge our illusions and fantasies, and help us to gain a better grasp on reality.[99] MacIntyre has set an admirable example of trying to learn from everyone, not only by publishing more than one hundred book reviews over the course of his career, but also by publishing appreciative responses to volumes of critical essays over the last three decades. On this point, perhaps his comparison between Emma and Hamlet should favor Emma. For Emma makes progress, however poorly she or, rather, Jane Austen might characterize it,[100] by taking counsel with her former governess and with her future husband, while Hamlet keeps his own counsel and ends in confusion.

If MacIntyre's theory of rationality is truthful, practicing the openness that he recommends will always require engagement with communities of enquiry that can help us to know ourselves, to understand our contemporaries on their own terms, to understand the rationalities that inform historical texts, and to explore the complexities of historical movements and events with courage and honesty.

Saint Meinrad Seminary and School of Theology
Saint Meinrad, Indiana

---

[98]Ibid., 130 (MacIntyre's response).

[99]See Alasdair MacIntyre, *Dependent Rational Animals: Why Human Beings Need the Virtues*, The Paul Carus Lectures 20 (Chicago: Open Court, 1999), 94–8.

[100]MacIntyre observes: "We of course can see that Jane Austen is merely replacing one interpretation by another, but Jane Austen herself fails to recognize this and so has to deprive Emma of this recognition too." MacIntyre, "Epistemological Crises," 6.

How I Think I Learned To Think Theologically

Stanley Hauerwas

Abstract: Stanley Hauerwas draws upon the Aristotelian philosophy of Alasdair MacIntyre and Charles Taylor to reflect upon his own approach to theology. Like MacIntyre and Taylor, Haurwas rejects the modern theoretical "position from nowhere" that demands "a ground that is unassailable." Instead he approaches theology as an exercise of practical rationality that takes seriously the varied "presumptions that shape the character" of different individuals and communities. Hauerwas reflects on the practical nature of theology by surveying his own attempt to work as a theologian. This seemingly self-reflexive exercise, however, does not lead to an implicit or explicit embrace of the privileged first person singular. Rather Hauerwas uses this exercise to reflect on the political character of theology in so far as the particularity of any theologian—any singular "I"—simply doesn't exist apart from the speech that makes her life and work both possible and intelligible. Attending to language and agency is another way to understand how the work of theology is at once practical and particular, meaning theology will always be political.

I.

Practicing Practical Reason. Toward the end of *Whose Justice? Which Rationality*, Alasdair MacIntyre makes a comment that I hope provides some justification for what I am going to do in this essay; that is, try to make explicit the way I have learned to think theologically. I am, of course, the declared enemy of any attempt to identify "a method" for doing theology and, in particular, any method for the way I do theology. But the denial of "method" can be understood to reflect some methodological commitments that can and should be made candid. By directing attention to MacIntyre's comment, I will try to make candid why I think to the extent there is a method for the doing of theology, and in particular the way I do theology, that method is best understood as an exercise in practical reason.

MacIntyre's comment came in response to the problem, a problem that is at the heart of *Whose Justice? Which Rationality?*, of how someone can act in a reasonable manner when faced by what seems to be the impossibility of deciding

©2014, *American Catholic Philosophical Quarterly*, Vol. 88, No. 4   pp. 641–658
doi: 10.5840/acpq201410237

between antithetical accounts of what is just and/or true. This is a person, according to MacIntyre, who has not yet given their allegiance to any tradition of enquiry; hence their inability in the face of alternative traditions to know what to do. The comment to which I want to direct attention is MacIntyre's suggestion that the initial response to such a person is quite straightforward: namely, the answer "will depend upon who you are and how you understand yourself."[1]

MacIntyre observes this is not the kind of answer that those who have had even an elementary introduction to philosophy expect from a philosopher. A philosopher, it is assumed, is to give an answer that would be persuasive to anyone at any time. MacIntyre argues, however, that this standard philosophical response is based on presumptions that are in fact false. The chief of those presumptions is that there are standards of rationality that provide adequate evaluation of rival alternatives that are equally available to all people, no matter the tradition in which they happen to find themselves. Once this presumption is questioned, it becomes clear that problems of justice and practical rationality are not the same for all people. What the problems are and how they are understood and resolved will vary not only with historical, social, and cultural contexts, but with the situation of the persons who have this or that particular set of problems.

Some worry that MacIntyre's response that "it will depend on who you are and how you understand yourself" implies a vicious relativism and/or subjectivism, but such an accusation simply reproduces the understanding of rationality MacIntyre argues is mistaken. For a person in the situation he describes has the possibility of self-recognition and self-knowledge because they have learned to speak and write some language in use. Accordingly, they will have some texts through which they can test certain kinds of argumentative interventions. They will, therefore, be able to assess, over time, their initial responses by testing those responses by arguments within an ongoing tradition as well as by debates of that tradition of enquiry with alternative traditions.[2]

MacIntyre is acutely aware that his account of a person capable of recognition that they are at home in a tradition is in marked contrast to the kind of person who thinks of themselves as alien to every tradition of enquiry. A person who thinks they are at home nowhere assumes that to be rational entails the attempt to provide neutral, impersonal, and independent standards of rational judgment. Such a view is the natural language of that strange individual associated with modernity, namely the cosmopolitan person, whose language seems to reflect a position from nowhere because it seeks to be everywhere.

MacIntyre well understands that for people who are formed by such cosmopolitan habits, nothing less than a conversion would be required if they were

---

[1]Alasdair MacIntyre, *Whose Justice? Which Rationality?* (Notre Dame, IN: University of Notre Dame Press, 1988), 391.

[2]Ibid., 394.

to acknowledge they represent a particular tradition. Being the good Aristotelian he is, MacIntyre argues such a conversion would require the person to recognize that as a person of practical reason they will be able to think for themselves only by thinking with others. Yet, that Aristotelian point, MacIntyre argues, must be disciplined by the Augustinian insight that a person of practical reason must also be ready to acknowledge they have ignored standards internal to their mind which make possible their ability to know their deficiencies.[3]

Below, I will try to show how MacIntyre's remark, "it will depend on who you are and how you understand yourself," is crucial for how I understand the work of theology as an exercise in practical reason. Theology so understood has no beginning and no end. The theologian always begins in the middle and their work is never finished. The discipline of theology so understood can be and often is quite frustrating because you often have no idea what you are or should be doing. But if theology is an exercise in practical reason there is no alternative. However, before I try to show what it means for theology, or at least the way I have tried to do theology, to be "practical" I need to say more about what I take to be the basic characteristics of practical reason.

II.

The Character of Practical Reason. In his *Self, World, and Time: Ethics as Theology*, Oliver O'Donovan observes that "practical thought is the most commonplace of human rational exercises, for action is the first and elementary of human existence."[4] O'Donovan argues, therefore, that morality is not about what we do, but about what we think about what we are to do. He suggests, however, that we must be awaken to our agency by acquiring the concepts and descriptions that shape our understanding of the way things are.[5] To be so awakened is to discover we are creatures of time, which means practical reason is an ongoing exercise in a narrative that implicates the interrelation of our agency and the world.[6]

I call attention to O'Donovan's account of practical reason not only because I am convinced he has given us one of the best accounts we have of practical reason, but also because I think his account helps us better understand MacIntyre's suggestion that it makes all the difference who a person is, as well as how they

---

[3] Ibid., 396.

[4] Oliver O'Donovan, *Self, World, and Time: Ethics as Theology*, vol. 1 (Grand Rapids, MI: Eerdmans, 2013), 3.

[5] Ibid.,11.

[6] O'Donovan argues, however, that as welcome as it is that narrative has been one of the ways a substantial place for agency has been reclaimed in ethics, that development has not been sufficiently on guard to avoid self-justifying bad faith. What is needed, according to O'Donovan, is not the narrative self as object, but the "responsible self-as-agent, emerging out of history precisely for the task that lies before it." Ibid., 37.

understand themselves, for how arguments are to be developed about what is the good and true. That O'Donovan and MacIntyre argue that it makes all the difference who we are for the exercise of practical reason is, in an interesting way, echoed by Charles Taylor's defense of practical reason as an exercise in *ad hominem* argument. Taylor's defense of *ad hominem* arguments is not meant to unleash criticisms of a person that are irrelevant to the matter at hand. Rather, by directing attention to the importance of *ad hominem* arguments Taylor is reminding us that we inhabit narratives that often are ignored but in fact make all the difference for the position a person holds.

By directing attention to *ad hominem* arguments, Taylor argues that the rise of modern skepticism is the result of despair in practical reason fueled by naturalistic presumptions that mistakenly assume that if practical reason is to avoid arbitrary judgments it must have a ground that is unassailable. By contrast, Taylor argues that an *ad hominem* understanding of practical reason is linked to our ability to effect purposes that makes possible the acquisition of "potential recipes for more effective practice."[7]

Taylor acknowledges that the differences between some cultures may be too great to make *ad hominem* argument possible, but there is no reason that attempts should not be made to develop arguments in which disagreements can be located. To make *ad hominem* arguments work requires an attempt to articulate the implicit presumptions that shape the character of those making the arguments. These presumptions will often take the form of a narrative whose complexity defies easy summary. Accordingly, Taylor argues, to discover where disagreements lie will be hard and slow work.

Taylor's (and MacIntyre's) understanding the character of practical reason owes much to Aristotle. In the *Nicomachean Ethics* Aristotle distinguishes between scientific knowledge and practical wisdom. The former deals with matters of necessity, whereas practical reason is about human concerns that are open to deliberation. Accordingly, practical wisdom not only entails universals but is also about particulars, "since it is concerned with action and action is about particulars. That is why in other areas also some people who lack knowledge but have experience are better in action than others who have knowledge."[8]

Aristotle thinks it very unlikely that practical wisdom will be found in the young because they have not developed the capacity to perceive or deliberate about particulars. The person of practical wisdom must have the understanding

---

[7]Charles Taylor, "Explanation and Practical Reason," in *The Quality of Life*, ed. Martha Nussbaum and Amartya Sen (Oxford: Oxford University Press, 1993), 220.

[8]Aristotle, *Nicomachean Ethics*, trans. Terrance Irwin (Indianapolis: Hackett Publishing, 1999), 1141b15–19. O'Donovan has an interesting discussion of how Aristotle's distinction between theoretical and practical reason became assimilated to the division between the cognitive and affective powers of the soul. See O'Donovan, *Self, World, and Time*, 22–3.

that gives them the capacity to judge last things, and judgments about ends are judgments about particulars. Such judgments Aristotle identifies as judgments of understanding because even though they are about matters that can be otherwise, they make possible the identification of universals through particulars.[9]

Therefore, the person of practical reason must have a capacity of perception of particulars that comes from being well trained. Though Aristotle sometimes sounds as if the end is a given, leaving only the question of the appropriate means to achieve the end, it is rather the case that the means are constitutive of the end. Training is required because the end and means are constitutive of one another, because for an action to be the kind of action that makes us virtuous we must not separate the end from the means. To be an agent of practical reason requires that we must be a person of virtue.[10]

Joseph Dunne, who provides one of the most careful and complete accounts we have of Aristotle's understanding of practical wisdom, suggests that for Aristotle there is an essential connection between character and practical wisdom (*phronesis*). According to Dunne, practical wisdom is a perfected form of experience because it is the virtue that makes the experience of some people not simply an accumulation of actions from the past, but "a dynamic orientation to bring this systematization into play and allow it to be tested by present circumstances, to draw from it what is relevant and to see where it does not fit."[11] Practical wisdom, therefore, is a habit of attentiveness that makes past experiences a resource that allows the present, in Dunne's words, "to unconceal" its peculiar significance.

Aristotle gave an account of the work of practical reason by drawing attention to the practical syllogism, but by its very nature the conclusion of the practical syllogism does not follow strict logic. MacIntyre suggests as much by arguing that every practical syllogism is a performance by a particular person on a particular occasion. The soundness of the practical syllogism will, therefore, depend on who utters it and on what occasion. This does not mean that a person must be able to formulate a practical syllogism before they act, but it does mean that they should act as someone would have done who had so deliberated. They must do so because they must be ready to answer the question, "Why did you

---

[9]In his very important article, "First Principles, Final Ends, Contemporary Issues," MacIntyre argues that first principles expressed as judgments are analytic, but that does not mean they are known *a priori*. Rather their analyticity, that is, that their predicates are essential properties of the subject, is discovered usually as the outcome of a prolonged process of empirical enquiry. This article can be found in Alasdair MacIntyre, "First Principles, Final Ends, Contemporary Issues," in MacIntyre, *The Tasks of Philosophy: Selected Essays* (Cambridge: Cambridge University Press, 2006), 143–79.

[10]Aristotle, *Nicomachean Ethics*, 1143a20–1143b5.

[11]Joseph Dunne, *Back to the Rough Ground: "Phronesis" and "Techne" in Modern Philosophy and in Aristotle* (Notre Dame, IN: University of Notre Dame Press, 1993), 305.

so act?" Indeed, one suspects that most moral judgments about what we do and do not do are retrospective.

Such retrospective judgments are not only possible but necessary, because even though the kind of practical rationality Aristotle describes is at odds with the modern tendency to separate the end from the means and reason from character, there are still contexts in which practical reason flourishes. We should not be surprised that there remain contexts that exemplify the work of practical reason, because such reasoning is not some esoteric achievement. In fact, our lives are constituted by activities shaped by practices recognizable as instances of the kind of wisdom MacIntyre thinks Aristotle so acutely describes. In the words of John Henry Newman, practical reasoning is "the exercise of a living faculty in the individual intellect."[12]

For example MacIntyre calls attention to the hockey player who, in the closing seconds of a crucial game, has the opportunity to pass to another player on his team who is better positioned to score the decisive goal. We think if the player has rightly perceived the situation they must make the needed pass. Mac-Intyre observes that our use of *must* to describe what the hockey player does or should do "exhibits the good of the person *qua* hockey player and member of that particular team and the action of passing, a connection such that were such a player not to pass, he or she must *either* have falsely denied that passing was for their good *qua* hockey player or would have been guilty of inconsistency or have acted as one not caring for his or her good *qua* hockey player and member of that particular team."[13]

MacIntyre comments on this example by observing that we recognize the necessity of rational action as integral to our social and political life just to the extent that those aspects of our life provide the structured roles necessary for the discovery of the goods needed to make our actions intelligible. Any account of practical reason that is faithful to Aristotle, therefore, entails a politics. For it was the *polis* that integrated the systematic activities of human beings "into an overall form of activity in which the achievement of each kind of good was given its due. . . . No practical rationality outside the *polis* is the Aristotelian counterpart to *extra ecclesiam nulla salus*."[14]

That practical reason entails a politics is central to Eugene Garver's important book on practical reason, *For the Sake of Argument: Practical Reasoning, Character, and the Ethics of Belief*. Garver observes that the philosophical presumptions of liberal political arrangements has resulted in severing the connection

---

[12]John Henry Newman, *An Essay in Aid of A Grammar of Assent* (Notre Dame, IN: University of Notre Dame Press, 1979), 240.

[13]MacIntyre, *Whose Justice? Which Rationality?*, 140–1.

[14]Ibid., 141.

between character and reason, with the result that the definitive resolutions of mathematicians and the battle of interest and power are the only alternatives. In particular, Garver calls attention to the use of "rational choice" theories of decision to legitimate and explain the behavior of modern states. Reason, so understood, seems suited to liberal democracies because reason so construed is formal rather than substantive, distinguished only, as MacIntyre suggested, by the marks of publicity, neutrality, impersonality, and universality.[15]

By contrast Garver draws on Aristotle's *Rhetoric* to argue for the essential connection between thought and character. By calling attention to rhetoric, Garver develops the political presumptions of practical reason by emphasizing that language makes possible a common life. The good person, therefore, must be a person of deliberation and persuasion able to avoid the temptation to engage in manipulative strategies. Rhetoric as a form of practical reason is constituted by contingency, emotion, and passionate interests, but is no less rational for being such.[16]

According to Garver, friendship is crucial for the flourishing of practical wisdom. Yet, it is friendship, Garver argues, that the modern state has abandoned in its quest to secure order and stability. Friendship has been abandoned in favor of trying to make justice the primary political virtue. Yet, it is only through political friendship that "practical reason can aim at truth while staying committed to public argument, because ethical arguments can be more powerful and more rational than arguments from reason alone."[17]

To be sure, practical reason in the concrete, and there is no other form than in the concrete, requires the acknowledgement of authority, but authority depends on the existence of an ethos that makes argument possible.[18] Such an ethos consists in narratives that constitute the memory of a community and help to establish its future. We become ethical agents through membership in such communities, through being schooled in the texts and exemplars that determine the character of our lives. Narratives are, therefore, invitations for inclusion into a community. Lives embedded in such narratives make possible the ongoing testing and revision of the narratives.[19]

---

[15]Eugene Garver, *For the Sake of Argument: Practical Reasoning, Character, and the Ethics of Belief* (Chicago: University of Chicago Press, 2004), 13.

[16]Ibid., 2–3.

[17]Ibid., 27.

[18]O'Donovan provides an illuminating account of the communicative character of action by reminding us of the role of advice for practical reason. Accordingly, the exercise of freedom depends on advice based on moral teaching that has the authority to give advice. Crucial for the exercise of authority is the resource of language for the framing of "nuanced discernment of reality." O'Donovan, *Self, World, and Time*, 56.

[19]Garver, *For The Sake of Argument*, 78–9.

Garver's emphasis on the rhetorical character of practical reason suggests that reason so understood can produce an "ethical surplus" that creates alternatives that would be missed by reason alone. Garver, for example, provides a close analysis of *Brown v. Board of Education*, the Supreme Court decision that ended the segregation of schools, to illustrate how practical reason can generate more powerful conclusions than the initial premises might seem to allow.[20] Given Garver's emphasis on the internal relation between character and practical reason, I assume he might also think that the source of "ethical surplus" is to be found in the lives of those who extend the narratives that constitute that community of discourse.

In summary, practical reason deals with matters that can be otherwise; that is, with the contingent. To reason well about matters that can be otherwise means that how one reasons cannot be abstracted from who is doing the reasoning. So understood, there can be no strong distinction between moral and non-moral reasoning, because the descriptions that form our worlds are various and interrelated. To act rationally and well is finally tested by our ability to provide a narrative that makes sense of who we are. We often get our stories wrong, but the good news, at least the good news of the story identified as Christian, is that we are not fated by our mistakes. Not to be so fated is the result of our belief that we are creatures destined to be friends with one another and God.

III.

How I Think I Think Theologically. By providing an account of practical reason, I hope I have prepared the ground to explore how I think I learned to think of theologically. To engage in such a project seems odd. Surely, I must know how I learned to think theologically, but I am not at all sure that is the case. Therefore, the first "I think" in the title of this essay is not an empty gesture, but rather indicates that I do not know without thinking how I think theologically. I think I am being honest when I confess I am not at all sure I have known how to say to myself or others what and how I have understood the work I have done a theologian. Of course, I have some ideas about how I have understood the task of theology, but I hope there is more in what I have done theologically than is in my understanding. This last remark I hope to make intelligible by calling attention to how what I have done is best understood as an exercise in practical reason.

Some may well think that I have already said how I learned to think theologically in *Hannah's Child: A Theologian's Memoir.*[21] I should like to think that is the

[20]Ibid., 9–11, 73–5.
[21]Stanley Hauerwas, *Hannah's Child: A Theologian's Memoir* (Grand Rapids, MI: Eerdmans, 2012). This is the paperback edition of the book with a new "Afterword" that I think will be of interest for those who are interested in practical reason.

case. In particular, I should like to think *Hannah's Child* suggests how I learned to think by being taught to read by great teachers. I think, moreover, that reading is an essential exercise in practical reasoning, but that is a subject for another time. What I hope to do in this essay, however, is to complement what I did in *Hannah's Child* by making articulate what could only be suggested in the memoir.

I confess I would feel much more comfortable to have avoided the first person singular.[22] I would prefer to have tried to characterize in general how to think theologically, but to do so would avoid MacIntyre's remark about who someone is and how they understand themselves if we are to address questions of the good and the truth. Certainly the "I" that is the subject of *Hannah's Child* in many ways exhibits the characteristics of MacIntyre's characterization of someone who knows not where they are. Thus, my oft repeated confession in *Hannah's Child* that I did not understand what I was doing in this or that circumstance until much later. The "I" of *Hannah's Child* I hope is the same "I" that seeks to understand how I learned to think theologically.

But the "I" of *Hannah's Child* or the "I" of this exercise is not unique to me. Hopefully, the "I" that is trying to tell the story of how I learned to think theologically others will recognize as not unrelated to how they have come to think theologically. If that is the case, then the story I have to tell is not just my story, but a story that helps us locate where we have been, as well as what our future may be. By trying to characterize my "I," however, I hope to make concrete how I learned to think theologically in a manner that defies a theology that seems to be but one more theoretical possibility.

There is certainly a place for attempts to say in general what theology is about, but I worry that too often such characterizations of theology fail to do justice to the politics that determine the shape of theology. I certainly think that there are crucial habits associated with how Christian convictions are to be understood in relation to one another—how Christological and Trinitarian commitments are interrelated—but I think it still to be the case that the Trinitarian and Christological doctrines are not done in the abstract but are part and parcel of the attempt by Christians to think through how they should live in the world in which they find themselves.

Another way to avoid the "I" is to report on how other theologians think. Much can be learned from such an exercise, but to attend to the work of particular theologians can give the impression that theology is the speculative work

---

[22]Yet, if William H. Poteat is right, and I think he is, the attempt to avoid the first person is an ontological mistake because what we mean by "the world" is appropriately understood only if the first person pronoun is seen as constitutive of what we should mean by "the world." Poteat's account of the significance of the first person is complex and subtle, deserving more than this footnote. See his collected essays: William Poteat, *The Primacy of Persons and the Language of Culture*, ed. James Nickell and James Stines (Columbia, MO: University of Missouri Press, 1993).

of an individual rather than an office of a community. The attempt to say what theology is in and of itself, as well as what particular theologians do, can and has produced quite useful accounts of the work of theology. But those accounts cannot help but reflect the particular theological perspective of the theologian who has provided those accounts. I am sure that by trying to provide an account of how I think I will make use of both these approaches for characterizing my work as a theologian.

It would be an act of hubris for me to claim that the way I have worked is the future of theology, but it would be an exercise in false humility to pretend I do not care that how I have tried to do theology may have implications for how theological work is done in the future. In particular, I have tried to think through how theology must be done such that it presumes the end of Christendom. Many have found the results of that effort quite odd if not out and out wrong, but I at least hope to suggest in this paper that there is a rationale for how I think that may be of use to others.

Taylor's defense of *ad hominem*, I should like to think, illumines what I am trying to do by directing attention to the way I have tried to think theologically. The *ad hominem* character of argument includes all who are participants in the exchange. Too often, I fear, we assume that Taylor's point applies only to those whose minds we are trying to change. But Taylor's argument about arguments means that all sides must try to identify the narratives that have shaped how and why they assume the stance they think is so important.

That said, it is still the case that I am hesitant to direct attention to how I have tried to do theology because I so dislike the narcissistic fascination with the self characteristic of so many intellectuals in the modern university. Our fascination with our work no doubt has everything to do with the fact that if we did not take our work seriously then no one would take our work seriously. Theologians at least have the advantage that, though we often end up writing for other academic theologians, we are at least committed to write for people who identify themselves as Christians. This means, however, that theology as an office of the church means the theologian does not get to determine what and how they think without reference to what and how theology has been done in the past. As I indicated above, when appropriately done the work of theology should reflect what has been done by other theologians.

Yet I do worry that by trying to understand how I have done theology I risk being self-absorbed in a manner that distorts the theological task. It is surely the case that the character of theology should demand that those engaged in the work of theology not take themselves overly seriously. Accordingly, no one should undertake the work of theology if they are devoid of a sense of humor and/or irony. Of course, one of the problems with that recommendation is, ironically, that those who have no sense of humor or irony often do not know they have no sense of humor or irony. This is not an insignificant challenge if the character of theology and the theologian are inseparable.

Thus, trying to think through, or at least make articulate, the way I have learned to do theology, I hope might be useful to others. I am aware that the way I have worked is hard to imitate. In fact, to try and imitate "my style" would mean that you have not learned the lessons I hope my way of doing theology entails. Thus, my infamous claim that I do not want students to think for themselves, but I want them to think like me. I do want them to think like me—only differently.

By trying to say how I think I think theologically, I need to make clear I am not trying to finally "pull it all together." I am old, but I am not about to write a "retractions" or respond to critics by "setting the record straight." Rather, I want to try to show that there has been some method to the madness of my work by directing attention to how what I have done has been an exercise in practical reasoning. I am aware that the way I have learned to think theologically cannot help but frustrate many readers. There is just so much of it and there is no one essay or book to be read in order to "get it."

Moreover, since my work has been in response to assignments, the diversity of topics I have addressed likely make those who specialize in one or another aspect of theology weary. I am an amateur in almost every subject I address, but I am not going to apologize for attempting to respond as constructively as I am able to requests that I think about subjects that may not seem to fall under the subject matter of theology or ethics. Seeing the connections makes all the difference and practical reason is all about seeing the connections. That I have written much and have written broadly I should like to think reflects my conviction that theology must be the ongoing effort to construe the world as God's good work.

That I understand the work of theology in this way is one of the reasons I have grudgingly been willing to be identified as an "ethicist." Ethics at least suggests that theology is a practical science, but the very distinction between theology and ethics can reproduce the deleterious distinction between theory and practice. I certainly do not mean to deny that theology properly understood has speculative, or I would prefer contemplative, moments, but I have tried to show that fundamental theological convictions about the Father, Son, and the Holy Spirit are inseparable from the work they do for the formation of a people set loose in and for the world. Accordingly, if you think Christians have "beliefs" that need to be applied, I assume that something has gone wrong in your understanding of the grammar of theology.

David Starling, in a very interesting paper entitled, "Theology and the Future of the Church," has called attention to my injudicious claim in *After Christendom* that "the very idea of systematic theology was a result of a church with hegemonic power that belied the very substance that made it the church to begin with."[23] Starling charitably observes that I am not dismissing theology per se, but rather the judgment I make about systematic theology reflects my general concern that Christian theology not be treated as a timeless system of belief. Theology so understood too often elides the politics that is the condition of the possibility for thinking theologically.[24] My worry about systematic theology, therefore, reflects my judgment that Christians must learn to live in a post-Christian world.[25]

Drawing on Paul's first letter to the Corinthians, Starling provides an account of the ecclesial presuppositions and corresponding narratives that shaped Paul's letter in a manner that can help us discern how we must learn to live and do theology in a post-Christian context. Starling, however, argues that Paul's theological commitments provided the material for the development of a kind of theological systematization that emerged in the centuries that followed Paul's missionary work. I could not agree more, but I do not think of the development of theology in the early centuries of the church to be "systematic" theology. Rather, I associate systematic theology with developments after the Reformation in which "doctrine" became an end in itself.[26]

That Starling draws attention to Paul's letter to the Corinthians as a source for reflecting theologically on the work of theology is very insightful. Paul's letters are occasional but their ad hoc character is held together, as Starling denotes, by Paul's understanding of what makes the church the church. Theology done as letters, or at least as reflection on letters such as the letters of Paul, has a concreteness that resists false universalizing tendencies. I should like to think, at least in terms of form, the way I have done theology is not unlike letters to the church.

---

[23]The quote Starling highlights is in *After Christendom* (Nashville, TN: Abingdon Press, 1999), 19. *After Christendom* was originally published in 1991. The 1999 edition has a new "Preface." For a more extended reflection on the character of systematic theology see Stanley Hauerwas, "Introduction," in *Sanctify Them In The Truth: Holiness Exemplified* (Nashville, TN: Abingdon Press, 1998). The first chapter of that book is also relevant dealing as it does with questions of the relation of doctrine and ethics.

[24]David Starling, "Theology and the Future of the Church," (lecture, New College Lectures, University of New South Wales, 2010).

[25]O'Donovan suggests that dogmatic theology stresses the impossible universality of sin, that is, sins significance as the defining qualification of the mis-relation between mankind and God. Moral theology concentrates on the possible contingency of sin to identify the horizon to be recognized and refused in each action we undertake. O'Donovan, *Self, World, and Time*, 83.

[26]See, for example, Brad Gregory, *The Unintended Reformation: How A Religious Revolution Secularized Society* (Cambridge, MA: Harvard University Press, 2012), 75–128. Gregory observes that doctrine prior to the Reformation was a Christian response to "life questions" such as "What should I live for and why?" or "What is meaningful in life?" After the Reformation doctrine became a marker for authority, but since there was no consensus on which doctrines were to be considered authoritative the way was prepared for the Enlightenment attempt to make "reason alone" the standard.

If theology is understood as something like the writing of letters then it should be clear that there is no place to begin or end the work of theology. Rather, you always begin in the middle. The demand for "method" is often an attempt to avoid this conclusion, but there is no method that can free theology of the necessity to respond to the challenges of trying to discern what being a Christian entails in this place and at this time. There is no prolegomena for all future theology. Indeed, there is no prolegomena period. It is performance all the way down. Thus, my presumption that letters, sermons, and essays may well be the central genres for theological reflection.

I need to make clear at this point that even though I am trying in this essay to understand how I have worked theologically I do not think the way I have done theology is the only way it can or should be done. I am sure, for example, I could not have worked the way I have worked if I had not known Barth's *Dogmatics*, McClendon's *Systematic Theology*, and Robert Jenson's *Systematic Theology* were available. A book that treats a specific topic, a book like Katherine Tanner's, *Christ the Key*, is invaluable. Theology comes in many shapes and sizes and we need most of those shapes and sizes.

In contrast to the way Barth, McClendon, Jenson, and Tanner have done theology, my work has been much more occasional. It is not by accident that most of my books are collections of essays. That character of my work, I suspect, drives some of my readers to distraction. Supporters and critics are often desperate to find a center that will make clear amid the chaos what I am really all "about." For example, I am often both praised and criticized for emphasizing the significance of the church as crucial for the work of theology, but I do not think that emphasis is a useful indicator of what I have been about. Some seem to think the animating center of my work revolves around the critique of liberalism, which from my perspective is clearly a side issue. Those with more friendly interpretations compliment me for reintroducing the importance of the virtues for understanding the moral life. The list could go on, but the truth is that there is no center to my work unless you count work itself as the center.

Those in the field of ethics, I suspect, are particularly frustrated that there is no easy way to sum up what I have been about. I refuse to focus on one characteristic to determine the content of Christian ethics. For example, love is often identified as the defining concept that makes an ethic Christian. From my perspective the attempt to put all the theological eggs in that basket usually makes fundamental theological concepts secondary. That is why I have always thought it a mistake to make love or justice the defining character of what it means to be a Christian. When love or justice is assumed to be what Christian ethics is allegedly about, Jesus often fades into the twilight.

My way of working, moreover, has got to be frustrating for those who associate theology and ethics with "having a position." I have worked very hard to avoid having a position. Of course I have positions about a host of matters. I believe that suicide is rightly understood negatively and that baseball should not be played in Florida in the summer. (Florida is for spring training.) But that is not what I mean by a "position." "Position" names the attempt by a theologian to develop a theological system that bears his or her name. Accordingly the "position" becomes more important than what the position is allegedly about: that is, God. Theology done with the ambition to produce a position appears more like modern philosophy.

Theologians do not need to have a position because we serve a confessional community that makes our reflections on church practice possible. That does means that theologians may and should take a critical attitude toward the church, but to do so means they must draw on resources that the church has made possible. That every Sunday the church is charged to attend to scripture means that the church cannot escape the judgment of the Holy Spirit. That is why, as I suggested above, one of the most fruitful genres for theology remains the sermon. Sermons that are faithful to scripture will defy any "positions."

I have been very fortunate to have had a long life and to have had responsibilities that have given me time to think and write about what I care about. I am sure, moreover, that there have been developments in my work that at the very least suggest different emphases. The stages Sam Wells identifies in his *Transforming Fate Into Destiny: The Theological Ethics of Stanley Hauerwas* I have always thought to be quite illuminating.[27] Yet I also think that the stages Wells identifies—that is, from quandary to character, from character to story, from story to community, from community to church—are exactly that, namely "stages," which mean the latter stages only make sense in the light of the beginnings.

This means, however, that the way I work continues to presuppose that the work I did very early is crucial for understanding why I am saying what I am now saying. Yet often those who have read what I am now saying have not, for quite understandable reasons, read what I wrote at the beginning of my work. For example, the claim that "you can only act in the world you can see and you can only see what you have learned to say" is only intelligible against the background of the work I did in *Vision and Virtue*,[28] a book that was first published in 1974. That claim, a claim that itself begs for further elaboration, is crucial if you are to understand my latter declaration that "the first task of the church is not to make the world more just but to make the world the world."[29]

---

[27]Samuel Wells, *Transforming Fate Into Destiny: The Theological Ethics of Stanley Hauerwas* (Cambria, UK: Paternoster Press, 1998).

[28]Stanley Hauerwas, *Vision and Virtue: Essays in Christian Ethical Reflection* (Notre Dame, IN: Fides Press, 1974).

[29]Stanley Hauerwaus, *Performing the Faith* (Grand Rapids MI: Baker/Brazos, 2004), 56.

I must ask the reader's patience for what can only seem a far too long exercise in throat clearing. But I felt I had to clear the swamp if I was to make explicit how I have learned to do theology as a form of practical reasoning. Now I must try to say how what I have said is best understood as an exercise in practical reason.

IV.

Back to the Beginning. When I began to write, and writing is more fundamental than thinking, I did not think what I was doing to be best understood as practical reasoning. In truth, I did not think about what I was doing when I begin to write—period. I do not mean I did not think I needed to have a "method" before I began. I was not that coherent. Rather, I just began doing what I thought needed to be done. But given the account of practical reason I have just given that is not a bad way to begin.

I did have something like a project. I was convinced that the current ways of thinking about ethics as a decision procedure failed to provide an appropriate account of the agent who was making the decision. Mark Ryan, in his extremely informative book, *The Politics of Practical Reason: Why Theological Ethics Must Change Your Life*, suggests that early on I sensed that agency is embedded in the life of a particular community which meant that practical inferences are licensed within communities of shared goods.[30] The strange mixture of topics in my first collection of essays, *Vision and Virtue*, a mixture that continued in subsequent books, was my way of trying to develop that understanding of agency.[31]

Ryan observes that, although my understanding of practical reason drew on Aristotle, I inflected Aristotle's account by stressing the importance of language. Thus my claim that "you can only act in the world you can see and you can only see what you have learned to say." I thought it at least a plausible suggestion that the church provides the habits of speech that shape how Christians see the world. Yet, Ryan suggests that my emphasis on the church as the source of Christian language can miss what is crucial about the developing account of practical reason in my work. In contrast to the presumption that language is a tool used to achieve specific ends or as something we can change as the occasion arises, Ryan suggests I followed "Wittgenstein in believing what is needed

---

[30]Mark Ryan, *The Politics of Practical Reason: Why Theological Ethics Must Change Your Life* (Eugene, OR: Cascade Books, 2011), 99.

[31]The topics addressed not only dealt with situation ethics, character, the narrative character of the self, abortion, death, children with mental disabilities, but also had chapters on Yoder, democratic theory, and what I can only describe as an attempt at theological journalism dealing with 60s. *Truthfulness and Tragedy* (Notre Dame, IN: University of Notre Dame Press, 1977) and *A Community of Character* (Notre Dame, IN: University of Notre Dame Press, 1981) have different agendas but I am clearly continuing to work on the same set of issues I began in *Vision and Virtue*.

is rigorous and disciplined attention to the constraints of grammar and its life-form-shaping rules."[32]

I call attention to Ryan's way of putting the matter because, as is so often the case, he has said better than I have been able to say what I think. In particular, he rightly says I learned from Wittgenstein that the relation of ethical deliberation to action is not external but internal and from Aristotle I learned to name this internal relation "character."[33] Interestingly enough, this meant I could not begin trying to do Christian ethics from a general anthropology. As Ryan observes, to do so would betray "the connection of Christian agency with the character-shaping language that sustains it, as well as deceptively imply that we can do ethics without language."[34]

Ryan's characterization of the essential presumption about agency in my early work nicely suggests that, though I was not explicitly trying to do theology as an exercise in practical reason, in fact, that is what I was doing. Moreover, that was the essential move that made me a theologian. I might have preferred to stay identified as an ethicist: that is, as someone in the field of ethics who entered the field because they did not want to have to attend to fundamental theological claims about, for example, the Trinity. But, given how I had learned to think that descriptions are everything, I could not avoid thinking theologically.[35] If, as I would come to say, theological convictions are meant to construe the world, then it must surely be the case that how Christians intend the world is different from those who do not talk the way we talk. That does not mean Christians and non-Christians share nothing in common, but it does mean that what they may share in common must be discovered rather than assumed.

That theology became for me an exercise in practical reason meant the church became central for how the world was to be understood. If you can only act in the world you can say, then the "saying" has to come from a determinative community with the habits of speech necessary for the discernment of difference. Thus "the first task of the church is not to make the world more just but to make

---

[32]Ryan, *The Politics of Practical Reason*, 101.

[33]Ibid., 109.

[34]Ibid., 101.

[35]In a similar manner, Oliver O'Donovan emphasizes the critical role of description for ethics. In particular he rightly objects to the characterization of practical reason as prescriptive rather than descriptive because moral reasoning, as he puts it, "has a vast stake in description. It describes particular things, describes their relations and purposes, describes the way the world as a world as a whole fits together. Without this descriptive exercise, practical reason would not be reason at all." O'Donovan, *Self, World, and Time*, 11. O'Donovan's account of time and narrative for constituting our "awakening" as agents I should like to think commensurate with how I have tried to think about these matters. If there is any difference, a difference that I do not think amounts to a disagreement, between O'Donovan and me about these matters I suspect it would have to do with my stress on the importance of language for how we learn to construe the world.

the world the world." Offensive as that claim may seem, it is but a way to make clear that the "world" cannot know it is the world unless an alternative linguistic community exists. The "world" so understood remains under God's providential care but exactly what makes it the world is the inability to acknowledge and worship the source of all that is.

This fundamental eschatological understanding of existence entails, or better, demands, that the church makes the world, which includes us, capable of being storied.[36] We are contingent creatures and we exist contingently. To say we are contingent beings is but a way to say we are creatures who did not have to exist but who do exist. The very description, "creature," is itself a story that provides a truthful account of our lives. One of the tasks of theology is to help us discern how our lives may be possessed by unacknowledged stories that make our ability to live in gratitude for the gift of our existence impossible. Worship is crucial for such discernment.

It was, of course, the work of Karl Barth and John Howard Yoder that gave me the resources necessary to emphasize the centrality of the church for discerning the challenges facing Christians in our day. The general stance of the liberal Protestant establishment, particularly in America, assumed that the church was an agent to make democracy work. In the name of being tolerant such a view presumed that Christians must find a way to engage the ethical and political challenges using language that was not specifically Christian. From my perspective, that was to give away the store.

My criticism of "liberalism" has not primarily been directed at "liberals," but rather at Christians who assume that our fundamental linguistic habits can be translated into the idiom of liberalism. My worry about that strategy is not only that in the process Christians lose the significance of the church as a political reality, but that they lose the story that shapes how Christians intend the world. Thus, my perhaps too-simplistic claim that liberalism names the project of modernity to create people who have no story except the story they chose when they had no story. That story reflects, as I suggested above, a view of rationality that cannot help but distort the situated character of practical reason.

I have tried to display how practical reason will by necessity reflect a determinative narrative by trying to show the connections between the gospel and everyday practices such as marriage, the birth and care of children, the commitment to the ill, being present to the dying, the demands of friendship, the disavowal of violence, the challenge of those physically and mentally disabled, the refusal to lie, and the refusal to abandon the poor. I have done so in the hope that

---

[36]For a fuller account of my understanding of the eschatological character of Christian theology and ethics see Stanley Hauerwas, *Approaching the End: Eschatological Reflections on Church, Politics, and Life* (Grand Rapids, MI: Eerdmans, 2013).

the worship of God is seen as constitutive of a way of life that would otherwise be unintelligible if in fact the God we worship does not exist. Ryan characterizes this aspect of "my method" as the employment of narrative in a manner that bridges rather than divides our reflective lives and our practical lives by showing how practical reason is no less rational for being particular and embodied.[37]

In effect "my method" is to show how theological language in good working order reframes what we take to be necessities by helping us see that who we are makes all the difference. For example, the justification of violence is often shaped by the assumption that in some situations there is no alternative to violence. That we must resort to violence can, therefore, be justified as a lesser of two evils. But the very existence of a people schooled by the gospel should make possible, even if it means they must suffer and die, the reality of an alternative to the assumed necessity of violence. The creation of such an alternative at least begins with a people who have learned to say "no." That "no" may well be the exemplification of Garver's understanding of what an ethical surplus looks like.

A theology so conceived may find that from time to time it is impossible to avoid polemics. If, as Taylor suggests, practical reason is an exercise in *ad hominem* argument, it is not surprising that the work of theology will involve polemics. The identification and location of enemies, which often entails our ability of self-recognition, is an ongoing task. The world does not want the presumption that it is intelligible without God challenged. So the Christian theologian cannot help but come into conflict with established conventions because the fundamental presuppositions that sustain the everyday are often at odds with the narrative Christians believe is true—that is, God was in Christ so that the world might be saved.

Finally, I discovered that the work of theology could not be separated from the friendships constitutive of the task itself. In particular, friendship with graduate students has been crucial for the way I have done theology. Graduate students are not only smarter than I am, but more importantly, graduate students bring with them reading habits that constantly force me to "catch up." By being forced to catch up I've learned better how to think once Foucault, for example, had been read. A reminder that reading, as I suggested above, is a form of practical reason just to the extent the reader is able to recognize an argument or a remark that is significant because of what a friend, which may be a book, has taught them.

If I were to give any final comment on how I think I learned to think theologically it would be that, through the work of theology, I have discovered friends I did not know I had. For what more could anyone ask?

Duke Divinity School
Durham, North Carolina

---

[37]Ryan, *The Politics of Practical Reason*, 125.

The Thomism of Alasdair MacIntyre: Which Ethics? Which Epistemology?

Christophe Rouard

Abstract. This article studies the Thomism of Alasdair MacIntyre. On the ethical level, it highlights the importance of the thesis of the unity of the virtues in the philosopher's work. This thesis is linked to an underlying epistemology the article clarifies. The God of the *Prima Pars* constitutes the Archimedean point of that epistemology, which the distinctions made in the *De Veritate* and *De Ente and Essentia* explain philosophically. This epistemology is at the heart of MacIntyrean thought, which is opposed in that to Hilary Putnam, an important foil in his work. The article shows how. It presents the way in which Alasdair MacIntyre moves beyond the internalist impasse while honoring the relativity of all rational investigation. It likens his thought to that of Charles Sanders Peirce while shedding light on the Thomistic specificity of the MacIntyrean theory of truth. It positions Alasdair MacIntyre's work within the context of contemporary Thomism.

I.

Introduction. On the publication of MacIntyre's *Three Rival Versions of Moral Enquiry*, Richard Rorty wrote that, in his book, Alasdair MacIntyre offers "the most persuasive recent restatement of the Thomist position on the relation of metaphysics to morality."[1] In many respects, MacIntyre appears as one of the most listened to representatives of the Thomist school today. The goal of this article is to understand MacIntyrean Thomism.

Between 1984 and 1987, MacIntyre's philosophy gradually drew nearer to Thomas Aquinas's. By late 1984, a change of tone can clearly be perceived. "Does Applied Ethics Rest on a Mistake?,"[2] published in October 1984, already evidences a degree of sympathy for Aquinas. In 1985, the rapprochement grew.

---

[1] Richard Rorty, in Alasdair MacIntyre, *Three Rival Versions of Moral Enquiry: Encyclopaedia, Genealogy and Tradition* (Notre Dame, IN: University of Notre Dame Press, 1990), back cover page.

[2] Alasdair MacIntyre, "Does Applied Ethics Rest on a Mistake?," *The Monist* 67 (1984): 498–513.

©2014, *American Catholic Philosophical Quarterly*, Vol. 88, No. 4   pp. 659–684
doi: 10.5840/acpq201492535

The review of Slote's work *Goods and Virtues*[3] written for the April 1985 issue of *Faith and Philosophy* testifies to his high regard for Thomas. In "Which God Ought we to Obey and Why?,"[4] published in the October 1986 issue of the same review, he is granted a place of choice. He is cited not only as an author of reference, but also as a thinker who brought discriminative and determinant elements to reflection. In that text MacIntyre seems to profess allegiance to Aquinas for the first time. In *Whose Justice? Which Rationality?*,[5] which appeared in 1988, but whose foreword, usually written after the corpus of a text, dates to April 1987, MacIntyre openly presents himself as a disciple of Thomas Aquinas.

Why? Antonio Allegra and John Haldane have reproached MacIntyre's thought for its lack of foundation. For Allegra,[6] it should have been founded not on the concept of narrativity but on a more radical ontology. For Haldane, MacIntyre's historicist version of Thomism should be supplemented by complementary work devoted to the development of certain metaphysical theses, "perhaps under the title *The Truth in Thomism*, or more generally, *The Requirements of Truth*."[7] For a time MacIntyre considered writing a work on truth and truthfulness: he spoke of it in an interview granted to Dmitri Nikulin, published in 1996,[8] but abandoned the project.[9]

Allegra's and Haldane's criticisms point towards essentials. But neither of them has seen that what is decisive in MacIntyre's intellectual evolution is precisely the progressive development of a science of foundations dealing with concepts like truth, the nature of the human being, and other questions of a metaphysical sort. Kent Reames, for his part, understood that:

> One way of stating the continuity among MacIntyre's work is that throughout he has been trying to be clear about the relationship of universality to particularity: the universality of the claim to truth, and the particularity of the person making the claim. . . . On my reading,

---

[3]Alasdair MacIntyre, "Review of *Goods and Virtues* by Michael Slote," *Faith and Philosophy* 2 (1985): 204–7.

[4]Alasdair MacIntyre, "Which God Ought We to Obey, and Why?," *Faith and Philosophy* 3 (1986): 359–71.

[5]Alasdair MacIntyre, *Whose Justice? Which Rationality?* (Notre Dame, IN: University of Notre Dame Press, 1988).

[6]See Antonio Allegra, "Nietzsche, Kuhn e San Tommaso: le Incertezze di Alasdair MacIntyre," *Rivista di Filosofia Neo-Scolastica* 89 (1997): 48–81.

[7]John Haldane, "MacIntyre's Thomist Revival: What Next?," in *After MacIntyre: Critical Perspectives on the Work of Alasdair MacIntyre*, ed. John Horton and Susan Mendus (Notre Dame, IN: University of Notre Dame Press, 1994): 91–107, at 92.

[8]See Dmitri Nikulin, "Wahre Selbsterkenntnis Durch Verstehen unserer Selbst aus der Perspektive Anderer: Interview von Alasdair MacIntyre," *Deutsche Zeitschrift für Philosophie* 44 (1996): 671–83, at 682–3.

[9]Alasdair MacIntyre, personal correspondence, December 8, 2006.

his writings from *After Virtue* through *First Principles* are continuous in affirming the former claim and denying the latter; the works differ only on the relative *stress* laid on the affirmation and the denial. *After Virtue* concentrates nearly all its energies on the denial; the affirmation is mostly implicit, and is made explicit in the "Postscript" to the second edition, where MacIntyre argues that a moral scheme that has survived many comparisons with rival formulations of morality gives us "the best possible reason to have confidence that the future challenges will also be met successfully, that the principles which define the core of [the] moral scheme are enduring principles." But apart from that hint, *After Virtue* gives no specification of the meaning of the enduringness of such principles, or the sense in which they can be called "true." That is rectified in *Whose Justice? Which Rationality?*, in which MacIntyre argues that traditions that successfully resolve epistemic crises are thereby enabled to make claims to truth understood as correspondence to reality. Similarly, in *Three Rival Versions*, he argues that a person like Aquinas who stands in two traditions at once, *must* understand truth as correspondence to reality; the insufficiency of mere warranted assertibility as an account of truth is obvious to such a person. It is thus not a new development in MacIntyre's thought when *FP* argues for an understanding of truth as the mind's correspondence to reality.[10]

The reasons why MacIntyre came to profess allegiance to Thomas Aquinas are best sought in the light of these broad rational investigations into the subject of foundations. In this respect, there is a profound continuity in his mature work. The discontinuity which occurred when he moved from Aristotle to Thomas should be understood as a deepening and progress in the continuous narrative he has been engaged in ever since *After Virtue*, a deepening which has led him to anchor his moral philosophy in a science of foundations of a metaphysical sort. At this crucial moment of his intellectual history, MacIntyre has thus himself lived what he thematizes in his texts in presenting rational investigation as a narrative that progresses in enlarging itself so as to be able to overcome difficulties encountered.

II.

Which Ethics? What difficulties led MacIntyre to pass from Aristotle to Thomas? What was his epistemological crisis? In *After Virtue*,[11] Thomas is only

---

[10]Kent Reames, "Metaphysics, History, and Moral Philosophy: the Centrality of the 1990 Aquinas Lecture to MacIntyre's Argument for Thomism," *The Thomist* 62 (1998): 419–43, at 430–1.

[11]Alasdair MacIntyre, *After Virtue* (Notre Dame, IN: University of Notre Dame Press, 1984).

662 AMERICAN CATHOLIC PHILOSOPHICAL QUARTERLY

one medieval thinker among many others, whose options are rather feature-less moments in a narrative spanning the entire Middle Ages, and he is even regarded as atypical within that tradition. In *Whose Justice? Which Rationality?*, MacIntyre honors Thomas Aquinas's success and confers on the reconciler of Aristotle and Augustine the title of the best thinker of practical rationality and the moral life until now. And, Christopher Thompson notes, "from the vantage point of the Thomistic tradition, the Christian revelation complemented the Aristotelian enquiry by supplying a more adequate characterization of the nature of the end of practical rationality. It had also (principally through the efforts of St. Augustine) reformulated the process by which one achieves that end."[12] An integration of the Aristotelian and Augustinian traditions was thus accomplished through a re-evaluation of two concepts key to the theory of virtues developed in *After Virtue* in Aristotelian terms: the *telos* and goods internal to practice. The *telos* is now a hereafter. For Aristotle, beatitude is a divine ideal that men only espouse to the extent they can humanly here below. Thomas is rather talk-ing about the beatific vision in the hereafter, to which men are called. As for goods internal to practice, for Aquinas they are accomplished by a will which knows that it is fundamentally badly oriented, even if it is very well informed. This double finitude is at the centre of the narrative pursued in *Whose Justice? Which Rationality?*

We are greatly indebted to Augustine for our understanding of the second finitude. There is a fundamentally dramatic dimension in Augustinian thought, due to the fact that the human individual is profoundly inhabited by a will in-clined towards evil. Aristotle never imagined that dramatic condition. Augustine lived through it and thematized it, while Thomas embraced it wholeheartedly. In so doing, he was more realistic about man than Aristotle. This Augustinian, dramatic contribution provides his thought a greater degree of realism, and for the author of *Whose Justice? Which Rationality?* is one of its strengths. MacIntyre's allegiance to Thomas is to be explained in terms of a realistic criterion. On this subject, Thompson offers a quite beautiful formula on the tribunal of reality. Thompson underlines that, at the time MacIntyre wrote *Whose Justice? Which Rationality?*, MacIntyre believed "all traditions of enquiry must submit their theses to the tribunal of reality. It is the untameable character of *esse* which pre-vents any tradition from exercising a hegemony on truth. Reality will inevitably rear its ugly head in defiance of any inadequate conception of it."[13]

The *telos* of human life's being displaced towards the hereafter and the hu-man will's being discovered to be inclined to evil results in the understanding

---

[12]Christopher S. Thompson, "Benedict, Thomas, or Augustine? The Character of MacIntyre's Narrative," *The Thomist* 59 (1995): 379–407, at 395.

[13]Ibid., 402.

of practical rationality being decentred from man. A sort of wound has been inflicted on human pride, which called for a decentring and a greater dependence on grace. It is grace that obtains charity, which ultimately allows the practice of justice. MacIntyre explains this in *Whose Justice? Which Rationality?*:

> The central human experience of the natural law . . . is of our inability to live by it; and what we know of justice as or more often finds application in its flouting and disregard as in its observance. Hence it is . . . no accident that the discussion of law in Aquinas in the *Prima Secundae* leads straight into the treatment of grace, the only remedy for disobedience to law, and that the account of the natural virtues in the *Secunda Secundae* had to have as its prologue an inquiry into the supernatural virtues. For just as and because justice is continually the victim of the vice and sin of pride, so justice cannot flourish, cannot indeed, so it turns out, even exist as a natural virtue, unless and insofar as it is informed by the supernatural virtue of *caritas*. Charity is the form of all virtues; without charity the virtues would lack the specific kind of directedness which they require. And charity is not to be acquired by moral education; it is a gift of grace.[14]

Hence, the following question arises: should we maintain the Aristotelian and/ or Thomistic thesis of the unity of the virtues? In *After Virtue*, MacIntyre reproached Aquinas for his thesis on the unity of the virtues. He clearly set that reproach aside in his second masterwork where, already in its short foreword,[15] he devotes a whole paragraph to setting his earlier critique aside. This evolution is capital in his thought and his work. Christopher Lutz explains this in his study on tradition in MacIntyre's ethical philosophy. The thesis of the unity of the virtues is at the heart of the enunciation of the moral philosophies of Aristotle and Thomas. They are integrally constructed so as to promote good and avoid evil. Now the unity of the virtues necessarily serves that end. Without unity, one cannot attain that end. Rejection of the thesis of the unity of the virtues in *After Virtue* is, hence, rather problematical. It amounted to "a rejection of the Aristotelian practical syllogism that MacIntyre wanted to recover in *After Virtue* because it separates prudent reasoning from virtuous action."[16] It also evacuates all substantial moral content discriminating the virtues, "reducing them to enabling qualities."[17] Detached from the virtue of prudence, which is their compass, the other virtues are disoriented and denatured, so that one might end up interpreting a murder as an act of courage.

---

[14]See MacIntyre, *Whose Justice? Which Rationality?*, 205.

[15]Ibid., x.

[16]Christopher Stephen Lutz, *Tradition in the Ethics of Alasdair MacIntyre: Relativism, Thomism, and Philosophy* (Lanham, MD: Lexington Books, 2004), 100.

[17]Ibid.

In this respect, it is highly significant that in the two editions of *After Virtue*, MacIntyre admits the possibility of bad practices. This passage is very revealing:

> I want to allow that there *may* be some practices—in the sense in which I understand the concept—which simply are evil. . . . I do have to allow that courage sometimes sustains injustice, that loyalty has been known to strengthen a murderous aggressor and that generosity has sometimes weakened the capacity to the good. . . . That the virtues need initially to be defined and explained in reference to the notion of a practice thus in no way entails approval of all practices in all circumstances.[18]

Consequently, "the definition of virtue in *After Virtue* truly falls prey to charges of relativism."[19] The height of irony for its author, who began his work in diagnosing the impasse the contemporary world has fallen into: a diffraction of sense due to the coexistence of multiple irreconcilable positions with no apparent criterion of discernment, a situation confining us to relativism in the area of ethics. Lutz sees major consequences in MacIntyre's rehabilitation of the thesis of the unity of the virtues. "The unity of virtue makes it possible to invoke a distinction between real and apparent virtues that can overcome the relativism of MacIntyre's definition of virtue in terms of practices, and render practices and virtues amenable to fruitful moral criticism. Once the unity of virtues is recognized, the content of the virtues becomes objective (even if that content is not fully understood), and two limitations on what can count as practices arise that render the rest of the *After Virtue* account of practice and virtue serviceable."[20] The first limitation is that no authentic practice can be intrinsically bad. The second is that the virtues will never support bad practices. Objectivity in ethics is saved. The truth of moral action can be advanced with coherence in the face of a diffraction of sense, which plunges the contemporary world into coerced indecision.

Moreover, Thomas's broadening of the Aristotelian thesis of the unity of the virtues to include the Christian virtue of charity lets him account for the possibility of man's attaining his supernatural end in the hereafter, towards which the Augustinian contribution displaced the moral action's centre of gravity, a decentring MacIntyre has taken fully into account. Aquinas explains this in his *Summa Theologica*:

> In so far as [human works] produce good works in proportion to a supernatural last end, thus they have the character of virtue, truly and perfectly; and cannot be acquired by human acts, but are infused by

---

[18]MacIntyre, *After Virtue*, 200.
[19]Lutz, *Tradition in the Ethics of Alasdair MacIntyre*, 99.
[20]Ibid., 102.

God. Such like moral virtues cannot be without charity. For it has been stated above (A. 1; Q. 58, AA. 4, 5) that the other moral virtues cannot be without prudence; and that prudence cannot be without the moral virtues, because these latter make man well disposed to certain ends, which are the starting-point of the procedure of prudence. Now for prudence to proceed aright, it is much more necessary that man be well disposed towards his ultimate end, which is the effect of charity, than that he be well disposed in respect of other ends, which is the effect of moral virtue. . . . It is therefore evident that neither can infused prudence be without charity; nor, consequently, the other moral virtues, since they cannot be without prudence.[21]

In rehabilitating the Aristotelian and Thomistic thesis of the unity of the virtues, MacIntyre made a major correction in his work. That correction avoided his falling into the fatal inconsistency of encouraging a theory of the virtues, which would have been confined to relativism, which would have represented a complete failure for him. Thanks to the thesis of the unity of the virtues, he has been able to answer the question whose justice? which rationality? in his manner . . . and continue his work.

III.

Which Epistemology? If grace, which begets charity, ultimately allows the practice of justice, a God of a certain type is required to account for practical reason. This leads us to consider another major change between *After Virtue* and *Whose Justice? Which Rationality?*. In the second work a metaphysical and even theological dimension appears in the argumentation, a dimension absent in the first. In *After Virtue*, MacIntyre willingly does without any metaphysical or theological references. He rejects Aristotle's metaphysical biology. He even rejects any teleology of nature. In *Whose Justice? Which Rationality?*, he consistently founds his moral theory above all on the narrative strength of a tradition. But metaphysics and theology intervene within the narrative argument—which remains primary. They are present as domains wherein a tradition can show its strength and find new paradigms, which enable it to overcome the epistemological crises it may encounter and testify to its relevance and its perenniality vis-à-vis the difficulties it must inevitably confront. In *Whose Justice? Which Rationality?*, metaphysics and theology have an unquestionable importance and the passage from Aristotle to Thomas is in part played out on their level.

In regard to what? For Aristotle, God is the unmoved mover and the metaphysical theology which serves as a framework for the moral enterprise ensures

---

[21]Aquinas, *ST* I-II, q. 65, a. 2.

a certain order of the world, of the cosmos. For Thomas, we are dealing with another God. MacIntyre does not go into too much detail concerning that God. We know that it is a God who gives grace, the supernatural virtue allowing us do right, a God who is such that, to practice justice, we have to believe in his existence and goodness, a God who identifies himself with Justice . . . a God who, all things said, is as Thomas describes him in the *Prima Pars* of his *Summa Theologica*. In *Whose Justice? Which Rationality?*, MacIntyre clearly establishes the link between his conception of ethics and the God of the *Prima Pars*.

> On Aquinas's view religion is a moral virtue, being that part of the car-
> dinal virtue of justice concerned with what we owe to God in the way of
> honor, reverence, and worship. Since perfected obedience to the natural
> law requires the virtue of justice in full measure (*ST* IIa-IIae, 79, 1), it
> is difficult to understand how someone who did not believe that God is
> and that his attributes make him worthy of honor, reverence, and worship
> could be perfectly obedient to the natural law. It is then important to my
> interpretation of Aquinas's positions that I understand his positions on
> practical knowledge and practical reasoning, let alone those on justice, as
> always presupposing the type of rational knowledge of God exemplified
> in the conclusions of the *Prima Pars*.[22]

That link appears for the first time in MacIntyre's work in his 1986 article *Which God Ought We to Obey and Why?* In that text, the God of Thomas, Creator and Judge, is considered superior to Aristotle's, which implies a re-evaluation of the conception of justice, the passage "from a conception of that type of human life which is the good and the best as consisting in the life of the political virtues, supplemented in its later stages by the contemplation of the Unmoved Mover, to a conception of it as consisting in rational friendship and therefore ultimately in friendship with God,"[23] the passage from Aristotle to Thomas.

This passage from one God to another is of capital importance in MacIntyre's intellectual history. It provides an interpretational key to a correct reading of his work, and particularly, his moral philosophy. More than one commentator has rightly underlined the bond that exists for him between practical reason and knowledge of the God of Thomas. For Joan Franks, what, in the Aristotelian moral tradition and particularly in its medieval and modern versions, guarantees moral objectivity is "confidence in the existence of God, one of whose functions is to provide accessibility to the moral order of the universe through the natural law,"[24] and, more than anyone else, it is Thomas Aquinas who is responsible for

---

[22]MacIntyre, *Whose Justice? Which Rationality?*, 188.

[23]MacIntyre, "Which God Ought We to Obey, and Why?," 369.

[24]Joan M. Franks, "Aristotle or Nietzsche?," *Listening: Journal of Religion and Culture* 26 (1991): 156–63, at 160.

the extension of the Aristotelian moral scheme needed for this divine function, "confronting and reconciling, as MacIntyre so ably notes, the Aristotelian and Augustinian traditions."[25]

This extension implies a new theology, rich in a new doctrine: that of a Christian creator God. Thompson observes that for MacIntyre "to grasp truly what is, is to grasp at the same time what it is to be a responsible creature within the drama of the created order. It is in the theology of the good creation that one finds the conditions of our moral enquiry."[26] The development of the argumentation carried out in *Three Rival Versions of Moral Enquiry* owes much to Augustinian creation theology, which provides an essential bond between the MacIntyrean option for Thomist realism and the narrative quality of the moral experience.

Thomas Hibbs has studied this new understanding of the relationships between man and God in the work of MacIntyre with great acuity. In his article entitled "MacIntyre, Tradition, and the Christian Philosopher," he offers some clarifications on the role of certain distinctions made by Thomas in the *De Ente et Essentia*:

> In the theoretical sphere, there is the teaching of the *De Ente et Essentia*, which MacIntyre rightly perceives as a seminal text. In it, Thomas provides a metaphysical and logical analysis of the terms *ens* et *essentia*. In so doing, he articulates the logical and metaphysical bases of the analogy between created and uncreated being. These teachings, which pervade Thomas's corpus, enable him to resolve the conflict between the traditions of Augustine and Aristotle through contextualization, subordination, and mutual qualification.[27]

In another article, "MacIntyre's Postmodern Thomism: Reflections on *Three Rival Versions of Moral Enquiry*," Hibbs is particularly insightful on the importance of MacIntyre's references to the *De Ente et Essentia* and *De Veritate*. He draws attention to the fact that in *Whose Justice? Which Rationality?*, resolution of the conflict between Aristotelianism and Augustinianism involves a new conception of truth, intimately bound to the doctrine of creation. In this way, Hibbs establishes the link between Aquinas's two treatises:

> In *Whose Justice? Which Rationality?*, MacIntyre argued that the conflict "could be resolved on the basis of a systematic conception of truth which enabled Aristotelian and Augustinian theses to be reformulated within one

---

[25] Ibid.

[26] Thompson, "Benedict, Thomas, or Augustine?," 407.

[27] Thomas S Hibbs, "MacIntyre, Tradition, and the Christian Philosopher," *Modern Schoolman* 68 (1991): 211–23, at 222.

and the same framework" (*WJWR*, 171). MacIntyre thinks that Aquinas developed the systematic conception of truth in the *De Ente* and the *De Veritate*. In these texts, Thomas provides an analysis of the causal and analogical relationships between key terms such as "truth" and "true," "being" and "essence." Behind these relationships stands the Christian doctrine of creation.[28]

This clarification sheds light on the architecture of MacIntyre's thought, thoroughly structured by the Christian doctrine of creation at its very core. On a philosophical level, the distinctions made in the *De Ente* and *De Veritate* explain that doctrine, around which his thought is articulated. That is why he refers to them so regularly in citing them as key texts for him, as in this extract from *Whose Justice? Which Rationality?*, where he discusses the role of distinctions made in Thomas's two treatises:

> But given my present purposes, it is impossible to avoid taking note of the function of those distinctions in enabling Aquinas to give an account of that reality by reference to which the terminus of all intellectually adequate explanation and understanding, whether theoretical or practical, has to be specified and in relation to which the ordering of all subordinate explanation and understanding has to be carried through. That reality, providing, as it does, the terminus for all understanding *ex hypothesi*, cannot itself be explained in respect of its nature and characteristics by anything beyond itself. Nothing can make it be other than what it is; necessarily, therefore, it is whatever it is and in the necessity of its being and action contrasts with the contingency of all other being or action. So it has to furnish the final *telos* for other beings in respect of their final causality.[29]

The role of the distinctions made in the *De Ente* and *De Veritate* is to explain the reality which is on the horizon of all intellectual activity, whether it be theoretical or practical, and in relation to which any attempt to give meaning must be made. That reality, for Thomas, is none other than God, the God of creation. How do these distinctions play their role? What space do they designate for human intellectual activity?

Let us study these distinctions more closely. The best way of proceeding in this is to study the question of truth, which MacIntyre dealt with much more than that of being. In *Three Rival Versions of Moral Enquiry*, important specifications are provided on the Thomistic theory of truth. MacIntyre has more to say here than elsewhere on how Aquinas synthesizes the Aristotelian and Augustinian

---

[28]Thomas S. Hibbs, "MacIntyre's Postmodern Thomism: Reflections on *Three Rival Versions of Moral Enquiry*," *The Thomist* 57 (1993): 277–97, at 286–7.

[29]MacIntyre, *Whose Justice? Which Rationality?*, 171.

theories in his analogical theory of truth. Aristotle, he explains, locates truth in the relation between the mind and its objects. Augustine distinguishes *veritas* from what is *verum*, and identifies *veritas* with God. He thus locates truth "in the source of the relationship of finite objects to that truth which is God."[30] In the *De Veritate* and *De Ente et Essentia*, Thomas synthesizes these two positions in a new theory.

> Both the questions *De Veritate* and *De Ente et Essentia* are philosophical dictionaries in which in the one case the various uses of "true" and "truth" are spelled out and related both to each other and to other key terms, and in the other, similarly, the various uses of "being" and "essence." In both works there is an underlying recognition not only that each of these sets of uses is related analogically, but that there is a primary application of each and that it is to God. It is from God as truth, *veritas*, that all other "truths" and "trues" flow; it is from God as being, *esse*, that all that is, insofar as it is, derives. But it is from the derivative that *we* have to begin. So in coming to understand the ordering of each being and each truth or true towards that which is first in being and first in truth, we reverse and retrace the causal order by which they were generated. To understand the analogical relationships is also, so it will turn out, to understand both the causal relationships in terms of which the present states and changes of all finite beings are made intelligible and the practical relationships through which and by means of which all finite beings move towards their perfected end. So finite beings are made intelligible, both as moved and as moving, and the structures through which they are made thus intelligible are those which in a variety of aspects relate all beings to their first cause as unmoved mover, itself not further determined or determinable by anything else.[31]

Hence, Thomas distinguishes various levels of truth. It is primarily in God, and secondarily in the human intellect. It may be said to be in things, but secondarily and improperly, to the extent that things are such as they are thought by the mind making a true judgment in regard to them. This doctrine makes the divine intellect in act the proper place of truth. Thomas explains it with the following reasoning: "Even if there were no human intellects, things could be said to be true because of their relation to the divine intellect. But if, by an impossible supposition, intellect did not exist and things did continue to exist, then the essentials of truth (*ratio veritatis*) would in no way remain."[32]

---

[30]MacIntyre, *Three Rival Versions of Moral Enquiry*, 110.
[31]Ibid., 122–3.
[32]Thomas Aquinas, *The Disputed Questions on Truth*, vol. I (Chicago: Henry Regnery Compagny, 1952), 11.

That shows the extent to which the divine viewpoint is essential to the definition of truth for Aquinas. That viewpoint is as it were an Archimedean point in
his conception of truth. It is he who authorized its realist definition in terms of
adequation between intellect and thing, which MacIntyre understood quite well.

Lutz has commented on this Thomistic doctrine in pointing out that if, *a
contrario*, "there were no God, but human intellects existed, as many contemporary thinkers hold, then according to Thomas Aquinas, things would have no
ontological truth *per se*."[33] MacIntyre is particularly sensitive to this. He indicates
that without this reference to God, the realism of truth fades, and with that
the possibility of discriminating between various rival traditions disputing their
pretensions to truth. Deprived of that absolute reference, truth must finally be
understood in the internalist terms of the possibility of justified assertion, as
it notably is by Hilary Putnam, a privileged interlocutor in MacIntyre's work.

A fundamental antagonism exists between MacIntyre and Putnam. Hence
the comparison of the two contemporary philosophers that I shall now undertake should consequently prove enlightening for understanding MacIntyrean
Thomism. It will enable us to grasp why, for MacIntyre, "it is from God as truth,
veritas, that all other "truths" and "trues" flow; it is from God as being, *esse*, that
all that is, insofar as it is, derives. But it is from the derivative that *we* have to
begin"[34], so as to attain the goal that the distinctions made in *De Ente* and *De
Veritate* are designed to reveal.

As Crispin Wright noted in 2000, Putnam's philosophy is characterized by
two major changes of opinion: the passage from the first—semantic—realism
"to the 'internalism' of the late 1970's and 1980's, and then, in the last decade,
back to a qualified—'common-sense' or 'natural'—realism supposedly innocent
of the objectionable features against which internalism had justly reacted."[35]
MacIntyre initially reacted to Putnam's first realism in the 1970s. He did so in
his important 1978 contribution to the Hastings Centre Studies "Objectivity
in Morality and Objectivity in Science."[36] In that essay, MacIntyre resolutely
distanced himself from Putnam's semantic realism for reasons that already reveal a
desire to overcome the semantic perspective in advocating a more robust realism.

In the 1980s, the opposition grew keener. The author of *After Virtue* measured himself against the internal realism of Putnam who, in *Reason, Truth and*

---

[33]Lutz, *Tradition in the Ethics of Alasdair MacIntyre*, 123.

[34]MacIntyre, *Three Rival Versions of Moral Enquiry*, 122.

[35]Crispin Wright, "Truth as Sort of Epistemic: Putnam's Peregrinations," *The Journal of
Philosophy* 97 (2000): 335–64, at 335.

[36]Alasdair MacIntyre, "Objectivity in Philosophy and Objectivity in Science," in *Morals,
Science and Sociality*, ed. Tristram Engelhardt Jr. and Daniel Callahan (New York: The Hastings
Center, 1978), 21–39.

History (1981), distinguished two radically opposed viewpoints on truth. The viewpoint Putnam calls externalist is that of metaphysical realism, holding that the world consists of a fixed ensemble of objects independent of mind, and that there exists only one true description of how the world is made, and that truth is a kind of correspondence relation between words or symbols of thoughts and things or ensembles of external objects. That point of view prefers to adopt a perspective amounting to God's point of view. The internalist viewpoint maintains that the question, "what objects is the world made of?" only makes sense within a theory or description. It can lead to a pluralism in the area of true conceptions of the world:

> "Truth," in an internalist view, is some sort of (idealized) rational acceptability—some sort of ideal coherence of our beliefs with each other and with our experiences as those experiences are themselves represented in our belief system—and not correspondence with mind-independent or discourse-independent "states of affairs." There is no God's Eye point of view that we can know or usefully imagine; there are only the various interests and purposes that their descriptions and theories subserve.[37]

The first text to be cited there is *Whose Justice? Which Rationality?*, where Putnam intervenes in the chapter devoted to Thomas Aquinas's overcoming the inter-tradition conflict between Aristotelianism and Augustinianism. As MacIntyre explains there, should one refuse reference to a reality external to our conceptual and belief systems, as Hegel, Green, and Putnam do, one falls into an internalism such that truth is, so to speak, never again understood, in practice and rather often in theory too, other than in terms of the idealization of the concept of rational assertability. "For on this view we can have no criterion of truth beyond the best warrants that we can offer for our assertions."[38]

Subsequent reference to Putnam appears in MacIntyre's *First Principles, Final Ends and Contemporary Philosophical Issues*. There Putnam is likened to Jacques Derrida. The latter is presented as the contemporary philosopher who most clearly incarnates rejection of the concepts of first principles and final ends that MacIntyre wants to restore to honour, concepts that he considers being at the foundations of the teleological, metaphysical narrative deployed in the Aristotelian-Thomistic tradition. For Derrida, admitting those concepts would be admitting realities outside speech, which Derrida denies, declaring that there is nothing outside the text. "Notice," MacIntyre comments, "the instructive resemblances between Derrida's denials and Hilary Putnam's attacks on what

---

[37]Hilary Putnam, *Reason, Truth and History* (Cambridge: Cambridge University Press, 1981), 49–50.
[38]MacIntyre, *Whose Justice? Which Rationality?*, 169.

he calls external or metaphysical realism."[39] Indeed, both of them emancipate themselves from reference to an exterior real so dear to Aristotelian-Thomistic metaphysical realism.

In the important "Moral Relativism, Truth and Justification," MacIntyre again distances himself from Putnam's internal realism. To understand the practices of rational justification, we must, MacIntyre argues, understand them as belonging to the ensemble of human activities which tend towards truth. When these practices are systematically organized in the context of long traditions of rational investigation, as is notably the case in the sciences, "their goal-directedness towards what is more and other than any particular form of rational justification is all the more evident."[40] In his *Metaphysics*, Aristotle expresses this teleological character of rational investigation, altogether focussed towards its *telos*, which is none other than truth. When rational investigation is completed—meaning, when truth is attained—the investigator then sees clearly that certain assertions justified in a particular context no longer are in the light of truth. And here Aristotelian metaphysics appears as the alternative to Putnam's internalism. This metaphysics is presented as expressing the teleology proper to the rational investigation which underlies the MacIntyrean conception of truth as a principle of intelligibility.

Putnam is cited again in the essay "Philosophy Recalled to its Task," first published in 2006 in *The Tasks of Philosophy*. This occurs in a passage where MacIntyre opposes the anti-metaphysical and antirealist perspectives of many contemporary philosophical schools to Thomas Aquinas's. The task of re-categorization and re-conceptualization carried out with a view to obtaining more adequate categorical and conceptual plans and judgments, he argues, leads us to recognize that categorized and conceptualized realities remain the same realities and exist independently of our categories and concepts. Thus, Thomistic Realism has an irrefutable answer for an antirealism of Putnam's type. Further along, allusion to Putnam can still be discerned when MacIntyre underlines the fact that the teleological character of rational investigation is related to man's very nature, and is only understandable if we make reference to God as the first and final cause. Hence we are dealing with a "God's eye view of things,"[41] recalling Putnam's well known God's Eye point of view.

---

[39]Alasdair MacIntyre, *First Principles, Final Ends and Contemporary Philosophical Issues* (Milwaukee: Marquette University Press, 1990), 19.

[40]Alasdair MacIntyre, "Moral Relativism, Truth and Justification," in *Moral Truth and Moral Tradition: Essays in Honour of Peter Geach and Elizabeth Anscombe*, ed. Luke Gormally (Dublin: Four Courts Press, 1994), 6–25. Reproduced in MacIntyre, *The Tasks of Philosophy* (Cambridge: Cambridge University Press, 2006): 52–73, at 58.

[41]Alasdair MacIntyre, "Philosophy Recalled to its Tasks: a Thomistic Reading of *Fides et Ratio*," in *The Tasks of Philosophy*, 179–96, at 191.

Thus there is a profound continuity in MacIntyre's defense of metaphysical realism against the Putnamian tendency to challenge any such realism. MacIntyre does not seem to have considered the turn taken by Putnam after 1990. That is because, for him, it is the second Putnam who has the appearance of playing a watchdog role in the world of contemporary philosophy in presenting his own conception of truth.

In the Putnamian critique of MacIntyre's thought, the difference between the attitude criticized by Putnam and MacIntyre's actual position is subtle—and rather revealing. Timothy Mosteller devoted his doctoral thesis in philosophy, defended at the University of Miami in 2002 and published in 2006, to the question of relativism in contemporary American philosophy, based on a comparative study of the works of MacIntyre, Putnam, and Rorty.[42] He isolates three texts[43] where Putnam addresses critical remarks to MacIntyre. Three criticisms are expressed in a rather cursory fashion on the occasion of developments which do not primarily relate to MacIntyre's philosophy as such, but which are no less rich in information.

The second criticism, via comparison, gives us a better understanding of how MacIntyre conceives truth. It is formulated in an article published in 1990 and entitled "A Reconsideration of Deweyan Democracy." Therein Putnam reproaches MacIntyre for defending a philosophy of the golden age, which immunizes institutionalized oppression against criticism, and expresses two reservations as to the rationality of the MacIntyrean traditions. "First, although rationality is relative and historical (perhaps *too* relative and historical!), in MacIntyre's view, there is a fixed principle governing rational discussion *between* paradigms, which allows one paradigm to sometimes 'rationally defeat' another. It is in the application of *this* principle that MacIntyre is forced back upon what amounts to 'What Is Agreeable to [MacIntyre's] Reason.'"[44] Putnam locates the hiatus existing between his position and that of his counterpart quite accurately. Because, according to MacIntyre, there is indeed a fixed element in virtue of which discriminations can be made between rival traditions. That fixed element, which for Putnam introduces an arbitrary factor into MacIntyrean thought, is, for MacIntyre,

[42]Timothy Mosteller, *Relativism in Contemporary American Philosophy* (London-New York: Continuum, 2006).

[43]*The Many Faces of Realism. The Paul Carus Lectures* (Chicago: Open Court, 1987), 48, 50; "A Reconsideration of Deweyan Democracy," *Southern California Law Review* 63 (1990), reproduced under the chapter title "Pragmatism, Relativism, and the Justification of Democracy," in *Campus Wars. Multiculturalism and the Politics of Difference*, ed. John Arthur and Amy Shapiro (Boulder, CO: Westview Press, 1995): 264–73, at 268; *Renewing Philosophy* (Cambridge, MA: Harvard University Press, 1992), 185–6. MacIntyre responds to the third text in "Politica, Filosofia e Bene Commune," *Studi Perugini* 3 (1997): 9–30, at 29.

[44]Putnam, "Pragmatism, Relativism, and the Justification of Democracy," 268.

external reality itself, in whose light diverse traditions are measured during their respective histories, not an epistemological principle but the tribunal of reality. The second reason that Putnam cannot accept MacIntyre's position involves the question of experimentation and falsification. Based on a comparison with Charles Sanders Peirce, whom Putnam considers to be quite close to MacIntyre in certain respects, he judges that whereas Peirce honoured experimentation and falsification as unavoidable epistemological principles, MacIntyre fails to do so and reverts to what Peirce denounced as "what is agreeable to reason" but has not passed the scrutiny of experimentation and falsification. However, "Peirce's fallibilism requires that one see experimentation, in the widest sense of that term, as the decisive element in rational paradigm change."[45]

This rapprochement to Peirce is particularly fortunate. Peirce and MacIntyre are indeed quite close to one another. And the proximity between Peirce and MacIntyre is even greater, so it seems, than Putnam suspected, blatantly minimizing the importance of falsification for MacIntyre. In this way, in *First Principles, Final Ends and Contemporary Philosophical Issues*, Peirce is cited, along with Karl Popper, as one of the philosophers whose conception of the investigation's being open to falsification is compatible with a legitimate revindication of truth.[46] In the interview he granted to Giovanna Borradori, MacIntyre cites Peirce as an author from whom, had he known him earlier, he could have learned the lessons he drew in his youth from his relationship to Marxism: the importance for any theory to be maximally open to falsification.[47]

Comparing MacIntyre and Bernard Lonergan is interesting here. Michael Maxwell sheds light on differences between the two Thomists. Both are conscious of the fact that rationality is always developed in a tradition, but whereas for MacIntyre an understanding of rationality implies that the norms expressing that understanding are themselves subject to a possible re-evaluation as the Thomist tradition advances, Lonergan considers those norms, the first principles of reason, to be constitutive of the rationality of all traditions of rational investigation, trans-traditional and standard for any rational enquiry. On the contrary, "MacIntyre argues that Thomism, as an ongoing tradition of enquiry, always remains open to dialectical revision of its understanding of rationality, either through a dialectical development internal to the Thomist tradition itself or through a dialectical encounter with a competing tradition informed by a more adequate

---

[45]Ibid.

[46]See MacIntyre, *First Principles, Final Ends*, 39.

[47]See Giovanna Borradori, "Nietzsche O Aristotele?," in *Conversazioni Americane*, ed. Giovanna Borradori (Roma-Bari: Editori Laterza, 1991), 169–87. English translation reproduced in *The MacIntyre Reader*, ed. Kelvin Knight (Notre Dame, IN: University of Notre Dame Press, 1998), 255–66, at 259.

understanding of rationality (*WJ*, 172–76, 360, 364; *TRV*, 124–5)."[48] That also amounts to saying that if MacIntyre's overture to falsification is maximal, the Putnamian charge is falsified.

How exactly does MacIntyre envisage rational investigation? The September 1994 foreword MacIntyre wrote for Frederick L. Will's work appears decisive at this stage of our reflection. There MacIntyre stresses the importance of Will's essays in the context of refuting Cartesianism and hails the fact that, while rejecting Descartes, Will does not fall into the trap of abandoning the theory of truth-as-correspondence and his own realism, a trap so many have fallen into. He praises Will and places him in the wake of Peirce in terms that reveal his own proximity to Peirce: "Both in his continuing allegiance to a conception of truth as correspondence and in his use of the notion of ampliation Will has been continuing, correcting, and extending the philosophical enterprise of the greatest of all American philosophers, C. S. Peirce."[49]

Ampliation is to be distinguished from deduction by the fact that what is ampliative is social, incarnated in practice, and may sometimes only be recognized as having been used after the events, as in ampliative logic, where the norm itself may be transformed over the course of its applications to particular cases. Or, further, it may happen that one can only correctly characterize a problem whose solution was sought after application of a norm. Continuing to profess allegiance to the traditional conception of truth-as-correspondence without being deductive—like a Descartes—but rather ampliative—like Will, heir to Peirce—that is the option favoured by MacIntyre.

Distancing himself from any Cartesianism, "it is from the derivative that *we* have to begin"[50] and not some absolute perspective, his approach to the real is not the Cartesian approach Bernard Williams considered the most remarkable attempt ever at pure rational investigation. For MacIntyre, man's access to reality is always accompanied by what I will call an inevitable conceptual idiosyncrasy which he takes rigorously into account in his work. In his thought, the concept of tradition invariably coexists with that of absolute truth, the *telos* of human investigation, whose ultimate guarantor is God. This is present in germ in his work from the late 1960s on and is thematized in *Whose Justice? Which Rationality?*

In that masterwork, MacIntyre wished to underline that the mind we are talking about in connection with the traditional truth-as-correspondence theory

---

[48]Michael P. Maxwell, "A Dialectial Encounter between MacIntyre and Lonergan on the Thomistic Understanding of Rationality," *International Philosophical Quarterly* 33 (1993): 385–99, at 390.

[49]Alasdair MacIntyre, "Foreword," in Frederick L. Will, *Pragmatism and Realism*, ed. Kenneth R. Westphal (Lanham, MD: Rowman & Littlefield Publishers, 1997), ix–xii, at xi–xii.

[50]MacIntyre, *Three Rival Versions of Moral Enquiry*, 122.

is not the sort Descartes imagines. The conception of mind presupposed is not Cartesian. "It is rather of mind as activity, of mind as engaging with the natural and social world in such activities as identification, re-identification, collecting, separating, classifying, and naming and all this by touching, grasping, pointing, breaking down, building up, calling to, answering to, and so on."[51] In *First Principles, Final Ends and Contemporary Philosophical Issues* MacIntyre takes great care to distinguish Aristotelian-Thomistic epistemology from Descartes's. He cites Aristotle who considers that "'it is difficult to discern whether one knows or not' (*Posterior Analytics* I, 9, 76a26),"[52] and Aquinas who comments on the phrase in specifying the scope: "whether we know from appropriate principles, which alone is genuinely scientific knowledge (*Commentary on the Posterior Analytics*, lib. I, lect. 18),"[53] or not. Hence, adds MacIntyre, for Thomas, we can know without knowing that we know, whereas for the Cartesian, "it is always reference backwards to our starting-point that guarantees our knowledge and, hence, it is only through knowing that we know that we know. By contrast, for the Thomist our present knowledge involves reference forward to that knowledge of the *archê/principium* which will, if we achieve it, give us subsequent knowledge of the knowledge that we now have."[54] Far from the Cartesian who hopes to deduce the ensemble of his knowledge from an assured starting point, the Thomist advances in a certain clarity-obscurity. He does not know the extent to which the present bases of his knowledge are assured. He knows that they are not perfectly so. But he knows that in advancing towards truth, he also advances towards a more assured and solidly based knowledge, also more conscious of the foundations and principles underpinning the progress of his investigations—and his science.

Here we find the full role of the intentionality integral to Aquinas's noetic delineated, thereby distinguished from Cartesian thought. *First Principles, Final Ends and Contemporary Philosophical Issues* is a key text in this respect since there, for the first time, MacIntyre introduces the concept of intentionality between rationality and truth. The whole lecture is rhymed by the rationality-intentionality-truth triad, recurring like a refrain. Intentionality plays the role of intermediary there, between rationality, always situated and relative, as opposed to truth which, for its part, is eternal. Yet intentionality is not defined as such in that lecture.

However, intentionality is much more so defined in the review MacIntyre wrote for the English translation of the Thomist Yves René Simon's doctoral dissertation for the *American Catholic Philosophical Quarterly* in 1991. In his view,

---

[51]MacIntyre, *Whose Justice? Which Rationality?*, 357.
[52]MacIntyre, *Three Rival Versions of Moral Enquiry*, 13.
[53]Ibid.
[54]Ibid., 14.

Simon's thesis is highly topical and offers "the correct grounds for dissenting from . . . the type of account of knowledge as justified true belief which has so often been defended in the last half-century among analytic philosophers."[55] The thesis does this by means of an analysis of what knowledge is—which is quite different from belief, a simple state of mind—and the most intimate relationship knowledge maintains with truth. Knowledge is a relationship of mind with what is known, a relationship which, once achieved, perfects a movement of the intellect in actualizing it. And, as in *First Principles, Final Ends and Contemporary Philosophical Issues*, the key concept establishing the link between knowledge and its end is intentionality. According to Simon, mind maintains a relationship of intentionality with the objects it knows. And those objects, in becoming objects of knowledge, become intentional objects. Those intentional objects, MacIntyre specifies, do not have just a mental existence as Descartes or Husserl thought. "An intentional object is, on Simon's Thomistic view, not something other than a physical object (or whether other object, existing independently of some knowing mind, is an object of knowledge to that mind). It is the physical object itself, but as conceived and known."[56]

We thereby understand the importance of the senses' experience in the knowing process. On this subject, "Simon's exposition lays emphasis on how the work of precognitive abstraction from sense experience stimulates the intellect to thought directed towards further exploration of its object, so that in turn further precognitive abstraction elicits yet further conceptual elaboration in extending the activities and the types of activity of the intellect. So the objects of experience are at more than one level intentionally integrated into the mind's ongoing constructive activity, and all knowledge is the knowledge of some mind in progress, moving forward beyond what it had hitherto achieved."[57] This mode of knowledge is far removed from that of computers, and, MacIntyre specifies, "it may not be entirely a mistake to ascribe to machines an essentially Cartesian consciousness; what they cannot have are minds understood as Thomists understand them."[58]

Machines might resemble the brains Putnam imagines placed in vats and linked to computers which would furnish them information convincing them that everything is normal. But for a Thomist like MacIntyre, humans will never resemble such machines. In other words, those machines could not be Thomistic minds, for which the body is indispensable, for it is the place where you learn about the real, carried on in decisive dependence on the body; nor could they be

---

[55]Alasdair MacIntyre, "Review of *An Introduction to the Metaphysics of Knowledge* by Yves René Simon," *American Catholic Philosophical Quarterly* 65 (1991): 112–4, at 113.

[56]Ibid.

[57]Ibid., 113–4.

[58]Ibid., 114.

minds like those described in *Whose Justice? Which Rationality?*, involved in the natural and social world in various activities notably involving the body, minds which cannot escape MacIntyrean conceptual idiosyncrasy.

MacIntyre explains this idiosyncrasy at length in presenting his rationality of traditions in *Whose Justice? Which Rationality?* In a key chapter of a work, which brings together the confluent currents of many earlier texts and is prolonged by many later texts, he distances himself from two pitfalls: Descartes and Hegel. The starting point of a rational tradition, he explains, is contingency and the categorical character of an ensemble of established beliefs. Of course a tradition can provide itself with first practical or metaphysical principles. But they will never be unfalsifiable. They will never be self-sufficient. They are not "self-justifying epistemological first principles."[59] If they exist within a tradition, the justificatory genus they belong to "is at once dialectical and historical. They are justified insofar as in the history of this tradition they have, by surviving the process of dialectical questioning, vindicated themselves as superior to their historical predecessors."[60] This is incompatible with the Cartesian method. Moreover, in its end goal, an investigation constituted by a tradition is anti-Hegelian since a tradition will at no time be able to claim a total adequation between mind and its objects. From the viewpoint of the rationality of traditions, absolute knowledge is a chimera. "No one at any stage can ever rule out the future possibility of their present beliefs and judgments being shown to be inadequate in a variety of ways."[61]

In avoiding Cartesian and Hegelian pitfalls, MacIntyre defines the space his rationality of traditions is situated in. It is a space that is anything but absolute, a space relative to a particular idiosyncrasy and ever open to the possibility of falsification. Far from any relativism, this also involves a space where progress is real, where man advances towards truth inasmuch as his gaze is strengthened by acquisitions he has garnered in his search for adequation with the real, and provided he does not lose sight of the goal of his investigation. In this space, the world is always seen by man from a certain point of view, the world is always interpreted by man. As MacIntyre writes at the end of his review of Gadamer's *Wahrheit und Methode*, "we inhabit an interpreted world in which reinterpretation is the most fundamental form of change."[62] During this process of interpretation and reinterpretation man really advances, if all goes well, towards truth, that correspondence he seeks between his mind and reality, which is unveiled to him little by little. Isn't he, "in his actions and practice, as well as in his fictions,

---

[59]MacIntyre, *Whose Justice? Which Rationality?*, 360.
[60]Ibid.
[61]Ibid., 361.
[62]Alasdair MacIntyre, "Contexts of Interpretation: Reflections on Hans-Georg Gadamer's *Truth and Method*," *Boston University Journal* 26 (1980): 173–8, at 178.

essentially a story-telling animal" who becomes, "through his history, a teller of stories that aspire to truth"?[63]

Contrasting Putnamian conceptual relativity and MacIntyrean relativity proves to be particularly enlightening here. In her two articles "On the Right Idea of a Conceptual Scheme" and "The Heart of Putnam's Pluralistic Realism,"[64] Jennifer Case offers a very good explanation of Putnamian conceptual relativity: "the heart of my internal realism,"[65] as Putnam himself describes it. In *The Many Faces of Realism*, a title under which the Paul Carus Lectures delivered by Putnam in 1985 are published, conceptual relativity is presented as a phenomenon consisting in this: "There are ways of describing what are (in some way) the 'same facts' which are (in some way) 'equivalent' but also (in some way) 'incompatible.'"[66] Thus Putnam intends to position himself between relativism and a realism he calls external and metaphysical in arguing both for the existence of facts and equivalent and incompatible ways of describing them. He explains this coexistence in *Realism with a Human Face* (1990): "The doctrine of conceptual relativity, in brief, is that while there is an aspect of conventionality and an aspect of fact in everything we say that is true, we fall into hopeless philosophical error if we commit a 'fallacy of division' and conclude that there must be a part of the truth that is the 'conventional part' and a part that is the 'factual part.'"[67] Hence, Case insists here, conceptual relativity is a doctrine of interpenetration of fact and convention. In what we hold as true there is an interpenetration of fact and convention, which we would be wrong to want to disjoin.

For example,[68] we know that it is possible to identify points with sets of convergent spheres in correctly tracing all the geometric data, and that it is just as possible to consider the points as being primitive and to identify the spheres as sets of points. Hence, there is an element of convention here. And, as Willard Quine has shown in refuting the distinction between analytic truth and synthetic truth, in saying that, we unavoidably make appeal to "a diffuse background of empirical facts."[69] To support his thesis on the interpenetration of fact and convention, Putnam refers to Quine's celebrated article "Two Dogmas of Empiricism" here, where the thesis is maintained that "truth in general depends on both language

---

[63]MacIntyre, *After Virtue*, 216.

[64]Jennifer Case, "On the Right Idea of a Conceptual Scheme," *The Southern Journal of Philosophy* 35 (1997): 1–18; Case, "The Heart of Putnam's Pluralistic Realism," *Revue Internationale de Philosophie* 55 (2001): 417–30.

[65]Hilary Putnam, "Replies and Comments," *Erkenntnis* 34 (1991): 401–24, at 404.

[66]Hilary Putnam, *The Many Faces of Realism. The Paul Carus Lectures* (Chicago: Open Court, 1987), 29.

[67]Hilary Putnam, *Realism with a Human Face*, ed. James Conant (Cambridge, MA: Harvard University Press, 1990), x.

[68]See Hilary Putnam, *Representation and Reality* (Cambridge, MA: MIT Press, 1988), 112–3.

[69]Ibid., 113.

and extralinguistic facts"[70] and that maintaining a distinction between analytic judgment—that is founded on significations independently of facts—and synthetic judgment—that is founded on the facts—amounts to an "unempirical dogma of empiricists, a metaphysical article of faith."[71] On the contrary, in all truth a factual part and a conventional part are always intermingled.

At the heart of the Putnamian doctrine of conceptual relativity lies the idea of conceptual scheme, which must be understood correctly. One helpful example "is familiar as to run the danger of seeming trivial; we may partly describe the contents of a room by saying that there is a chair in front of a desk, and partly describe the contents of the same room by saying that there are particles and fields of certain kinds present. . . . *Both* descriptions are descriptions of the room as it really is."[72] Yet they are different because they belong to two different conceptual schemes: that of common sense and that of physical science.

Putnamian doctrine of conceptual relativity involves a plurality of different conceptual schemes. Even what are counted as facts depend on these conceptual schemes: they are never totally deprived of convention. This plurality of conceptual schemes is such that two judgments incompatible on the factual level may sometimes both be true. Yet it must not violate what Simon Blackburn calls the unity imperative, according to which the coherence of knowledge ought not be affected to the point of considering two contradictory propositions valid even if they express judgments that are incompatible on a factual level. How can we simultaneously maintain both of these requirements? Here Putnam makes appeal to a subtle distinction between meaning and use, thus revealing his pragmatic turn of mind. Two propositions with apparently different significations may both be true in different contexts of utilization, i.e., used in different ways. Hence Case explains, "ascertaining whether two statements that appear to be inconsistent are consistent requires ascertaining whether the words expressing those statements are being used in the same or different ways."[73]

What Putnam says about truth, MacIntyre says about rationality. For MacIntyre too, every human intellectual proposition contains a factual part and a conventional part; these parts may be different in terms of the conceptual schemes one is located in. Man lives in an interpreted world. He does not have direct access to facts purified of all convention. His knowledge is always related to a conceptual scheme, that of the tradition of which he's a part, a tradition that is always both factual and conventional. But—and this is what distinguishes

---

[70]Willard Van Orman Quine, "Two Dogmas of Empiricism," *Philosophical Review* 60 (1951): 20–43, at 34.

[71]Ibid.

[72]Hilary Putnam, "Simon Blackburn on Internal Realism," in *Reading Putnam*, ed. Peter Clark and Bob Hale (Oxford: Basil Blackwell, 1994): 242–8, at 243.

[73]Jennifer Case, "On the Right Idea of a Conceptual Scheme," 14.

MacIntyrean relativity from Putnamian relativity—two incompatible judgments on the experimental level can never both be true for MacIntyre. They may both be rational in the conceptual scheme within which they are formulated. And in this respect it might help to verify whether the words by which they are expressed are used in the same way or differently. But those two judgments can in no case both be true. Because, for MacIntyre, truth means adequation with the real, and there is only one real. The MacIntyrean rationality of traditions clearly distinguishes belonging to a particular conceptual scheme, which is understood univocally, from belonging to a particular historical tradition of rational investigation of truth itself. And MacIntyre unceasingly protected the Platonic distinction between "what's true" and "what seems true to so and so," as he did notably in "Relativism, Power and Philosophy."[74] What guarantees the fact that the truth of things is beyond the possibility of justified assertion within a conceptual scheme is God himself, the absolute Archimedean point on which the entire MacIntyrean theory of truth relies.

For MacIntyre, truth presents itself to man *in fine* as a truth one might describe as harmonic, even if MacIntyre never uses that term. In his essay "Truth as a Good," it is described in terms of the relations of various partial truths to the ultimate truth, which is in God. Each partial truth has its place in a general order of truth whose keystone, the luminous centre, is none other than God himself; just as each being has its place in the general order of beings, whose keystone is none other than the supreme being: God. The truth about a particular reality cannot even exist except for the existence of a general order of things in which every reality takes its place, an order of things in terms of which we can understand not only the truth about such and such a thing, but also the why of that truth.

> The mind that understands is such that its thoughts not only of how things are, but also of why they are as they are, are identical with how they are and with why they are as they are. . . . That is to say, a mind whose thoughts are adequate to the subject matter about which it thinks not only makes and is disposed to make true judgments and only true judgments about that subject matter, but it judges in such a way as to present that subject matter as intelligible. And the mind, when adequate to some subject matter, finds that subject matter intelligible only insofar as that subject matter is intelligible, is, prior to its being understood by you or me, apt to be understood in virtue of those characteristics which give its place in the order of things. For to explain some subject matter, to

[74]Alasdair MacIntyre, "Relativism, Power and Philosophy," *Proceedings and Addresses of the American Philosophical Association* 59 (1985): 5–22.

render it intelligible, just is to identify its place, function, and relationship within the overall order of things.[75]

Far removed from Putnam, all the rest of the theory holds thanks to an absolute point of view. It is with respect to it, to its truth that particular truths exist, that particular judgments are possible, that it is suitable to distinguish various levels of use of the terms "true" and "false" the way Thomas did in his *De Veritate*. In making truth judgments about particular realities, the human mind makes appeal to this absolute point of view. This point of view is also what makes the concept of the mind's movement as oriented towards an ultimate end which is truth itself understandable. For, without such a point of view, we might quickly conclude that no end of this type exists. The human mind advances nearer and nearer to this complete truth, the truth which is the *telos* of the rational investigation it carries out, including towards truth about the conception, i.e., the theory of truth itself. The investigation advances until it arrives at its final, perfect state, the perfect science, the ideal of Aristotelian-Thomistic science, where all beings are understood as necessarily being what they are, will be, and have been. Such a state is hierarchical. A mind that arrives at a perfect understanding in a particular domain represents what he has understood—in a form which necessarily coincides with the form of what he has understood—"by a deductive scheme in whose hierarchical structure the different levels of causal explanation are embodied."[76] In each domain, in each particular science, there consequently exists an ensemble of first principles "which provide premises for demonstrative arguments and which specify the ultimate causal agencies, material, formal, efficient and final for that science."[77] And, ultimately, the most fundamental sciences will specify this reality in terms of which everything can and must be understood, which is called God. Yet investigation never stops advancing . . .

In this regard, Lutz explains the importance of each of the two contributions—Augustinian and Aristotelian—to Aquinas's thought for MacIntyre. The integration of the two traditions, he notes, is paramount "because together these two kinds of adequation, a thing's adequation to the divine intellect, and a human intellect's adequation to a thing, define the situation and structural limitation of the human intellect in the pursuit of truth. The human intellect seeks to understand the world through the senses and through reason, but the truth about things includes their relationship to God which surpasses our understanding,

---

[75]Alasdair MacIntyre, "Truth as a Good: a Reflection on *Fides et Ratio*," in *Thomas Aquinas: Approaches to Truth: the Aquinas Lectures at Maynooth 1996–2001*, ed. James McEvoy and Michael Dunne (Dublin: Four Courts Press, 2002), 141–57. Reproduced in MacIntyre, *The Tasks of Philosophy*, 197–215, at 205–6.

[76]MacIntyre, *First Principles, Final Ends*, 28.

[77]Ibid., 29.

so while we may know what things are, we cannot fully comprehend them."[78] And since we are always located somewhere, we always know things in a way related to the place where we are. The role of the distinctions made in the *De Veritate* and *De Ente* is to present the geography of human rational investigation, its typical location, always relative, as well as its centre of gravity, which, for its part, is absolute.

MacIntyre considers truth as being eminently a good, the specific good of the human mind. He underlines that in *Truth as a Good*, where he also notes that Thomas Aquinas on more than one occasion considers truth to be the specific good of the human mind, notably in establishing the catalogue of intellectual virtues: they must render the human mind capable of achieving its good, knowing the truth.[79] Christopher Tollefsen stresses how for MacIntyre rational investigation is itself very much a practice which has its goods, its own excellences, and whose good par excellence is none other than truth conceived as its *telos*. "Enquiry is . . . a kind of search, whose *telos* is truth, whether theoretical or practical. Insofar, then, as one is engaged in the activity or practice of enquiry, truth is the supreme good, a good not weighable against other goods,"[80] whence the importance of certain virtues proper to the search for truth. Among them, honesty is obviously crucial: without it, research results do not hold up and have no value. Being honest requires a certain amount of courage, as well as other virtues. Prudence is notably indispensable to a rational investigation's progressing well, since it is precisely it "which rightly orients all our pursuits and virtues towards their end. Thus 'the lack of virtue in those who pursue, and those who teach others to pursue, enquiry is always in danger of depriving enquiry of the possibility of moving towards its *telos/finis*' (*FP*, 189)."[81] This brings us around to the rehabilitation of the thesis of the unity of the virtues, so crucial for MacIntyre. It is all interrelated in his thought.

IV.

Conclusion. MacIntyre's work certainly belongs in the third category of Thomisms distinguished by Serge-Thomas Bonino in his introductory contribution to the collection *Thomistes ou de l'actualité de saint Thomas d'Aquin* published in 2003,[82] the category of living Thomisms. MacIntyre does not strive

---

[78]Lutz, *Tradition in the Ethics of Alasdair MacIntyre*, 121–2.

[79]See MacIntyre, "Truth as a Good," in *The Tasks of Philosophy*, 210.

[80]Tollefsen Christopher, "MacIntyre and the Moralization of Enquiry," *International Philosophical Quarterly* 46 (2006): 421–38, at 430.

[81]Ibid., 433.

[82]Bonino Serge-Thomas, "Etre thomiste," in *Thomistes ou de l'actualité de saint Thomas d'Aquin* (Paris: Editions Parole et Silence, 2003), 15–26.

for an inspirational Thomism: he is not stirred by an apologetic urge to do in the present what Thomas did in his time, namely to express the Christian faith in the terms of contemporary philosophy. Nor does he work towards a fundamentalist Thomism: not suffering from an aversion to everything that considers the historical incarnation of the thought of Aquinas—far from it. He rather shows his constant concern to take both the history and historical context wherein Aquinas's thought was born into account, unceasingly working to update it. He does this in terms of the demands of the general cultural movement of the age he writes in, while developing the still implicit, though massively imposing, potentialities in Thomas's thought, thereby encountering certain contemporary questions the medieval thinker could never have envisaged.

As to the temperament coming through in his work, it is of a rather conservative type. Admittedly, in *After Virtue*, he rejects Aristotle's biological metaphysics while trying to extract another foundation for ethics from him. But he was not yet a Thomist. He only became one after 1981, for reasons which are precisely metaphysical for the most part. Once a Thomist, he no longer contributed to the kind of updating Bonino describes as risky and has assumed a rather prudent attitude.

MacIntyre is moreover rather critical of enterprises of the late nineteenth and early twentieth century that Bonino classifies among the works of living Thomism by authors with rather audacious temperaments. He explains his position in *Three Rival Versions of Moral Enquiry*, in a chapter entitled "Too many Thomisms?" If he distances himself from those attempts, it is because he considers that they were misled in seeking an impossible reconciliation between epistemological principles of a systematic type and a rather more historical type of rationality, such as that animating Aquinas's own work. That shows the extent to which a radically historicist accent characterizes MacIntyrean Thomism.

While opting for a non-systematic Thomism, always open to falsification and aimed at an end that is never perfectly attained, MacIntyre assents to the experience Thomas lived at the end of his life when he felt he could no longer write a single line. All the language Thomas had crafted over the years seemed to him then as straw beside what he had glimpsed of God in a mystical experience: truth is beyond all that.

Studium Notre-Dame de Namur
Namur, Belgium

Paradigms, Traditions, and History: The Influence of Philosophy of Science on MacIntyre's Ethical Thought

John C. Caiazza

Abstract. MacIntyre's mature ethical philosophy was the result of his becoming aware of trends in the philosophy of science in the 1970s when MacIntyre had reached a block in the development of his ethical theory. MacIntyre translated Kuhn's theory of "paradigms" and Lakatos's "research programmes" into his richly developed theory of ethical "traditions," which constitutes a *historicist* ethical philosophy. This point is argued by a detailed comparison of Kuhn's theory of *paradigms* with MacIntyre's *traditions*; emphasizing paradigms rather than research programs is more productive for highlighting the historicist aspects of MacIntyre's ethical philosophy. Paradigms and traditions are compared in four areas. Both philosophies deny the validity of the Enlightenment ideal of universal reason, and of social science. Kuhn never resolves the issues connected with the radical incomparability of paradigms. MacIntyre does derive a method of comparing ethical traditions in favor of the Augustinian/Aristotelian/Thomistic one. Questions of ontology remain.

I.

Th*he Influence of the Philosophy of Science in MacIntyre's Thought.* The thought of Alasdair MacIntyre on fundamental ethical issues has been expressed over several decades in a series of essays, but especially in several thoughtful and richly layered books which constitute an important legacy that not incidentally provide a record of the ethical, cultural and political controversies of the modern age. Teasing out separate themes and causes in an attempt to understand his thought and glean from it ideas that may be helpful in understanding the modern age, leads to understanding the effect of the philosophy of science on MacIntyre's thought.

That philosophy of science is not a minor or isolated thread in the development of MacIntyre's thought is testified to in his own words as he cites his colleagues at Boston University and particularly Marx Wartofsky who, along with physicist Robert Cohen, were the founders of the Philosophy of Science program at B. U. (It is now the B. U. Center for the Philosophy and History of

©2014, *American Catholic Philosophical Quarterly*, Vol. 88, No. 4
doi:10.5840/acpq201492536

Science). Wartofsky, now deceased, was an energetic, open-minded, and gregarious professor whose good humor and extensive acquaintance with current issues in philosophy, particularly in philosophy of science and left wing politics, made him popular among the graduate students; he published two books in his lifetime, on philosophy of science and on Feurbach. From 1972 to 1975, MacIntyre was the Chair of the Boston University Department of Philosophy, and while at B. U. came in contact with the current field of philosophy of science, including, by his own account, the thought of Thomas Kuhn and Imre Lakatos.[1] In the Preface to *After Virtue*, MacIntyre gives credit to Wartofsky, whose criticisms enabled him to develop his mature approach to ethical theory; he also thanks Boston University Professors Elizabeth Rappaport and Thomas McCarthy for reading the manuscript.[2] (Both MacIntyre and Wartofsky began their intellectual careers as advocates of Marxist theory which presumably provided a common basis for their discussions.) In the Preface to a collection of his essays published in 2006, MacIntyre describes the effect of becoming acquainted with the philosophy of science on the development of his thought. This volume contains the critical essay, "Epistemological Crises, Dramatic Narrative, and the Philosophy of Science," which was originally written after MacIntyre wrote his *A Short History of Ethics* but before he wrote and published *After Virtue* and which marks a critical passage in the development of MacIntyre's ethical philosophy, particularly as it presaged the development of his theory of *traditions*.[3]

> "Epistemological Crises, dramatic narrative, and the philosophy of science" marks a major turning-point in my thinking during the 1970s. . . . It was elicited by my reading of and encounters with Imre Lakatos and Thomas Kuhn and what was transformed by that reading was my conception of what it was to make progress in philosophy or indeed in systematic thought more generally. . . . What I learned from Kuhn, or rather Kuhn and Lakatos read together, was the need first to identify and then to break free from [the larger, shared, conceptual framework] and to enquire whether the various problems on which I had made so little progress had baffled me not or not only because of their difficulty, but because they were bound to remain intractable so long as they were

---

[1]Alasdair MacIntyre, "Epistemological Crises, Dramatic Narrative, and Philosophy of Science," in *The Tasks of Philosophy*, vol. 1 (New York: Cambridge University Press, 2006), viii.

[2]Alasdair MacIntyre, *After Virtue*, 2nd ed. (Notre Dame, IN: University of Notre Dame Press, 1984), x. Wartofsky was impatient with the popularity of Kuhn's thesis; other members of the Philosophy Department seemed to reject it as well, as I can personally attest. I was Wartofsky's Graduate Assistant for one year but was not any closer to him than many others, and I never met MacIntyre except for a very brief hallway conversation.

[3]See Christopher Lutz, *Tradition in the Ethics of Alasdair MacIntyre: Relativism, Thomism and Philosophy* (Lanham, MD: Lexington Books, 1984).

understood in the terms dictated by those larger assumptions which I shared with many of my contemporaries.[4]

The major turning-point to which MacIntyre refers occurred after he published *A Short History* in 1966 and prior to the publication of *After Virtue* in 1981. Prior to reaching his turning point, MacIntyre had been preoccupied with various issues in the social sciences, politics, and culture, and as a result his work in that time period up into the 1970s appears piecemeal (see section IV of this essay). In *Against the Self Images of the Age*, a collection of his shorter works written during this time, MacIntyre wrote that he could not provide an overall account of his thought because that "would require that I know how to tie those arguments together in a substantive whole. This I do not yet know how to do, but I regard learning how to do it as a prerequisite for further advancing inquiry into those questions."[5]

In the middle of the last century, philosophy of science developed into an identifiable and separate field of philosophy. It has developed its own journals (e.g., *The British Journal of the Philosophy of Science*) and its own institutes and programs in established universities, including Indiana University and Boston University. The development of a separate field reflected the acknowledged importance and influence of modern empirical science which had become especially noteworthy in the twentieth century due to the advancement of new comprehensive theories, but also due to enormous technological development which have affected and transformed, it is fair to say, all areas of human life from agriculture to electronic communication to birth control. What mainly intrigued philosophers of science as the field emerged was not the social effects of technological developments or the emergence of such theories as neo-Darwinism and Relativity, but the issue of what constituted the basic nature of scientific explanation and associated questions of scientific logic and proper methodology. Here the inspiration came largely from the positivism of the Vienna Circle and from philosophers such as Russell, Quine and Carnap whose philosophical approach relied heavily on the explication of the empirical philosophical implications expressed in terms of formal logical structures.[6]

This formal approach, which emphasized scientific methodology, was challenged, however, in the 1960s by the writings of several philosophers of science who imported into the field an approach based on the historical and social aspects of modern science. Most notable among these was Thomas Kuhn,

---

[4] Alasdair MacIntyre, "Epistemological Crises," vii–viii.
[5] *Against the Self Images of the Age* (New York, Schocken, 1971), x.
[6] For a detailed account, see John Caiazza, *The Disunity of American Culture*, chap. 7, "The Counter-Revolution in the Philosophy of Science" (Piscataway, NJ: Transaction Publishers, 2013), 87–100.

whose reflections on the history of science led him to a description of science as a process of the successive arrivals and overturnings of dominant theories ("revolutions") whose influence reached beyond the merely formal and logical to areas of social identity, research methodology, and assumptions of what constituted proper scientific explanation ("paradigms").[7] The conflict then occurring in philosophy of science during the time that MacIntyre was present at B.U. was that the positivistic influence of the Vienna Circle was being supplanted by the historicist influence of several authors including Paul Feyerabend, Michael Polanyi, Norwood Russell Hanson, Karl Popper, but especially Imre Lakatos and Thomas Kuhn.[8]

Another point in the development of MacIntyre's ethical doctrines occurs in a prior book that is important not only for the understanding of the how MacIntyre's thought was influenced by his appreciation of the philosophy of science but also in itself, for it is probably MacIntyre's second most influential book after *After Virtue*, namely *A Short History of Ethics*.[9] Although it is usual in attempting to understand MacIntyre's ethical theory to concentrate on three books—*After Virtue*, *Three Rival Versions of Moral Enquiry*, and *Whose Justice, Which Rationality*—the sequence for understanding his ethical theory should start with a reading of *A Short History of Ethics*. For MacIntyre states that it was between writing this book and *After Virtue* that the discovery of recent philosophy influenced on his thinking.[10]

But what would have appealed to MacIntyre from these philosophers of science and what was the effect on the development of his thought? As I have already characterized the process then ongoing, in general terms philosophy of science was turning from a positivistic and logicist understanding of science and scientific explanation to what can be called a historicist understanding. By "historicist" I mean that these philosophers of science did not only refer to historical examples from science such as new discoveries or controversies for purposes of illustration of, e.g., the "hypothetical-deductive method" or the confirmation or falsification of theories. Rather, this new school of philosophers more fundamentally and exactly defined science in terms of its history; that is, it was the historical exigencies and developmental patterns of science that more fully explained, and indeed defined, the essence of science. Science history was

---

[7]Thomas Kuhn, *The Structure of Scientific Revolutions*, 2nd ed. (Chicago: University of Chicago Press, 1970).

[8]MacIntyre, "Epistemological Crises," 15–23. While MacIntyre explicitly mentions the others, he nowhere cites Hanson, yet he relies on the concept invented or made popular by Hanson, i.e. "theory laden observation terms."

[9]Alasdair MacIntyre, *A Short History of Ethics*, 2nd ed. (Notre Dame, IN: University of Notre Dame Press, 1998).

[10]Alasdair MacIntyre, "Epistemological Crises," vii–viii. See n4 above.

for them, therefore, not merely a series of useful illustrations, but an ongoing history, directly attached to normal human concerns in actual personal, political, cultural, religious and technical contexts, and often explained in psychological and sociological terms.

There were several prominent contributors to the new, historicist turn in the philosophy of science. Polanyi emphasized the degree to which scientific knowledge was personal knowledge, tacitly known, and an acquired skill. Feyerabend attacked the ideal of scientific rationalism, forcefully denying that the events, procedures, and results that constitute the sciences have a common structure. Hanson discovered patterns of discovery, and invented the term, "theory laden observation terms" to emphasize the point that scientific observations were not neutral observations of experimentally discovered "facts." Popper, in effect, provided a halfway house between the old school of Vienna Circle positivism and the historicist perspective by the invention of a new criterion for the adequacy of scientific explanation, namely, "falsification" (replacing "verification"). Popper attempted to provide an explanation of how even the most well established theories can be overturned because scientific statements were positings that did not operate as final truths. The distinctive aspect of Popper's new account of science history, which he distinguished from what he termed "inductivism," was to have redefined scientific rationality. Science was no longer understood as the accumulation of theories and laws that were proven true in a continuing process of discovery; rather, scientific reason was now to be understood, according to Popper, as a method of providing statements and theories precise enough so that they could be tested, and falsified.[11] Overall, the new, historicist emphasis on the personal and the cultural which implied that scientific reason could no longer plausibly be thought to fit Enlightenment ideals, had a direct and major impact on MacIntyre's thinking at the point when he was at Boston University.

The specific influence is seen in the close resemblance between MacIntyre's concept of ethical traditions, Kuhn's theory of paradigms and Lakatos's theory of "research programmes" (referred to in the remainder of this paper as "research programs")[12] For all three, the means of explanation and exploration of the relevant issues in science and ethics (for MacIntyre) is understood in terms of overarching, dominant ideas, ideas, however, which cannot be understood without a description of the social and historical environment in which they exist, or, more exactly, in which they are manifested. However, it is apparent that

---

[11]Karl Popper, *The Logic of Scientific Discovery* (New York, Routledge, 2002 [originally in English in 1959]).

[12]Kuhn, *The Structure of Scientific Revolutions*; Imre Lakatos, "Falsification and the Methodology of Scientific Research Programmes," in *Criticism and the Growth of Knowledge*, ed. I. Lakatos and A. Musgrave (Cambridge,: Cambridge University Press, 1970), 91–196.

Lakatos's version of the history of science is less concerned with the sociological and historicist implications of a historical view of science than Kuhn's, as I explain in the next section below.

The influence of philosophy of science on MacIntyre's ethical philosophy is apparent beyond the influence of paradigms and research programs. It can be seen and studied in two areas: MacIntyre's brief against social science, and MacIntyre's attempt to develop, in his terms, a "metaphysical biology." First, however, a discussion of the role that history plays in the development of Mac-Intyre's thought, in the context of philosophy of science, is in order.

II.

A Role for History. MacIntyre mentions the influence of the philosophy of Kuhn and Lakatos when he was at Boston University; up to that point in his own philosophical career, however, MacIntyre had already decided on a historical approach to the understanding of ethical theory. This is very apparent as expressed in his *A Short History of Ethics*, the volume he wrote just prior to the publication of *After Virtue*. At the point he had finished his history, he had not apparently been able to make the historicism explicit or give his thought a definite intellectual grounding or clarity. Kuhn's theory of *paradigms* and Lakatos's account of *research programs*, however, provided MacIntyre with a means to make most clear his basic idea that ethical theory could not be properly understood without an intimate knowledge of the immediate social and historical contexts in which it was produced. Indeed, it was this emphasis on the historical contexts of the development of ethical theories in MacIntyre's account that enabled *A Short History of Ethics* to have significant influence: it has been translated into several languages and gone through three editions, and might be, on an international level, his most influential work. But proceeding from an historical account of the development of ethical theory to a theory of ethics based on an historicist point of view was a definite point of transition; after that point came the development of MacIntyre's theory of ethical traditions which, in broad form, translates paradigms and research programs from philosophy of science into the field of ethics.

In *After Virtue* and more so in his later book, *Whose Justice, Which Rationality?*, the resemblances between MacIntyre's fully developed theory of ethics expressed as traditions and Kuhn's historicist version of scientific reasoning expressed as paradigms are readily apparent. MacIntyre argues that the concepts and outcomes of ethical theories arise in their social settings, i.e. traditions, and that "the nature of moral community and moral judgment in distinctively modern societies was such that it was no longer possible to appeal to a moral criteria in a way that had been possible in other times and places."[13] Of particular note is the idea of "incommensurability," which MacIntyre uses to describe the current situation in the West where advocates of differing ethical and political positions cannot find common ground for their debates.

Since this paper will concentrate on the resemblance between MacIntyre's concept of traditions and Kuhn's theory of paradigms in some detail, and since MacIntyre seems in some ways to prefer Lakatos's formulation of research programs, an explanation is necessary. While Lakatos's theory of research programs broadly resembles Kuhn's paradigms and MacIntyre's traditions, this paper proceeds to argue that there is more to be learned about MacIntyre's thought in relation to the philosophy of science from Kuhnian paradigms than from Lakatosian "research programmes." However, contrary to this assertion, it is the case that in discussions of science history, that Lakatos's account of research programs is more often the focus than Kuhn's account of paradigms. This is the case notably in Christopher Lutz's book where in his treatment of the influence of the philosophy of science on MacIntyre's theory of ethical traditions, reference is made almost solely to Lakatos's research programs.[14] The appeal of Lakatos's theory is understandable, for it is clearly expressed in terms available to philosophy of science done in the positive and logical mode of the thought of the Vienna Circle. And, like his mentor Popper's, Lakatos's theory is a kind of a halfway house between the positivistic and historicist traditions of philosophy of science.[15]

In Lakatos's version, the history of science is described by means of a succession of research programs, each consisting of a "hard core" central theory of such comprehension, internal consistency, and wide applicability that it dominates a field of science. Around the hard core, according to Lakatos, exists a belt of auxiliary or subordinate theories, logically connected to the hard core, which take in anomalies and provides a basis for experimentation and research.[16] This aspect of Lakatos's theory enables it to account for the particular aspect of scientific history to which Kuhn brought attention and which contradicts the prior Enlightenment assumption that scientific progress is a reliably rational process, so that the discovery of contrary evidence does not necessarily or usually make scientists who hold a theory change their minds about its validity. Rather than dismiss a major theory to which they are committed, scientists develop

[13]Alasdair MacIntyre, *Whose Justice, Which Rationality?* (Notre Dame, IN: University of Notre Dame Press, 1988), ix.

[14]Lutz, *Tradition*, 47–52. Also see Nancey Murphy and George Ellis, *On the Moral Nature of the Universe* (Minneapolis, MN: Fortress Augsburg, 1996), 10–5.

[15]Popper's rejection of historicist philosophy is well expressed in the title and content of his book, *The Poverty of Historicism* (New York: Haroer Torchbooks, 1961).

[16]Lakatos, "Programmes," 132–8.

subordinate theories to account for observational or experimental evidence that is contradictory. Thus, in Lakatos's version, this uncomfortable fact of science history brought into focus by Kuhn is dealt with by means of a rationalist model, and the social-psychological fact of the refusal of scientists to recognize contrary evidence and drop their belief in a prominent theory is reduced, as it were, to a mere item of logical contradiction in a subsidiary theory, protecting in effect the main theory from rational contradiction.

Lakatos's motive for proposing his theory of research programs is indicated by his comment regarding Kuhn: "The clash between Popper and Kuhn is not about a mere technical point in epistemology. It concerns our central intellectual values, and has implications not only for theoretical physics but also for the underdeveloped social sciences, and even for moral and political philosophy."[17] Lakatos and Popper retain the rationality of science as its essential aspect, albeit in terms of science's methodology rather than in its putative truth telling capacity. However, MacIntyre is unsure by that allowance of methodological rationality whether Lakatos has not in fact lost the point that scientific rationality is constituted not by its method but by its history. In an intricate discussion toward the end of "Epistemological Crises," MacIntyre writes, "the appraisal is one of a *series* of *theories* rather than of an isolated *theory*."[18] For Lakatos, there remains the temptation to see science history as a (mere) succession of hard core theories, modified, discarded, or subsumed, but with no implication about the historical nature of scientific knowledge.

In this paper, it is argued that Kuhn's theory of paradigm commitment and the imbeddedness of scientific theories in a social and historical context more closely resembles MacIntyre's ideas about ethical traditions than does Lakatos's account of research programs.[19] For, despite MacIntyre's very critical analysis of Kuhn's theory, Kuhn never lost sight of the point that the essence of science lies in its history, a point which MacIntyre also never lost sight of after this encounter with late-twentieth-century philosophy of science. In the last sentence of "Epistemological Crises," he writes: "It is after all Vico . . . who has turned out to be in the right in approaching the relationship between history and physics."[20]

III.

Paradigms and Traditions Compared. An online search reveals that nothing has as yet been written that directly compares MacIntyre's *traditions* to Kuhn's *paradigms*. While there are four major points of resemblance that will be

---

[17]Ibid., 93.
[18]MacIntyre, "Epistemological Crises," 19, italics in original.
[19]Ibid., 21.
[20]Ibid., 23.

considered, the overall basis for comparison is that Kuhn and MacIntyre have turned their respective fields from a rationalistic, or a positivistic study to a post-Enlightenment or historicist study. The four specific points of comparison are that, first, for both MacIntyre and Kuhn the study of the history of their respective fields has been of central importance; second, paradigms and traditions play comparable roles in understanding science and ethics respectively; third, both Kuhn and MacIntyre reject the authority or validity of social science; fourth, both philosophers reject the Enlightenment ideal of reason and as a result have been accused of epistemic relativism, a charge that both reject.

First, it is notable that MacIntyre and Kuhn are serious historians of their respective fields. MacIntyre's *A Short History of Ethics*, as noted above, used a combination of historical and sociological approaches to describe the course of ethical theory in the West. Thus, after a preparatory chapter, "The Philosophical Point of the History of Ethics," the volume proceeds with a chapter on the "prephilosophical history of the 'Good'" which concentrates on the Homeric context that precedes the account of Athenian culture that begins in the next chapter on the Sophists and Socrates. Only then, after three historical chapters, does MacIntyre write about Plato's ethical theory in an examination of the *Gorgias*. MacIntyre's historical version of the course of ethical theory is further indicated by the long passages and whole chapters devoted to the topic in *After Virtue* and *Whose Justice, Which Rationality*. Not coincidentally, it is in *After Virtue* that MacIntyre first puts forth his theory of traditions, which is then further developed and defended in *Whose Justice, Which Rationality*, which contains detailed chapters on the history of ancient Greek culture, medieval theological ethics, the Scottish Enlightenment, and the modern liberal tradition. MacIntyre's detailed account of these individual topics are not intended, it appears, to provide a "neutral" account, but rather an interpretation to support the entirety of MacIntyre's thesis about the nature of ethical traditions.

Kuhn's *The Structure of Scientific Revolutions* begins with a chapter entitled "A Role for History," and while MacIntyre evinces an interest in the history of ethics as shown in various chapters in his later writings, Kuhn was a full-time historian of science. Kuhn's career at Harvard College began as an undergraduate and eventuated in his acquiring a doctorate in physics. Instead of becoming a research scientist or a theoretical physicist, Kuhn turned to the history of science as his interest under the influence of the then President of Harvard, himself a chemist and advisor to the federal government on scientific matters, James Bryant Conant.[21] After he left Harvard, Kuhn proceeded to write articles on the history

---

[21]On the History of Science program for Harvard liberal arts students, which Conant organized and in which Kuhn taught, see references in Kuhn, *Revolutions*, xi; and James Bryant Conant, *Science and Common Sense* (New Haven: Yale University Press, 1951), vi–vii.

of science, and his first book was *The Copernican Revolution*, which indicated his interest in the history of science during times of "revolutionary" change and prefigured his later development of the theory of paradigms.

In *After Virtue*, the resemblances between MacIntyre's fully developed theory of ethics and his idea of traditions, and Kuhn's historicist version of scientific reasoning and his theory of paradigms are easily noted. MacIntyre argues that the concepts and actions of ethical theories arise in their social settings, i.e. traditions, and that "the nature of moral community and moral judgment in distinctively modern societies was such that it was no longer possible to appeal to a moral criteria in a way that had been possible in other times and places." Kuhn describes paradigms as: "some accepted examples of actual scientific practice—examples which include law, theory, application, and instrumentation together—[that] provide models from which spring particular coherent traditions of scientific research."[22] Of particular note is the idea of "untranslatability" in his later volume *Whose Justice, Which Rationality*, which MacIntyre uses to describe the current situation in the West, where advocates of differing ethical and political positions cannot find common ground for their debates. MacIntyre's thought here directly reflects Kuhn's well known presentation of "incommensurability," a term which MacIntyre also uses.

Second, a more specific resemblance between MacIntyre and Kuhn lies beyond their knowledge of the history of their respective fields, in their subsequent characterization of *traditions* and *paradigms*. For both, their interest in the history of their fields is not that that they use history for illustrative purposes, but that the fields themselves are characterized by their histories. The shared quality of both traditions and paradigms is that they constitute in effect the essence of ethical thought and science respectively, in that their participants and advocates could not recognize contrary ideas and contradictory evidence, in Kuhn's terms, "incommensurability," in MacIntyre's, "untranslatibility." Thus, paradigms are strictly speaking incomparable to one another so that as between a Ptolemaic astronomer and a Copernican, there was a psycho-social barrier that prevented each from recognizing the rationality of the opposing theory. The underlying idea of the Ptolemaic system was underwritten by the cosmology of Aristotle and by reference to particular biblical texts. The underlying idea of the Copernican system was underwritten by its putative geometric simplicity and its usefulness in the creation of navigational tables for seamen. For Galileo, arguing for the Copernican astronomy required not only that he refer to astronomical observations such as the discovery of Jupiter's moons, but also that he criticize Aristotle's mechanics and theory of impetus, while also defending himself from the charge of heresy.[23]

---

[22]Kuhn, *Revolutions*, 10.
[23]MacIntyre, "Epistemological Crises," 10.

What the Copernican revolution was for Kuhn, the breakup of medieval social forms and the rise of modern European society is for MacIntyre. This too constitutes in Kuhn's terms a "revolution," for as MacIntyre describes it, the medieval structure of feudal lord, bishop, and commoners, and the reciprocal duties of each person within that structure, provided the basis on which to make moral judgments about someone's actions or a person's character. With the rise of capitalism and Protestantism came not only the dissolution of monasteries but the dissolution of the social fabric which underwrote pre-modern European ethics. The individual replaced the society as personal psychology rather than established social norms became the reference point of moral evaluation.[24] Thus, the two competing ethical traditions could not relate rationally to one another. In *After Virtue*, MacIntyre makes a distinctive claim, i.e. that modern moral philosophy is in a manner required by the replacement of pre-modern by modern culture, and also by implication, by the evacuation of Christian ethics from Western civilization. In a historicist understanding, the variegated and contradictory state of modern ethical thought from the Enlightenment period onward, is an almost necessary consequence of the discordant fabric that characterizes modern Western culture.[25]

This comparison highlights an important difference between Kuhn's theory and MacIntyre's: namely that for Kuhn, a single paradigm comes to dominate a field or subfield of science, which, in effect, precludes the availability of contrary theories. In other words, one paradigm at a time since Kuhn's project is to explain large theory change in science. By contrast, MacIntyre's project is to explain why contemporary and post-medieval Western civilization manifests such a discordant mix of ethical options, which he does by positing the contemporaneous existence of untranslatable traditions. For in MacIntyre's view traditions do not necessarily dominate their respective cultures, as in the present times when they exist side by side in a discordant manner. Unresolvable clashes are inevitable in our contemporary culture, given the untranslatability of prevailing ethical traditions.

Third, the historicist methodology that Kuhn and MacIntyre pursue rests not only on the description of the course of successive paradigms or traditions but in a description of their global aspect. That is, at each point in history that is pictured in terms of a paradigm or a tradition, these entities are, to use a term, "global wholes" since they are not only leading and dominant ideas on an intellectual level, but also, as described at length by Kuhn and MacIntyre, involve social identity, a deep sense of personal commitment, a methodology, a means of

---

[24]MacIntyre, *Short History*, 167.

[25]*After Virtue* is predicated throughout on the idea that "after virtue," i.e. after the breakup of the late medieval ethical consensus and following the Enlightenment, a cultural condition of constant ethical invention and inevitable disagreement follows; e.g., 256; see chaps. 1–6, 17, 18.

understanding (in effect their own system of rationality), and a tool kit for solving problems. Thus change from one global whole to another is a matter of personal conversion and/or social revolution. To generalize further, the methodology of a philosophical history—historicism—provides a well-established pattern, for analysis in terms of global wholes is readily apparent in the writings of Vico, Hegel, and Collingwood. While philosophical history is done in terms of deep patterns over time, successively replacing or completing with one another, such as Hegelian "weltgeists," such history is also done by describing each dominating element that constitute these patterns as holistic entities, that is as global wholes which dominate their respective cultures. Thus for Hegel, his description of the dominant global whole of his time included, besides "mind": law, morality, art, revealed religion, and philosophy.[26] The use of a global or holistic means of historical description is obviously apparent in MacIntyre's ethical traditions and Kuhn's scientific paradigms; however, they limit their analyses/descriptions to specific areas, an approach more likely to be philosophically effective than grandiose attempts at analyzing all of human history in all its aspects, historical patterns and global wholes included.

Fourth, as historicist philosophers of ethics and science respectively, MacIntyre and Kuhn reject the universal ideal of reason as exemplified in Enlightenment thinkers, e.g., Kant and Bacon. As described by contemporary defenders of that ideal, "the Enlightenment ideal of a unified epistemology . . . discovers the foundational truths of physical and biological phenomena and unites them with an accurate understanding of humanity in its psychological, social, political, and aesthetic aspects."[27] MacIntyre and Kuhn, however, argue that any concept of universal reason, at least in the Enlightenment sense, is instantiated in a particular tradition or paradigm: for a universal reason, if it exists, is not otherwise available to human beings and the human mind, aside from a tradition or paradigm. Referring to standard ways of explaining science, e.g., by means of its general method or in terms of its explanatory progress, Kuhn writes early in his book, "Rather than being elementary logical or methodological distinctions, which would thus be prior to the analysis of scientific knowledge, they now seem integral parts of a traditional set of substantive answers to the very questions upon which they have been deployed."[28] Kuhn argues that among the elements of a paradigm is a particular way of thinking about the problems dealt with in the period of "normal science"; indeed for Kuhn when scientific research is being done during non-revolutionary times, it consists of (mere) "puzzle solving," a

---

[26]Hegel, *Philosophy of Mind*, trans. J. N. Miller and A. V. Findlay (Oxford: Clarendon Press, 1976), 293–316.

[27]Paul R. Gross and Norman Levitt, *Higher Superstition* (Baltimore, MD: Johns Hopkins University Press, 1998), 72.

[28]Kuhn, *Revolutions*, 9.

term which seemed offensive to some of his most eminent critics.[29] MacIntyre makes the corresponding point, arguing that Enlightenment liberalism does not provide access to the universal reason by which to understand ethics and politics, for the ideal of universal reason is itself a tradition. In Chapter VII of *Whose Justice, Which Rationality?*, MacIntyre, after a long preparatory discussion, (finally) makes the point: "liberalism, which began as an appeal to alleged principles of shared rationality against what was felt to be the tyranny of traditions, has itself been transformed into a tradition whose continuities are partly defined by the interminability of the debate over such principles."[30]

Both MacIntyre and Kuhn must deal with the common sense claim that while theories and explanations are fine in their place, that such things must always be judged by irreducible facts, facts which cannot be denied or glossed over. Facts, in this common sense view, are pieces of incontrovertible data and are the fundamental elements that all theories, paradigms, traditions, and general explanations must bend to accommodate. As against this prevailing view, both MacIntyre and Kuhn deny that such facts actually exist—apart, that is, from human minds' comprehension of them, with MacIntyre going so far as to re-analyze the correspondence theory of truth.[31] In this manner, both MacIntyre and Kuhn argue for the prevalence of traditions and paradigms as the essential constitutive elements of ethical thought and scientific explanation.

As a consequence of their denial of the independent existence of facts, MacIntyre and Kuhn also deny the existence of a neutral language by which to compare paradigms with one another, and traditions also. Both men use the case of translation from one language to another as comparable to "translating" one paradigm or tradition to another, but conclude simply that no neutral observation language in scientific terms, or neutral stance in ethical terms, exists. Both philosophers assert that the idea that a universal point of view is possible is an assumption or an unexamined presumption originating in Enlightenment thought; each makes the point in the context of actual theory change by closely examining historical circumstances.[32]

MacIntyre, in an effort to rebut or finesse the charge of relativism, argues that the Aristotelian/Thomist tradition has advantages over all the others in play because it can survive dialectical criticism and is better able to provide a

---

[29]See, e.g., the contributions by Watkins and Popper and Kuhn's response in *Criticism and the Growth of Knowledge* 27–30, 54–56, 241–9. Kuhn's initial characterization is in Kuhn, "Normal Science as Puzzle Solving," in *Revolutions*, chapter IV.

[30]MacIntyre, *Whose Justice*, 335.

[31]Ibid., 356–7. Kuhn, *Revolutions*, 52–3.

[32]For Kuhn, see *Criticism*, 266–77. For MacIntyre, see *After Virtue*, chap. 7 and *Whose Justice*, 345–69.

historical narrative that comprehends the opposing traditions.[33] Kuhn, by contrast, does not invest in any particular paradigm nor does he describe any kind of universal methodology beyond the rise and fall of paradigms as constituting the essence of science, guaranteeing that his critics would continually press the accusation that Kuhn's theory is epistemologically relativistic; MacIntyre writes that it is irrationalistic.[34]

IV.

MacIntyre and Kuhn contra Social Science. Social science has been promoted as the means by which previous attempts to understand human nature, society, and politics—whether by religion, literature, or philosophy—have been surpassed. Kuhn and MacIntyre must meet this claim if their own method of historical study, sociological description and dialectical analysis is to be credited; each does so, albeit in a somewhat different manner.

Kuhn noted the difference that, on a historical basis, distinguishes the social sciences from the natural sciences, is that while discussions and debates about the fundamental ground of their particular field continue to be common among practitioners of the social sciences, such grounds are settled or taken for granted in the natural sciences.[35] Chemists do not debate the issue of valence or the use of laboratory analysis to determine the nature of compounds and physicists do not argue over the existence of atoms (as they did in the late nineteenth century) or how to accurately measure energy levels. In the natural sciences such fundamental issues once they arise are settled, and remain so. (It was only in a time of severe crisis in the theoretical basis of their field at the start of the twentieth century that physicists attempted to redefine space, time, gravity, and causality.)

In the social sciences, however, such fundamental issues remain open. In anthropology, the fundamental issue of whether explanation is better done on the basis of a materialistic understanding of human nature or a standard based on human intentions (e.g., Clifford Geertz) remains an open question. Likewise, psychology, which claims to provide a scientific understanding of human nature, encompasses such a disparately broad area of research and application that university departments of psychology are divided up into experimental and clinical sub-departments whose practitioners often cannot talk to one another with understanding. Such examples are easy to multiply, even without reference to the most technically accomplished and most quantitative field of social science, economics, where in any election year the field seems divided up between

---

[33]Alasdair MacIntyre, *Three Rival Versions of Moral Enquiry* (Notre Dame, IN: University of Notre Dame Press, 1991); *Whose Justice*, 400–3; Lutz, *Tradition*, 83–5, 179–82.

[34]MacIntyre, "Epistemological Crises," 16–20.

[35]Kuhn, *Revolutions*, vii–viii.

Keynesians on one side and (Adam) Smithians on the other. If a generalization is possible in surveying these debates, it seems as if the controversies within each field are generally between advocates of two opposing approaches: a strictly empiricist approach, relying on experimentation in a laboratory setting under standard protocols whose results are quantitatively accessed and which impels to a mechanistic account of human nature; and a humanistic approach relying on narrative, intentionality and personal interaction which implies a non-quantitative element characteristic of human nature and which places social science in a separate category apart from the material phenomena dealt with by the natural sciences. If this is so, then the debates about the grounds of each of the areas of the social sciences remain intractable, forever unsettled, as such debates are at their heart philosophical and beyond empirical resolution.

Although Kuhn's recognizing this difference is one of his major contributions, nonetheless in developing his paradigm theory he utilized the sociological and psychological research current at the time. This is apparent in two specific areas: first, in cognition, where he cited experiments on human subjects that showed how such things as perspective and ambiguous shapes could foster a variety of the interpretations or change the actual sense of what a subject had seen. Second, since paradigms exist as a communal rather than as an individual enterprise or entity, Kuhn paid much attention to the social aspects of scientific research in regards, e.g., to the influence of a great scientist's reputation or social identity generally.[36] In this manner, Kuhn may be said to have relied on contemporary research in social science—psychology, sociology, and anthropology—to erect his theory of paradigms, and so introduce a distinctively social and implicitly historicist turn into Anglo-American philosophy of science.

There is an additional point here, for even as Kuhn was influenced by contemporary social science, he in turn has had a large influence on it: he is constantly cited by students of the social sciences and political scientists especially for his explicit comparison of paradigm change to political revolutions (and religious conversion experiences).[37] Further, he made the essence of science seem understandable to students of the social sciences and the humanities who, for example, did not know the calculus or atomic theory, genetics or astrophysics, because it was now only necessary to understand that science did not stand apart from normal human concerns as an ideal or a practice of rational understanding.[38]

While Kuhn acquired his notion of the incompleteness of social science by comparison with the natural sciences, MacIntyre acquired his more complex

[36]Ibid., 24, 176–81; see also chap. 10, "Revolutions as Changes of World View," esp. 111–20.
[37]MacIntyre, "Epistemological Crises," 15.
[38]See the criticism of Gross and Levitt, "The Debasement of Science Education," in *Superstition*, 244–8, which might apply also to readers of Kuhn.

ideas from another direction: not by comparison but by direct involvement. From his earliest publications in the late 1950s at least up to the 1980s, MacIntyre has thought and written on a plethora of issues of social philosophy and social scientific theory. Although he wrote about, among others, Weber, Winch, Steiner and Polanyi, and dealt with the issues of *praxis* and the relationship between reasoning and moral action, the major arc of his thought was defined by his departure from the sere plains of Marxist theorizing into the realm of historical thinking. It was in the fifteen-year period between the publications of the *Short History* and *After Virtue*, that MacIntyre's thinking was piecemeal, as he stated in *Against the Self Images of the Age*, until, that is, he became influenced by Kuhn and Lakatos at Boston University. By that time, his view of social science at large had hardened, apparently because it could not give him an intellectual basis for a philosophy of ethics.[39]

As reflected in various parts of *After Virtue* and *Whose Justice, Which Rationality?* MacIntyre has criticized modern social science as unable to provide the degree of accuracy of prediction expected from or attributed to scientific accounts. MacIntyre's exact assertion that the social sciences fail to predict is foreshadowed (once again) in the earlier essay, "Epistemological Crises" even though it does not directly mention social science. Instead, MacIntyre considers the general case of individuals who have made mistaken appraisals of other people's beliefs or assessments of themselves—unexpectedly terminated employees, jilted lovers, etc. He illustrates his point by consideration of well known literary texts, namely *Hamlet* and Jane Austin's *Emma*, in which he points out that the main characters have to choose between two or three possible schemata or interpretations in order to explain the motives of other people, a condition which he argues is endemic in social life. MacIntyre goes on to state, "an epistemological crisis is always a crisis in human relationships."[40] Understanding the origin of epistemological crises as arising from social situations indicated that MacIntyre would not place unrestrained confidence in the predictive, or indeed analytic power of the social sciences. At the time he wrote "Epistemological Crises" MacIntyre was predisposed against the "predictive power" of social science.

In *After Virtue* MacIntyre attacks the overall competence of social science in a chapter entitled, "The Character of Generalizations in Social Science and their Lack of Predictive Power." He frames the issue, however, in terms of what kind of valid knowledge is required to legitimize the power and authority of bureaucracies, those social organizations which dominate policy making and

---

[39]For a critical account of MacIntyre's early and later thought, see Stephen Turner, "MacIntyre's Damascus: In the Province of the Philosophy of Social Science": http://faculty.cas.edu/sturner5/Papers/PracticePapers.

[40]MacIntyre, "Epistemological Crises," 5; see 3–8.

execution in the all nations in the modern world: "the aim of the social sciences is to explain specifically social phenomena by supplying law-like generalizations which do not differ in their logical form from those applicable to natural phenomena in general . . . [however ,] the salient fact about those sciences in the absence of the discovery of any law-like generalizations whatsoever."[41] This is an extraordinarily strong statement exceeding any criticism that Kuhn made, but to attempt to prove it, MacIntyre considers four examples of what appear to be successful predictions from "law-like generalizations" of the social sciences. In each of the four instances, he concludes that despite the claims for their success, they in fact failed the test of predictability. He adduces three reasons for their failure in order to make the case that in general the social sciences do not successfully predict: the refusal to countenance the importance of counterfactual evidence that contradicts the prediction of laws; that the laws of social sciences lack "scope modifiers" which would delimit their application to the intended phenomena in an exact manner; that the generalizations, i.e. laws, "do not entail any well defined set of counterfactual conditionals," in effect that the generalizations of social science are not falsifiable (to use Popper's term).[42]

He concludes this long and detailed chapter (much of the substance of which is not dealt with in this summary account) with the question: "Do we now possess that set of law-like generalizations governing social behavior of the possession of which Diderot and Condorcet dreamed?"[43] MacIntyre has previously answered this question, "For the salient fact about those sciences is the absence of the discovery of any law-like generalizations whatsoever."[44] Not to have derived any useful law-like generalizations is to have failed completely the putative aim of the social sciences, which is, as much as for the natural sciences, the ability to predict and ultimately control events in the areas which they study, i.e. the human psychological and social environment. MacIntyre goes on to pursue the question of why so much authority is ceded to bureaucrats who rely on the social sciences, given their overall predictive failure. He concludes that despite the element of inevitable unpredictability in human affairs, which he equates to Machiavelli's concept of "fortuna," that belief in the validity of the results of social science research are an established part of the social setting in modern society which depends on a regime of experts to guide the fortunes of men and women and the guide the governments under which they live.[45]

---

[41]MacIntyre, *After Virtue*, 88.
[42]Ibid., 90–1.
[43]Ibid., 87.
[44]Ibid., 87–8.
[45]Ibid., 107–8.

V.

Metaphysical Biology, History, and Ontology. To say that MacIntyre and Kuhn are post-Enlightenment thinkers seems obvious as they have made the point themselves, but, again speaking in broad terms, we can ask if they are *post-modern* thinkers in the sense that they deny the reality of truth in terms of a "master narrative." Given that they are so particular and detailed on the points of fact and common language, it would seem an inevitable if unwelcome conclusion that, to extend the point, both MacIntyre and Kuhn are relativists in their approach to ethics and science respectively. Both philosophers deny that implication; however, to overcome that criticism, it would seem ultimately necessary for each to describe in terms appropriate to their general subject matter a metaphysical underpinning, a methodology, or an ultimate ground of experience. It seems fair to say that Kuhn does not attempt to accomplish this, but that MacIntyre does.

Historicist accounts invite the inevitable question of what the nature of reality must be like in order to support such an account, for if reality itself must defined in terms of narrative or history then it may appear that the human mind creates its own reality, without reference to any external, or "real" reality. According to MacIntyre, Kuhn never escapes this dilemma because he never attempts to give an account of the nature of (physical) reality that undergirds the research activities of scientists, via paradigms. Like many critics of Kuhn, MacIntyre lights on the issue of incommensurability, arguing that Kuhn goes too far in emphasizing this admittedly important phenomenon, since it renders Kuhn's theory in effect an argument for irrationalism: "It is not just that the adherents of rival paradigms disagree [for Kuhn], but that *every* relevant area of rationality is invaded by that disagreement." MacIntyre expands on the point at length, citing in conclusion, "Kuhn's disregard for ontological truth."[46]

Aware of the dilemma, how does MacIntyre, within the terms and concepts of his own historicist theory of ethics, overcome it? To answer this question in the most general terms, i.e. in terms of historicism and ontology, is beyond the scope of this paper (indeed of the scope of this writer).[47] The ultimate

---

[46]MacIntyre, "Epistemological Crises," 17; cf. 21.

[47]The question arises for MacIntyre, does his rejection of the Enlightenment ideal of universal reason also imply a rejection of natural law doctrine as exemplified, e.g., in Aquinas? While at one point, in response no less to a papal request made of the University of Notre Dame to examine the issue of natural law, MacIntyre did attempt to deal with the issue, his essay is, in this writer's opinion, not very useful. MacIntyre's contribution in the volume was to set up a position that was commented on by other scholars, but it is a reprise of his earlier writings and does not significantly develop his thought in this direction. See MacIntyre, *Intractable Disputes about the Natural Law* (Notre Dame, IN: University of Notre Dame Press, 2009), 1–52. Lutz, writing from a Thomistic perspective, provides a detailed analysis: Lutz, *Tradition*, 141–52.

reference in regard to discovering an ontological basis for MacIntyre's traditionalist/historicist theory of ethics is, appropriately enough, the thought of Aristotle. Aristotle, though he was conversant with the history of philosophy that had been developed up to his own time was most notably a biologist, the first to make up a classification of life forms and the first to do systematic recording of dissections and observations of animal species (e.g., *Parts of Animals*). The link between Aristotle's biology and his ethics is the concept of teleology, for he referred in his biological observations to the functions of internal organs (such as the liver) and external (such as hooves) and ultimately asked as the principal question of ethics: what is the good for mankind in terms of enquiring what mankind's ultimate end is (or what is the purpose of human existence).[48] Writing of ends and purposes was Aristotle's way of providing a comprehensive understanding of biology, ethics, human nature, and nature as a whole. Thus, in approaching the issue of an ontological basis for his ethical theory, MacIntyre refers to Aristotle's "metaphysical biology" and attempts his own version in a short but resonant book, *Dependent Rational Animals*.

In MacIntyre's treatment of the issue, however, he does not in fact attempt a precisely "metaphysical" biology of his own, *a la* Aristotle. His approach in *Dependent Rational Animals* is to note two aspects of human nature. First, the close relationship between the human and animal species—a point well noted by both Aristotle and Darwin; MacIntyre dotes on dolphins, the sleek aquatic mammal with advanced cognitive abilities. Second, MacIntyre, in an implicitly Christian vein, brings attention to the physical and emotional vulnerabilities of people and their mutual interdependence—the adults guiding the young, the able-bodied assisting the disabled, the well-to-do helping the poor, the clear-headed instructing the confused—in effect, a discourse on human dependency and weakness.[49] This approach is more, as it were, Augustinian than Thomistic, since MacIntyre does not offer a philosophy of nature as such and is based more on a meditational approach than on a description of metaphysical architecture.

In general, MacIntyre's attempt at a biological basis of ethics seems to miss the point by not burrowing deeply enough into the question so as to be able to erect a philosophical substructure which can support his historicist ethics. One reason for this, it is possible to infer, is that MacIntyre accepts the premise of modern biology that excludes teleological explanation whatever, and that he accepts this limitation of Darwinian biology. (In this respect, it is notable that MacIntyre cites approvingly Arnhart who wrote a philosophical attempt at a

---

[48]Aristotle, *Nichomachean Ethics*, bk. I, ch. 1–4.

[49]Alasdair MacIntyre, *Dependent Rational Animals: Why Human Beings Need the Virtues* (LaSalle, IL: Open Court, 1999).

naturalistic basis for "natural right" explicitly comparing Darwin to Aquinas.)[50] Given this limitation, MacIntyre, primarily an ethicist, derives characteristics—the animal ancestry and inherent weakness of human beings—that are of intrinsic interest to an ethicist's understanding of human nature but which do not provide an ontology.

This lack of an ontological view, if it is such, can hardly be due to MacIntyre's insufficient knowledge of Aristotle's doctrine or the history of scientific ideas but may finally be related to what was adverted to above, namely the resistance to or lack of necessity to provide an ontology when doing philosophy from a historicist perspective. For in a completely historicist manner of doing philosophy it will be argued that a trans-historical view of things such as presented in a metaphysical ontology is inherently presumptuous, probably false, and certainly unverifiable; for no such general idea or "form" can be provided in a manner which transcends historical conditions. In this way, historicists refuse in effect to develop a general metaphysics or an ontology, which is as true of Vico and Collingwood as it is of Kuhn and MacIntyre.

Yet MacIntyre goes beyond Kuhn by providing within his view of traditions what Kuhn does not in his view of paradigms: namely, a recognition that adherents of a traditions have of the critical nature of their own commitments and of their ability to compare their tradition with others. It is the knowledge of the possibility of internal contradiction which forces reliance on dialectic and criticism which is as it were the method MacIntyre utilizes, so that unlike *paradigms*, adherents to a *tradition* may self-criticize, anticipate contradictions to their own tradition, cross-talk with adherents to competing traditions, and finally make a definitive comparison.[51] For MacIntyre, in defiance of postmodernist strictures, defends and relies on a master narrative, namely the Thomistic/ Aristotelian tradition—which is not an ontology but rather a history of the one competing tradition which is more comprehensive and with more explanatory power than its competitors. But does this then provide a general method, a means perhaps of transcending the relativistic epistemology of postmodernism? In his critical analysis of traditions, which applies to historicist global wholes generally, MacIntyre has gone further in providing a solution to this question than Kuhn, certainly, and any historicist philosopher since Hegel.

Rivier University
Nashua, New Hampshire

---

[50]MacIntyre, *Dependent Rational Animals*, 12, 125. See Larry Arnhart, *Darwinian Natural Right: The Biological Ethics of Human Nature* (Albany: SUNY Press, 1998).
[51]See MacIntyre, "The Rationality of Traditions," in *Whose Justice*, 349–69.

Alasdair MacIntyre as a Marxist and as a Critic of Marxism[1]

Paul Blackledge

Abstract. This essay reconstructs Alasdair MacIntyre's engagement with Marxism with a view both to illuminating the co-ordinates of his mature thought and to outlining a partial critique of that thought. While the critique of Marxism outlined in *After Virtue* is well known, until recently Marx's profound influence on MacIntyre was obscured by a thoroughly misleading attempt to label him as a communitarian thinker. If this erroneous interpretation of MacIntyre's mature thought is now widely discredited, the fact that he has distanced himself from several of the arguments he previously gave for rejecting Marxism both reduces the theoretical space between his mature thought and his early Marxism and highlights a consistent theme in his critique of Marxism since the 1960s to which this essay is addressed: his dissatisfaction with the ethical dimension of Marxist attempts to theorise the relationship between socialist militants and the working-class movement from below.

I.

Introduction. In his 1995 introduction to *Marxism and Christianity*, Alasdair MacIntyre claimed that Marxism "is the only secular post-enlightenment doctrine to have" a metaphysical and moral scope comparable to that of Christianity.[2] This was not meant as a mere academic point,

---

[1]This essay extends arguments first outlined in several earlier essays including Paul Blackledge, "Freedom, Desire and Revolution: Alasdair MacIntyre's Early Marxist Ethics," *History of Political Thought* 25, no. 4 (2005): 696–720; Blackledge, "Morality and Revolution: Ethical Debates in the British New Left," *Critique* 35, no. 2 (2007): 203–220; Blackledge, "Alasdair MacIntyre's Contribution to Marxism: A Road not Taken," *Analyse and Kritik* 30, no. 1 (2008): 215–27; and Paul Blackledge and Neil Davidson, "Introduction: The Unknown Alasdair MacIntyre," in *Alasdair MacIntyre's Engagement with Marxism: Essays and Articles 1953–1974*, ed. Paul Blackledge and Neil Davidson (Leiden: Brill, 2008), xiii–l.

[2]Alasdair MacIntyre, "Introduction, 1953, 1968, 1995: Three Perspectives," in *Marxism and Christianity*, 2 ed. (London: Duckworth, 1995), vi, republished as Alasdair MacIntyre, "Three Perspectives on Marxism: 1953, 1968, 1995," in *Ethics and Politics* (Cambridge: Cambridge University Press, 2006), 145–58, at 146.

©2014, *American Catholic Philosophical Quarterly*, Vol. 88, No. 4   pp. 705–724
doi: 10.5840/acpq201491127

for *Marxism: An Interpretation* (the title of the first, 1953, edition of *Marxism and Christianity*) was written as a contribution to what he hoped would be a renewal of Christianity. MacIntyre was drawn towards Marxism because, as he saw it, Marx's political theory converged with his vision of critical Christian ethics: "Marxism is of first-class theological significance as a secularism formed by the gospel which is committed to the problem of power and justice and therefore to themes of redemption and renewal which its history cannot but illuminate."[3] Moreover, he perceived a parallel between the situation faced by Marx in the early 1840s and that encountered by contemporary [1950s] Christians. Whereas Marx "was faced with a stark antithesis" between both Hegel's and Feuerbach's visions of human freedom, and the reality of the world of work and suffering, contemporary Christianity accepted a split between the sacred and the secular such that it had lost any critical perspective on the world. Indeed, because modern Christianity had reduced faith to a matter of personal taste, it no longer concretely criticised social injustice and thus did not interfere with daily secular existence. MacIntyre believed that Christians would do well to learn from Marx's turn to politics in his attempt to overcome the gap between reality and the vision of freedom in Hegel's system.[4]

The point made by MacIntyre in 1953 illuminates the leftist backdrop to his later claim that "my critique of liberalism is one of the few things that has gone unchanged in my overall view throughout my whole life. Ever since I understood liberalism, I have wanted nothing to do with it—and that was when I was seventeen years old."[5] MacIntyre's critique of liberalism was profoundly influenced by Marx and his intellectual evolution over the past six decades has been marked by this influence alongside his Christianity. Indeed, it is very interesting that he eventually came to reject Marxism not so much for its revolutionary substance but rather for its failure fully to disassociate itself from inherited aspects of liberal theory, particularly liberal moral theory.[6]

MacIntyre's criticisms of liberal moral theory are well known and need only be briefly restated. In *After Virtue* he famously argued that in the modern world moral arguments could be reduced to "masks for expressions of personal

---

[3]Alasdair MacIntyre, *Marxism: An Interpretation* (London: SCM, 1953), 18. For the relationship between MacIntyre's youthful Christianity and his Marxism see Peter McMylor, *Alasdair MacIntyre: Critic of Modernity* (London: Routledge, 1994) and McMylor, "Marxism and Christianity: Dependencies and Differences in Alasdair MacIntyre's Critical Social Thought," *Theoria* 55, no. 116 (August 2008): 45–66.

[4]MacIntyre, *Marxism: An Interpretation*, 45, 10.

[5]Alasdair MacIntyre, "Interview with Professor Alasdair MacIntyre," *Kinesis* 20 (1994): 34–47, at 43

[6]Alasdair MacIntyre, *After Virtue: A Study in Moral Theory* (London: Duckworth, 1985), x.

preference,"[7] whose premises often proved incommensurable. Indeed, he suggested that Marx was "right when he argued against the English trade unionists of the 1860s that appeals to justice were pointless, since there are rival conceptions of justice formed by and informing the life of rival groups."[8] Furthermore, though he disagreed with Marx's suggestion that contestations over the nature of justice were secondary social phenomena, he believed that Marx was "fundamentally right in seeing conflict and not consensus at the heart of modern social structure":[9] "modern politics is civil war carried out by other means."[10]

Nonetheless, though MacIntyre expected Marxists would be sympathetic to a great deal of the critique of liberal individualist (bourgeois) morality outlined in *After Virtue*, he believed that they would reject his "realistic" political alternative to the status quo. This realism grew in part out of a critique of Marx's alternative to capitalism. Against Marxism, MacIntyre argued, first, that in the century since Marx's death, insofar as Marxists had taken "explicit moral stances" they tended to fall back on either one form or another of Kantianism or utilitarianism. Second, Marx failed to conceptualise the means through which his vision of "a community of free individuals" was to be constructed. Third, Marxists in power had tended to become Weberians. Fourth, Marx's political optimism was undermined by capitalism's tendency to morally impoverish the human resources necessary to renew society. Additionally, he insisted that anyone who took Trotsky's mature analysis of the Soviet Union seriously would be drawn to embrace a form of political pessimism that was incompatible with Marxism.[11] Finally, he argued that, in conditions of moral impoverishment, Marxists were wont to construct their own "versions of the *Übermensch*": for instance, "Lukács's ideal proletarian" or "Leninism's ideal revolutionary."[12]

More recently, MacIntyre has added the claim that, while workers may have embodied in their practice a revolutionary ethics of emancipation, at certain moments in history, the process of proletarianization, by contrast with Marx's

---

[7]Ibid., 19.

[8]Ibid., 250.

[9]Ibid., 252–3.

[10]Ibid., 113.

[11]One problem with this argument is that Trotsky's understanding of the class nature of the Soviet Union was, as MacIntyre had previously argued, in a process of change at the time of his death. See Alasdair MacIntyre, "Trotsky in Exile," in *Alasdair MacIntyre's Engagement with Marxism*. For a sense of Trotsky's evolving position see, Leon Trotsky, "The USSR in War," in *In Defense of Marxism* (New York: Pathfinder, 1990). For a discussion of the contradictions between Trotsky's analysis of the Soviet Union and his broader interpretation of Marxism see my "Results and Prospects: Trotsky and his Critics," in *Permanent Revolution: Results and Prospects 100 Years On*, ed. Bill Dunn and Hugo Radice (London: Pluto Press, 2006), 48–60.

[12]MacIntyre, *After Virtue*, 261–2; see also Alasdair MacIntyre, *A Short History of Ethics* (London: Routledge: 1967), 214.

expectations to the contrary, simultaneously made resistance a necessary part of the lives of the working class while robbing this resistance of its emancipatory potential. Proletarianisation "tends to deprive workers of those forms of practice through which they can discover conceptions of a good and of virtues adequate to the moral needs of resistance."[13] Consequently, whereas MacIntyre had, in the late 1950s and early 1960s, argued that working class struggles could provide the basis for the creation of a truly human community, in the 1980s he saw no alternative to liberal individualism except as a form of virtue ethics rooted in the practices of small communities.

There is much to commend in MacIntyre's critique of Marxism, particularly his claim that Marxists have tended to oscillate between Kantian and utilitarian justifications for their politics. Conversely, he has outlined a powerful and appealing critique of liberal ethics that draws deeply, as Fredric Jameson points out, on the rich legacy of the Marxist tradition.[14] This Marxist influence on his work marks a continuity with his youthful writings where he suggested a Marxist route out of the dead ends of Kantian and utilitarian ethics while, contra more recent analytical contributions to debates about Marxism and morality, remaining true to Marx's revolutionary political project.[15] The reasons for MacIntyre's rejection of this project in the 1960s, included, as I have argued elsewhere, his dismissal both of Marx's theory of economic crisis and any essentialist theories of human nature.[16] Interestingly, he has recently signalled a change of heart on both these issues. Thus, whereas the arguments of *A Short History of Ethics* and *After Virtue* similarly involved refusals of the concept of human nature, *Dependent Rational Animals* includes the argument that the theses of these books were weakened by their shared supposition of the possibility of "an ethics independent of biology."[17] Moreover, his introduction to the 1995 edition of *Marxism and Christianity* suggests that he had previously been too harsh on Marx's labour theory of value, and by implication his theory of crisis.[18] In thus reappraising his relationship to Marx's economic theory and more general theories of human nature, MacIntyre has significantly reduced the theoretical space between his mature thought and his early Marxism.

---

[13]Alasdair MacIntyre, "The Theses on Feuerbach: A Road Not Taken" in *The MacIntyre Reader*, ed. Kelvin Knight (Cambridge: Polity, 1998), 232.

[14]Fredric Jameson, "Morality versus Ethical Substance," in *The Ideologies of Theory: Essays 1971–1986*, vol. 1, ed. Fredric Jameson (Minneapolis: University of Minnesota Press, 1988), 181.

[15]See Paul Blackledge, *Marxism and Ethics* (New York: SUNY Press, 2012), 150–7, 179–89.

[16]Paul Blackledge, "Freedom, Desire and Revolution: Alasdair MacIntyre's Marxist Ethics" *History of Political Thought*, 26, no. 4 (2005): 696–720.

[17]Alasdair MacIntyre, *Dependent Rational Animals* (London: Duckworth, 1999), p. x.

[18]Alasdair MacIntyre, "Introduction," in *Marxism and Christianity*, xx; MacIntyre, "Three Perspectives on Marxism," 152.

This shift is evident in the 2004 preface to his 1958 study of Freud: *The Unconscious*. In this essay he reasserts the necessity of linking psychoanalysis and politics through the concept of desire in a way that is reminiscent of his early Marxism, but which stands in sharp contrast to the general trajectory of his thought from the 1960s to the 1980s.[19] While a large gap remains between MacIntyre's contemporary moral and political thought and Marxism, his changed perspective at least opens up the possibility of a renewed dialogue between the two.[20] It is with a view to facilitating such a dialogue that this essay traces the contours of MacIntyre's relationship with Marxism in the 1960s. In particular, I want to interrogate MacIntyre's claim that Marxism's moral flaws stem from its liberal inheritance through the lens of his discussion of the problem of organised socialist agency within the class struggle. Indeed, I argue that this problem, the problem of socialist leadership, sits at the core of MacIntyre's critique of Marxism.

II.

MacIntyre's Early Marxism. There is a contradiction at the heart of Marxism. On the one hand, Marx holds to an ultra-democratic conception of socialism as a process of proletarian self-emancipation; while, on the other hand, he insists that the dominant ideas in society are at any given time the ideas of the ruling class.[21] Simply put, the latter claim seems to negate the possibility of the former. This contradiction has been expressed by many Marxist intellectuals through a fundamental misconception of the role of socialist militants within the workers' movement. Whereas some have downplayed this role through a fatalistic assumption about the victory of socialism being guaranteed by the laws of history, others have effectively embraced a voluntaristic view of history in which militants play the role of anti-Nietzschean supermen (who are unfortunately characterised by all the negatives of the original but without their sense of self-awareness!).

That this contradiction has roots in reality does not detract from the fact that it presents a very real problem for Marxists. To the extent that Marxists have engaged with this issue they have tended to address it as a political, rather than a moral, concern—usually through the medium of a contrast between Lenin's vanguardist model of socialist leadership and Rosa Luxemburg's defence of the spontaneous creativity of working-class struggle.

---

[19]Alasdair MacIntyre, *The Unconscious: A Conceptual Analysis* (London: Routledge, 2004), 27, 114.

[20]See, for instance, MacIntyre's reply to his critics, including myself, in "Where We Were, Where We Are, Where We Need to Be," in *Virtue and Politics*, ed. Paul Blackledge and Kelvin Knight (Notre Dame, IN: University of Notre Dame Press, 2011).

[21]Tony Cliff, "Revolution and Counter-Revolution: Lessons for Indonesia," in *International Struggles and the Marxist Tradition* (London: Bookmarks, 2001), 311–26, at 317.

Though this is a largely caricatured debate,[22] its polarities express important aspects of social reality. Who would want, for instance, to reject the ideas either of leadership or of spontaneity when assessing the recent revolutionary movement in Egypt? In the third of his theses on Feuerbach, Marx addressed this contradiction through the concept of revolutionary practice: "the coincidence of the changing of circumstances and of human activity or self-changing can be conceived and rationally understood only as *revolutionary practice.*"[23] Though this claim can clearly be interpreted as leaning towards Luxemburg's interpretation of Marxism, it is not difficult to find quotations from Marx that equally prefigure Lenin's writings: for instance, in the 1850 March Address, he wrote, "the workers' party, therefore, must act in the most organised, most unanimous and most independent fashion possible."[24]

In relation to moral theory, while fatalism, like pre-Marxist materialism, leaves little space for free will and morality, voluntarism points in the opposite direction toward an abstract conception of agency that, like Kantian morality, doesn't know real sensuous human activity as such.[25] It is unsurprising that among revolutionary socialists who have embraced a variant of political voluntarism, including perhaps most famously Karl Liebknecht, there has been a tendency to reduce socialist morality to a form of Kantianism. And though Liebknecht won MacIntyre's admiration—"one Liebknecht [is worth] a hundred Webers"[26]—the path to Kant was clearly not one he was likely to follow. Conversely, Karl Kautsky, who tends to play the role of Liebknecht's "fatalistic other" within the annals of the international socialist movement, has rightly been dismissed by MacIntyre for the opposite error of deifying history as the arbiter of moral judgement.[27]

At one level, these are unoriginal criticisms of voluntaristic and fatalistic variants of Marxism. Neither does MacIntyre's originally lie in the generalisation

---

[22]See Paul Blackledge, "What was Done," *International Socialism* 111, no. 2 (2006): 111–26, at 116.

[23]This is the third of Marx's famous theses on Feuerbach. See Karl Marx, "Theses on Feuerbach," in *Early Writings* (London: Penguin, 1975), 421–3.

[24]Karl Marx and Frederick Engels, "Address of the Central Authority to the League: March 1850," in Marx and Engels, *Collected Works*, v. 10 (New York: International Publishers, 1978), 278.

[25]Thus, in the third thesis on Feuerbach, Marx wrote that, "[t]he chief defect of all hitherto existing materialism—that of Feuerbach included—is that the thing, reality, sensuousness, is conceived only in the form of the *object or of contemplation*, but not as *sensuous human activity, practice*, not subjectively. Hence, in contradistinction to materialism, the *active* side was developed abstractly by idealism—which, of course, does not know real, sensuous activity as such." Karl Marx, "Theses on Feuerbach."

[26]Alasdair MacIntyre, "Causality and History," in *Essays on Explanation and Understanding*, ed. Juha Manninen and Raimo Tuomela (Boston: D. Reidel, 1976), quoted in Kelvin Knight, *Aristotelian Philosophy* (Cambridge: Polity, 2007), 127.

[27]Alasdair MacIntyre, *Marxism and Christianity* (London: Duckworth, 1968), 101.

of these criticisms to Marxism as a whole. Indeed, his 1973 critique of Lenin for embracing an "ideology of expertise" in which the revolutionary "cannot avoid in himself the very elitism which he attacks in others"[28] is uninteresting insofar as it rehearses what Lars Lih calls the "textbook interpretation" of Leninism.[29] Rather, MacIntyre's importance as a critic of Marxism stems from his awareness of the ethical implications of this criticism; in particular his claim that Lenin's failings reflect the sedimentation within Marxism of aspects of the liberal inheritance that Marxists have never adequately addressed.

What is particularly interesting about MacIntyre's critique of Marxism is the route through heterodox Trotskyism by which he came to these conclusions. Elsewhere,[30] I have traced the process whereby he intervened within an ethical debate within the British New Left after 1956 to articulate a distinct and novel Marxist ethics of liberation in opposition to both Kantian and consequentialist alternatives. Briefly summarised, this debate had Edward Thompson and Harry Hanson play the roles of consequentialist and Kantian respectively, while Mac-Intyre intervened from a position strongly influenced by Marx's dialectical sublation of materialism and idealism. Thompson, in his 1957 essay "Socialist Humanism," criticised the Stalinists for the inhumanity of their system, but tacitly accepted their consequentialist frame of reference, when he commented that, although they had employed bad means, the Russians had gone some way towards realising, at least aspects of, socialism.[31] Conversely, Hanson denounced the Stalinist experiment *tout court* as an assault on basic human rights.[32] If Hanson criticised Thompson's moral consequentialism without providing a viable alternative to it, Charles Taylor argued that Thompson's attempt to retrieve a vibrant Marx from the carcass of Stalinism elided over deep problems within Marxism itself. For Marx's understandable impatience with abstract moral criticisms of capitalism, and his counter-position of proletarian virtue to bourgeois morality could easily slip into a justification for the type of revolutionary elitism that had morphed into Stalinism. The party, according to Taylor, could imagine itself as the embodiment of proletarian virtue against the real inadequacies of the proletariat.[33]

---

[28]Alasdair MacIntyre, "Ideology, Social Science and Revolution," *Comparative Politics* 5, no. 3 (July 1973): 340–2.

[29]Lars Lih, *Lenin Rediscovered* (Leiden: Brill, 2006).

[30]Blackledge, "Morality and Revolution: Ethical Debates in the British New Left."

[31]Edward Thompson, "Socialist Humanism," *The New Reasoner* 1 (Summer 1957): 105–43.

[32]Harry Hanson, "An Open Letter to Edward Thompson," *The New Reasoner* 2 (Autumn 1957): 79–91.

[33]Taylor, Charles, "Marxism and Humanism," *The New Reasoner* 2 (Autumn 1957): 92–8; Cf. Taylor, Charles, "Socialism and Intellectuals—Three," *Universities and Left Review* 2 (Summer 1957): 18–9.

In his contribution to this debate, MacIntyre sought to defend the essence of Thompson's socialist humanism so that it was no longer susceptible to the types of critique mounted by Hanson and Taylor. The resulting essay, "Notes from the Moral Wilderness," reads in many ways as a precursor to the thesis of *After Virtue*, but without the concluding dismissal of Marxism. In opposition both to Stalin's teleology of historical progress and to Kant's ahistorical categorical imperative, MacIntyre suggested that we should look for a "theory which treats what emerges in history as providing us with a basis for our standards, without making the historical process morally sovereign or its progress automatic."[34] He went on to argue that if Marxists were to make human actions intelligible then they should, contra Kant, follow Aristotle in linking ethics to human desires.[35]

Nevertheless, MacIntyre followed Marx in accepting that human desires had been remoulded by capitalism such that it was important to ask, first, if this remoulding was absolute, and, second, if it was not absolute was it possible that it might be transcended? To understand these issues historically it is necessary to ask if a form of human nature could emerge in the modern world such that the needs and desires of individuals are not felt to be in simple atomised opposition one to the other? Marx, according to MacIntyre, comprehended both the deep historical and sociological content to this question when he suggested that "the emergence of human nature is something to be comprehended only in terms of the history of class-struggle. Each age reveals a development of human potentiality which is specific to that form of social life and which is specifically limited by the class-structure of that society." In particular, under advanced capitalism, "the growth of production makes it possible [for man] to re-appropriate his own nature." This is true in two ways: first, the increasing productivity of labour produces the potential for us all to lead much richer lives, both morally and materially; and second, capitalism also creates an agency—the proletariat—which, through its struggles for freedom, embodies a new collectivist spirit, out of which individuals come to understand both that their needs and desires can best be satisfied through collective channels, and that they do in fact need and desire solidarity.[36] According to MacIntyre in 1958–1959, the proletariat, in its struggles against capital, was beginning to create the conditions for the solution of the contemporary problems of morality; it embodies the practice that could overcome the "rift between our conception of morality and our conception of desire."[37]

---

[34]MacIntyre, "Notes from the Moral Wilderness" in *Alasdair MacIntyre's Engagement with Marxism*, 57.

[35]Ibid. 58–60.

[36]Ibid., 64.

[37]Ibid., 63.

III.

On Self-Emancipation and Socialist Leadership. Though MacIntyre believed that the link between socialism and proletarian practice was inscribed within capitalist relations of production, at the turn of the 1960s he did not accept that the socialist potential of the struggles of the working class could be realised independently of some form of political organisation. In an argument strongly influenced by perspectives developed in the French Marxist journal *Socialisme ou Barbarie*, he claimed that socialist ideas where not to come, pace Kautsky and Lenin, from without the working class, but would be rooted in worker's consciousness of the spontaneous struggles against capital at the "point of production." He argued that a revolutionary socialist party should therefore orientate towards these struggles because it was at this level that the dominance of bourgeois ideas began to be challenged and thus where people in "our society . . . begin to act and think for themselves."[38]

Edited by Cornelius Castoriadis and Claude Lefort, *Socialisme ou Barbarie* was one of a number of groupings to emerge out of the post-war crisis of Trotskyism. These factions were united in agreeing, negatively, that Trotsky had been wrong to classify the Soviet social formation as a degenerate workers' state, and, positively, that Stalin's Russia was a form of state capitalism. Alongside Castoriadis's French grouping, this international milieu included the American Johnson-Forrest Tendency led by Raya Dunayevskaya and C. L. R. James and the British *Socialist Review/International Socialism* group led by Tony Cliff and Mike Kidron.[39] Interestingly, by placing Marx's concept of proletarian self-emancipation at the centre of their criticism of orthodox Trotskyism, all three of these groups were drawn towards questioning the relationship of Leninism to Marxism.

MacIntyre's attempt to come to terms with the dialectic of spontaneity and leadership within the socialist movement was profoundly influenced by these debates. In "Breaking the Chains of Reason," he insisted that freedom cannot be won by telling the masses to do what the elite desires they do, but only by helping "them move where they desire. The goal is not happiness, or satisfaction, but freedom. And freedom has to be both means and ends. The mechanical

---

[38]MacIntyre, "The 'New Left,'" in *Alasdair MacIntyre's Engagement with Marxism*. Cf. Cornelius Castoriadis, "The Proletariat and Organisation," *Socialisme Ou Barbarie* 1959, reprinted in Castoriadis, *Political and Social Writings*, vol. 2 (Minneapolis: University of Minnesota Press, 1988).

[39]According to Marcel van der Linden all three of these groups broke with orthodox Trotskyism between 1948 and 1951 and kept in contact with each other over the next decade: cf. Marcel van der Linden "Socialisme ou Barbarie: A French Revolutionary Group (1949–65)," *Left History* 5, no.1 (1997): 7–37.

separation of means and ends is suitable enough for human manipulation, not human liberation."[40] Moreover, for MacIntyre, emancipatory politics emerge spontaneously through the struggles of the working class against capitalism.[41] Because freedom is both the means and end of socialist activity, such activity, contra the Kantians, required a strong anchorage in contemporary history, while, contra the consequentialists, it was not a reified end that could be inaugurated by any one of a variety of means. MacIntyre concluded, "the philosophers have continued to interpret the world differently; the point remains, to change it."[42]

MacIntyre's most important contribution to the debate on socialist strategy, "Freedom and Revolution," articulated a broader socialist politics rooted in the experience of workers at the point of production. Published in *Labour Review* early in 1960, this essay challenged the negative liberal understanding of freedom that was common within New Left criticisms of Leninism through the medium of the Hegelian argument that human freedom can only be realised through some form of social organisation. He suggested that because capitalism constrains human freedom, the struggle for freedom must involve a struggle against capitalism. Moreover, this struggle demanded a "vanguard party" because the working class, on whose conscious agency socialism depended, could not achieve socialist consciousness "spontaneously." The role of the vanguard party was, therefore, not to build freedom, but to move "the working class to build it."[43]

To the extent that MacIntyre complemented this insight with a concrete discussion of the mechanisms through which the party might interact with the working class in this process, he merely noted that it should act as an organisation of "continuous education" through which it would "enable its members to withstand all the pressures of other classes and to act effectively against the ruling class." Moreover, he noted that this function required some form of discipline through which the party might guard itself against "alien class pressures." Thus, against the tendency within the New Left to equate their break with Stalinism with a fundamental critique of Leninism, MacIntyre defended the applicability of Leninism to an authentic socialist practice.[44]

Amongst MacIntyre's interlocutors on the revolutionary wing of the New Left, Cliff Slaughter criticised him for his inadequate conceptualisation of conscious "political leadership." Against MacIntyre's suggestion that the party would

---

[40]MacIntyre, "Breaking the Chains of Reason," in *Alasdair MacIntyre's Engagement with Marxism*, 163.

[41]Ibid. 165.

[42]Ibid., 166.

[43]MacIntyre, "Freedom and Revolution," in *Alasdair MacIntyre's Engagement with Marxism*, 132.

[44]Ibid.

merely mediate against the pressures of conformism inherent in bourgeois life, Slaughter insisted that it must be more than this: "it must be the vanguard of revolutionary action" who would pass socialist theory "from bourgeois intellectuals" to the working class "from outside."[45]

Slaughter's criticism of MacIntyre was tangential to the main focus of his essay, which was intended as a critique of the ideas of Cornelius Castoriadis's journal *Socialisme ou Barbarie*. Castoriadis characterised capitalism through the idea of a "permanent crisis," which "owes its origin to the conflict at the point of production."[46] Prefiguring arguments outlined by MacIntyre in "Freedom and Revolution," Castoriadis suggested that the "proletariat's struggle against capitalism . . . begins at the point of production" where there exists "an autonomous development of the proletariat towards socialism."[47] Castoriadis believed that the role of socialists was, contra Lenin and Kautsky, not to bring consciousness to the working class from without, but to express and give shape to the struggle from below.[48]

As we have noted, it was to this model of socialist leadership that MacIntyre was drawn at the turn of the 1960s. And as against Slaughter's elitism, he repeatedly quoted the third of Marx's theses on Feuerbach: "The materialist doctrine that men are products of circumstances and upbringing, and that, therefore, changed men are products of other circumstances and changed upbringing forgets that it is men that change circumstances and that the educator must himself be educated. Hence this doctrine necessarily arrives at dividing society into two parts, of which one is superior to society."[49] Commenting on these lines, MacIntyre wrote:

> As Marx saw it, this doctrine implies the sharpest of divisions in society between those who know and those who do not, the manipulators and the manipulated. Classical Marxism stands in stark contrast to this: it wants to transform the vast mass of mankind from victims and puppets into agents who are masters of their own lives. But Stalinism treated Marxist theory as the discovery of the objective and unchangeable laws of history, and glorified the party bureaucrats as the men who possessed the knowledge which enabled and entitled them to manipulate the rest of mankind.[50]

---

[45]Cliff Slaughter, "What is Revolutionary Leadership?," *Labour Review* 5, no. 3 (Oct./Nov. 1960): 93–6, 105–11 at 107, 109.

[46]Castoriadis, "Proletariat and Organisation I," in *Political and Social Writings*, 195. This essay was first published in *Socialisme ou Barbarie* in 1959.

[47]Ibid., 195, 199.

[48]Ibid., 211.

[49]Karl Marx, "Theses on Feuerbach," 421–3 .

[50]MacIntyre, "Communism and British Intellectuals," *Alasdair MacIntyre's Engagement with Marxism*, 119. cf. MacIntyre, "Breaking the Chains of Reason."

Despite his affinities to *Socialisme ou Barbarie*, in 1960 MacIntyre joined the editorial board of the journal *International Socialism*. Associated with the ideas of Tony Cliff and Mike Kidron, *International Socialism* stood alongside *Socialisme ou Barbarie* in attempting to rethink the problem of socialist leadership through the lens of Marx's concept of proletarian self-emancipation. However, whereas Castoriadis made a fairly absolute break with Lenin, Cliff's criticisms were much more measured.[51] This was true even in 1959 when he published a short study of Rosa Luxemburg's Marxism in which he argued that "for Marxists, in advanced industrial countries, Lenin's original position can serve much less as a guide than Rosa Luxemburg's, notwithstanding her overstatements on the question of spontaneity."[52] A year later, he extended this argument to position himself some way between Castoriadis's spontaneism and Slaughter's elitism in which he argued that, "the revolutionary party must conduct a dialogue with the workers outside it. The party, in consequence, should not invent tactics out of thin air, but put as its first duty to learn from the experience of the mass movement and then generalise from it."[53] Against a top-down model of socialist leadership, Cliff insisted that "the revolutionary party, while conscious of its leading role, must beware of slipping into a way of thinking that the party is the fount of all correct thoughts and deeds, while the working class remains an inert mass without initiative."[54] At this juncture Cliff's arguments were very close to those of MacIntyre, who in the pamphlet "What is Marxist Theory For?," suggested that "the only intellectual who can hope to aid the working class by theoretical work is the one who is willing to live in the working-class movement and learn from it, revising his concepts all the time in light of his and its experience."[55]

Over the next few years MacIntyre attempted to flesh out this conception of socialist leadership. In a response to "The Case for Left Reformism" penned by Oxford labour historian Henry Collins,[56] he argued that reformism was less a coherent response to the problems that beset the working class than it was a reflection of a particular moment in the history of capitalism. It arose "within a

---

[51]See Ian Birchall, *Tony Cliff: A Marxist for his Time* (London: Bookmarks 2011), 182.

[52]Tony Cliff, "Rosa Luxemburg," in *International Struggle and the Marxist Tradition* (London: Bookmarks, 2001), 113.

[53]Tony Cliff, "Trotsky on Substitutionism," in *International Struggle and the Marxist Tradition*, 129. This essay was originally published as, "The Revolutionary Party and the Class, or Trotsky on Substitutionism," *International Socialism* 2 (1960).

[54]Cliff, "Rosa Luxemburg," 77.

[55]MacIntyre, "What is Marxist Theory For?," in *Alasdair MacIntyre's Engagement with Marxism*, 100.

[56]Henry Collins, "The Case for Left Reformism" *International Socialism* 6 (1961): 15–9.

capitalism which has learnt some degree of rationalisation and control."[57] Against Collins's claim that revolution was predicated, primarily, upon the impoverishment of the working class, MacIntyre suggested that socialism emerged as the experience of capitalism forced workers, first, to recognise their own unfreedom, and, second, to "combine with other workers" to set themselves free. MacIntyre argued that the role of revolutionaries was to develop programmes that brought "together three elements in our social life": "the deep and incurable dissatisfaction with social life which capitalism breeds"; "the recurrent state of objective crisis in capitalist social order"; and "socialist theory."[58]

But how would this model work in periods when workers believed that they had, in the famous words of Harold Macmillan, "never had it so good" in part because they were living through an economic boom that appeared to falsify Marx's claim that capitalism was an essentially contradictory and thus crisis prone system? By 1963, MacIntyre came to believe that contemporary economic trends had created barriers to the diffusion of socialist class consciousness across the working class. Specifically, post-war capitalism had been transformed by the "conscious, intelligent innovation" of the bourgeoisie and its representatives.[59] Furthermore, the working class had become increasingly fragmented: "there is a sad case for saying that being in an economically strong position today against the employers in certain industries at least, means that the issues on which you are likely to fight and even possibly win are just the issues that are going to divide you from less skilled workers."[60] A few years later he reinforced this claim through the suggestion that the attitudes of the British working class had been fixed within a reformist world-view since the nineteenth century: "They were not concerned with advancing the claims of one way of life against another; they were concerned with making claims for so much an hour."[61]

Prefiguring, as it does, the arguments of "The *Theses on Feuerbach*: A Road Not Taken," this analysis appeared to imply damning consequences for the Marxist political project. Nevertheless, MacIntyre concluded "Prediction and Politics" with a call to arms. Paralleling arguments first outlined on the pages of *Socialisme ou Barbarie*, MacIntyre argued that the condition for the fall of

[57]MacIntyre, "Rejoinder to Left Reformism," in *Alasdair MacIntyre's Engagement with Marxism*, 190.

[58]Ibid., 196. Cf. Castoriadis, "Modern Capitalism and Revolution" in *Political and Social Writings*, vol. 2 (1988).

[59]MacIntyre, "Prediction and Politics," in *Alasdair MacIntyre's Engagement with Marxism*, 256.

[60]MacIntyre, Unpublished paper given to *International Socialism* day school, in *Alasdair MacIntyre's Engagement with Marxism* 226. cf. MacIntyre, "Herbert Marcuse," in *Alasdair MacIntyre's Engagement with Marxism*.

[61]Alasdair MacIntyre, *Secularization and Moral Change* (Oxford University Press, 1967), 27.

capitalism was the growth in socialist class consciousness within the proletariat, and, as this growth was neither inevitable nor impossible, it "depends upon us" to make that change in consciousness.[62]

This voluntaristic conclusion represents a frankly astonishing *volte-face* for MacIntyre. The arguments he had articulated in 1959–1960 clearly resonated with Marx's claim that "Communism is for us not a *state of affairs* which is to be established, an *ideal* to which reality [will] have to adjust itself. We call communism the *real* movement that abolishes the present state of things. The conditions of this movement result from the premises now in existence."[63] In 1963, by contrast, his perspective resembled nothing so much as the type of moralistic call to arms that Marx, following Fourier, had dismissed as "impotence in action."[64]

It was against the voluntarism of this conclusion that Tony Cliff insisted that *International Socialism* republish Hal Draper's convoluted 1947 essay, "The 'Inevitability of Socialism,'" within which Draper attempted to square the demands of political activism with a highly deterministic interpretation of Marxism.[65] Accordingly, Draper's essay was editorially introduced with the comment that it was being published "as part supplement and part reply to Alasdair MacIntyre's 'Prediction and Politics.'"

Interestingly, MacIntyre's next two contributions to *International Socialism* seemed, eclectically, to combine voluntarist and fatalist elements. First, in a paper presented to an *International Socialism* day-school in 1963,[66] he followed Trotsky in suggesting that revolutionary leadership involved formulating a series of transitional demands which, while nominally reformist, could, in practice, only be realised through a revolutionary transformation of society. Second, in his last major article for *International Socialism*, he argued that revolutions emerge not from proletarian immiserisation, but rather out of "period[s] of rising expectations." Revolutions occur when "the established order cannot satisfy the expectations which it has been forced to bring into being. The new capitalism cannot avoid calling into being a new working-class with large horizons."[67] Not that he believed such revolutions would automatically lead

---

[62]MacIntyre, "Prediction and Politics," 261. On *Socialisme ou Barbarie's* voluntarism see Alex Callinicos, *Trotskyism* (London: Open University Press, 1989), 68.

[63]Marx and Engels, "The German Ideology," in Marx and Engels, *Collected Works*, v. 5 (New York: International Publishers, 1976), 49.

[64]Marx, "The Holy Family," in Marx and Engels, *Collected Works* v. 4 (New York: International Publishers, 1975), 201.

[65]Hal Draper, "The 'Inevitability of Socialism,'" *International Socialism* 15 (1963): 21–9. This article was first published in *New International* 13, no. 9 (December 1947): 269–79.

[66]MacIntyre, Unpublished paper given to *International Socialism* day school.

[67]MacIntyre, "Labour Policy and Capitalist Planning," in *Alasdair MacIntyre's Engagement with Marxism*, 289.

to the socialist transformation of society. As he had done in *Prediction and Politics* he again argued that there was nothing inevitable about the proletariat's ability to realise the potential generated by the new situation: "Whether it will or will not founder on this contradiction depends in part on the forms of our present activity."[68]

One problem with this scenario is that the transitional demands, through which he hoped socialists might bridge the gap between the struggles in and against capitalism were an inadequate response to the challenges posed by a form of capitalism which, he believed, had escaped the boom-slump cycle. Indeed, whereas Trotsky had formulated the "Transitional Programme" in conditions of deep economic crisis, it was not at all clear how similar demand in the context of massive economic growth would generate a revolutionary consciousness within the working class.[69]

It was in belated recognition of the hopelessness of this situation that MacIntyre eventually broke with Marxism in the mid to late 1960s. Interestingly, if *Marxism: An Interpretation* (1953) marked the moment of his own turn to politics, the second edition of that book, *Marxism and Christianity* (1968), marked his despair at the prospects for that project. Indeed, this is where he first condemned Marxism *tout court*, rather than Stalinism specifically, for its failure to sublate the limitations of liberalism or of what Marx would have called the standpoint of civil society. For though Marxism had promised to transcend the materialist and idealist modes of thought characteristic of bourgeois society, in practice, because the revolutionary practice through which this sublation was to be realised failed to materialise, Marxists tended to revert back to one or other pre-Marxist mode of thought.[70]

Thus, in *Marxism and Christianity*, MacIntyre argued that Marx's mature writings were guilty of a crime he sought to critique in others: the model presented in *Capital* acted as a barrier to understanding the modern world because it reified capitalism as an imminently "self-destructive" system in which the wills of proletarians and entrepreneurs are "fixed and unalterable," such that individual capitalists were unable to do what they had in fact managed to do in the post-war period—"become conscious of those workings in a way that enables him to modify them."[71] Moreover, this new development undermined Marx's revolutionary politics. Because Marx's political predictions were predicated upon, first, a model of deepening economic crisis coupled with, second, the growth in self-consciousness of the working class, once capitalists became conscious of the

---

[68]Ibid.; cf. MacIntyre, "Prediction and Politics."
[69]See John Molyneux, *Leon Trotsky's Theory of Revolution* (London: Harvester, 1981), 182.
[70]MacIntyre, *Marxism and Christianity*, 128, 99–101.
[71]Ibid., 81–4.

system and reshaped it accordingly, then revolution would cease to be on the agenda. In this situation, an unbridgeable gulf opened between the reformist coordinates of contemporary politics and the revolutionary rhetoric of Marxists. MacIntyre concluded that Marxism offered two inadequate answers to this question: those proffered by Kautsky and Lukács. As I noted above, he claimed that the former was effectively drawn to deify history in his attempt to theorise human agency. This is true enough, but because Marxism tends to be reduced to a version of Kautskyism only in second-rate textbooks, few actual Marxists would be troubled by the limitations of his interpretation of Marx's ideas. Indeed, even in his lifetime Kautsky's fall was dramatic. From being the "Pope of Marxism" prior to the First World War, by the 1920s he was an isolated individual. Because he had tried to stem the growing polarisation between left and right within social democracy up to and after the War, once this polarisation matured into a split, Kautsky's influence quickly waned.[72]

Lukács is an altogether more contentious target. His *History and Class Consciousness*[73] is without doubt the most important work of twentieth-century Marxist philosophy. Indeed MacIntyre acknowledges that this book is not merely "a brilliant interpretation of Marx" but more importantly it "made of Marxism what the Marxism of the Second International [pre-eminently Kautsky's Marxism] was not, something to be reckoned with philosophically, even by those who rejected its claims."[74] According to MacIntyre, Lukács argued that Marxism was the self-consciousness of capitalism as realised through the proletariat. However, there was a process of mediation in this argument such that class consciousness is actually embodied through the Communist Party. And while MacIntyre recognises the nuances in Lukács position—his model of the Communist Party was open and democratic and embodied through actual proletarians—he is also aware that because Lukács believed that the actually existing Communist Parties of the Third International under Stalin were such parties, when he was denounced by the Third International as a heretic he accepted the leadership's criticisms of his view and succumbed to party discipline.[75] Thus despite the power of Lukács actual arguments, in practice he did come to substitute the Communist Parties for the working class in his model of Marxism. On this basis MacIntyre concludes his survey of contemporary Marxism with the claim that the gap between the actual movement of the working class and the revolutionary aspirations ascribed to it by Marxists can only be solved

---

[72]Paul Blackledge, "Karl Kautsky and Marxist Historiography," *Science and Society* 70, no. 3 (2006): 337–59.

[73]Georg Lukács, *History and Class Consciousness* (London: Merlin, 1971).

[74]Alasdair MacIntyre, *Edith Stein: A Philosophical Prologue* (London: Continuum, 2006), 171–2.

[75]MacIntyre, *Marxism and Christianity*, 97–100.

theologically, either through Lukács's "deification of the Party," or Kautsky's "deification of history."[76]

This is all very plausible but for one problem: to fully substantiate his claim MacIntyre needs to show not that Lukács capitulated to Stalinism, but that this act was more than a contingent fact of his biography. But, to take a related example suggested by MacIntyre, the exemplary virtues exhibited by Trotsky surely include his refusal to capitulate to Stalinism.[77] This was a commendable act in part because the pressures to capitulate were so very great, and these pressures were certainly strong enough in and of themselves to explain Lukács behaviour in the 1920s and 1930s.[78] Of course, some have explained Lukács behaviour in terms of his understanding supposed reification of the Communist Party. However, MacIntyre signals problems with this approach even if he doesn't explore it.

He did not explore this issue, in part, because Lukács's argument was predicted upon Marx's claim that capitalism was a crisis prone system, and MacIntyre had come to believe that this model was no longer operative. Given this assumption, Lukács position is at best utopian. MacIntyre's dismissal of Lukács is nevertheless unfortunate both because the subsequent history of capitalism has tended to confirm Marx's account of its crisis prone essence[79] and, more positively, because Lukács did point towards a means of overcoming weaknesses with MacIntyre's earlier conception of socialist political activity. Whereas Cliff Slaughter had rehearsed an elitist form of revolutionary politics which certainly did tend to deify "the party," the position MacIntyre outlined in 1959–1960 had the strength of being rooted in the real movement from below. Unfortunately, MacIntyre was so keen to distance himself from the dualistic conception of leadership expressed by Lenin's epigones that he erred in the opposite direction. So in contrast to Slaughter's sectarian perspective, MacIntyre's approach tended to justify liquidating the socialist party into the working-class movement. And because his model of leadership tended merely to reflect the movement from below, it was susceptible to crisis if and when this movement ebbed. This weakness was, of course, the flipside of its strength—it would tend to rise and fall with the ebb and flow of the real movement.

In a sense, MacIntyre's conception of revolutionary leadership can be understood as paralleling weaknesses with Edward Thompson's notion of class. In a brilliant counter to the reified abstractions of Stalinist historiography, Thompson, in his groundbreaking classic, *The Making of the English Working*

---

[76]Ibid., 101.

[77]MacIntyre, *After Virtue*, 199.

[78]On Lukács's Marxism and his capitulation to Stalinism see John Rees, "Introduction," in Lukács, *Tailism and the Dialectic: A Defence of History and Class Consciousness* (London: Verso, 2000).

[79]Chris Harman, *Zombie Capitalism* (Chicago: Haymarket, 2009).

Class, attempted to reinsert human agency into historical materialism. However, despite the undoubted strengths of his approach, because he tended to reduce social class to class consciousness his method obscured the salience of class in periods when class consciousness was at a minimum.[80] Similarly, MacIntyre's conception of socialist politics was weakened by its seeming embrace of an inadequately mediated relationship to the "the *real* movement that abolishes the present state of things." When the movement was on the up, MacIntyre's approach could easily express its confidence. Conversely, his own pessimism grew as a direct consequence of the decline of the movement. And this pessimism was reinforced by the way he conceived the economic boom as a consequence of deliberate (Keynesian) policies. In a sense MacIntyre's approach was too Hegelian: his focus on the idea of proletarian self-emancipation informed a weak conception of the mediated relationship between the socialist party and the "real movement" of things. This meant he did not have the theoretical resources necessary to stand against the temporary shift to the right that occurred in the mid 1960s. Indeed, he effectively reified the non-revolutionary context in which he operated. Unfortunately, though other theorists associated with *International Socialism* did have the theoretical resources necessary to make sense of the transient character of this context,[81] MacIntyre remained unconvinced by their arguments in part because they were hitched onto Draper's unsuccessful defence of the inevitability of socialism.

By contrast with MacIntyre's conception of socialist leadership, it is a great strength of Lukács's position that he recognised that "the class consciousness of the proletariat does not develop uniformly throughout the whole proletariat."[82] Consequently, a communist party could "only be created through struggle" and in particular through the "interaction of spontaneity and conscious control."[83] So, while Lukács distanced his ideas from those sectarians who deified the party as "the representative of the 'unconscious' masses," he did so without flipping over into the opposite error of embracing a simplistic deification of spontaneity.[84] Thus his use of the most contentious term in *History and Class Consciousness*: "imputed consciousness."[85] While often presented as the means through which he did deify the party, this term is best understood as the corollary of Marx's

---

[80]E. P. Thompson, *The Making of the English Working Class* (London: Penguin, 1980), 8–13. compare Thompson's approach with Geoffrey de Ste. Croix, *The Class Struggle in the Ancient Greek World* (London: Duckworth, 1983).

[81]Mike Kidron, "Reform and Revolution" *International Socialism* 7 (1961): 15–21, at 15.

[82]Lukács, *History and Class Consciousness*, 304.

[83]Ibid., 317.

[84]Ibid., 322.

[85]Ibid., 323.

essentialist model of social class.[86] Far from allowing Lukács to slip back towards a form of dualism, it opened a space within which he was able to conceptualise socialist political intervention within the class struggle in a non-emotivist yet activist way by means of the generalisations about class interests that could be made on the basis of the *history* of workers' struggles. For instance, to say that workers have an objective interest in challenging racism even in the absence of an anti-racist movement does not imply imposing the idea of anti-racism onto the working class. Rather, it functions as a generalisation about objective interests made on the basis of previous moments of struggle. This way of thinking about politics opens the door to an interventionist conception of political leadership that escapes the emotivist substitutionism of self-appointed vanguards without liquidating the left into a (retreating) movement.[87]

IV.

Conclusion. In 1960, Edward Thompson argued that MacIntyre's stress on politics at the point of production was the ABC of Marxism with the B and C left out.[88] With this argument, Thompson highlighted a central flaw in MacIntyre's politics. In the 1960s, MacIntyre's conceptualisation of the role of revolutionary leadership was innocent of either a concrete analysis of the complex nature of the class struggle suggested by Thompson, or of a concrete model of the role of revolutionaries within that struggle. Unfortunately, to the extent that a coherent approach to politics was formulated within *International Socialism*, it was philosophically underpinned by Hal Draper's untenable defence of the inevitability of socialism. While MacIntyre was justified in rejecting the kind of inevitabilism Draper shared with Kautsky, his rejection of Lukács's much more sophisticated defence of revolutionary socialism is less convincing. This is important because the pessimistic political conclusions to which he evolved in the 1960s were deeply informed by his weak model of the role and nature of political leadership in the emergence of proletarian socialist class consciousness. In the late 1950s and early 1960s, the limitations of MacIntyre's conceptualisation of socialist leadership were masked by the upturn in the political struggle that gave rise to the first New Left and Campaign for Nuclear Disarmament. However, with the defeat of these movements in the early 1960s, the inadequacies of his increasingly voluntarist model of socialist politics were brought into sharp relief by his inability to provide a socialist explanation for the limits of mass proletarian apathy.

---

[86]Ibid., 325.

[87]Alex Callinicos, "Leninism in the Twenty-First Century?" in *Lenin Reloaded*, ed. Sebastian Budgen et al. (Durham, NC: Duke University Press, 2007), 26; Alex Callinicos, *Resources of Critique* (Cambridge: Polity, 2006), 119.

[88]Edward Thompson, "The Point of Production," *New Left Review* 1 (1960): 68–70.

When, in the 1970s, Marxists again debated the issue of morality, MacIntyre's contribution to this debate was largely overlooked, in part because of his subsequent political evolution.[89] This is unfortunate, for MacIntyre's break with the revolutionary left was informed by the very seriousness with which he understood Marxism. He could no more embrace utopian Marxism, à la G. A. Cohen,[90] than he could Kantianism; his Aristotelianism provided a political way out of his interpretation of the impasse of socialist politics. If we are to maintain a commitment to revolutionary politics while avoiding MacIntyre's pessimism, it is incumbent upon us to formulate a better model of the relationship between struggles in and against capitalism and the role of socialists within them. So, while MacIntyre's recent rethinking of the concepts of desire and human nature and the labour theory of value have created a space through which Marxists might reengage with his ideas, to realise its potential such a dialogue must reengage with the limitations as well as the strengths of MacIntyre's critique of Lenin and Lukács.

Leeds Metropolitan University
Leeds, United Kingdom

---

[89]See, for instance, Perry Anderson, *Arguments Within English Marxism* (London: Verso, 1980), 108.

[90]G. A. Cohen, *If You're an Egalitarian, How Come You're So Rich?* (Cambridge, MA: Harvard University Press, 2000).

History and Plurality[1]

Kelvin Knight

Abstract. Alasdair MacIntyre has long believed that philosophy should be conducted with reference to its past. Since *After Virtue*, he has argued that philosophy's past should be understood in terms of rival traditions. This essay attempts to chart the development of MacIntyre's historical thinking about ethics against the longer development of liberalism's rival tradition of thinking about history, drawing contrasts with what was said by Immanuel Kant on progress, R. G. Collingwood on civilization, and John Rawls on pluralism.

Alasdair MacIntyre's "problem is with the practice of liberalism . . . not with its ideals. It is with the extent to which the practice of liberalism is a betrayal of its ideals." That betrayal is committed by "political, financial, and media elites," and by the "oppressive and deceitful institutions" through which they rule.[2]

Historically, "belief in liberal values . . . was forged in the struggle against the *ancien regime*" and MacIntyre happily acknowledges that in "what it was *against*, the Enlightenment was often right," so that, "insofar as its values are defined as denials they are generally compelling."[3] His issue is that Enlightenment denials of arbitrary claims to authority were unaccompanied by affirmations of any "teleological understanding of human action and human relationships." It is because "the thinkers of the Enlightenment" were precluded by "earlier sixteenth- and seventeenth-century rejections of Aristotelian modes of thought"

---

[1] I thank Alasdair MacIntyre for comments on the original form of this paper, and especially on its second part. Readers are warned that he might still consider that second part to exaggerate his commonality with Collingwood.

[2] Alasdair MacIntyre, "Replies," *Revue Internationale de Philosophie* 67, no. 2 (2013): 201–20, at 202, quoting Bernard Williams.

[3] Alasdair MacIntyre, "Where We Were, Where We Are, Where We Need to Be," in *Virtue and Politics: Alasdair MacIntyre's Revolutionary Aristotelianism*, ed. Paul Blackledge and Kelvin Knight (Notre Dame, IN: University of Notre Dame Press, 2011), 325–6; MacIntyre's emphasis.

©2014, *American Catholic Philosophical Quarterly*, Vol. 88, No. 4   pp. 725–750
doi: 10.5840/acpq201491529

from such an understanding that "the larger social hopes of the Enlightenment
. . . have not been realised."[4]

The Enlightenment's largest social hope, and liberalism's highest ideal, is
Immanuel Kant's kingdom of ends, in which "deceptive methods can never be
used."[5] As an ideal, this is certainly attractive. As MacIntyre once noted, even
Karl Marx sometimes wrote "as though communism will be an embodiment
of the Kantian kingdom of ends."[6] Now, when he tells us of the persistence of
his "Marxism" alongside his "Thomistic Aristotelianism,"[7] he recounts that,
when drawing "upon the resources of Marxism," he has always been "critical
not only of Marx's Hegelian inheritance and of the doctrines of historical and
dialectical materialism, but also of the residual liberalism in Marx's portrayal of
communism."[8]

The doctrines of historical materialism are of a piece with those of both
Enlightenment historiography and liberal idealism, insofar as they portray
history as the progress of reason toward freedom. Kant proposed that progress
toward the kingdom of ends was caused by conflict between "asocially social"
individuals and between states, whereas Marx explained progress toward
communism as propelled by conflict between classes. MacIntyre agrees with
neither. He too perceives conflict to be pervasive, in the past as in the present,
but refuses to theorize such conflict as any cause of a future harmony. In *this*
sense—rather than in the sense of such values as liberty, equality or justice—he
refuses liberalism's ideals, along with modernity's account of its own history as
a progress toward them.

MacIntyre may have no quarrel with liberalism's ideals, but, since he is no
liberal, he nonetheless refuses to begin from them. His own way of thinking is
very different. Whereas liberals have often theorized some moral ideal and then
proposed their present politics as the means to its future actualization, he refuses
any such privileging of theory over practice. Liberals' characteristic way of theorizing what ought to be apart from what already is must always be betrayed by
liberal practice, because it renders politicians' ideals superior to the practices of
ordinary actors, such that those actors ought to be managed and manipulated
in order to achieve progress toward the liberal ideal.

---

[4]Ibid.

[5]Alasdair MacIntyre, "Truthfulness and Lies: What Can We Learn from Kant?," in *Selected Essays*, vol. 2: *Ethics and Politics* (Cambridge: Cambridge University Press, 2006), 129, quoting Christine Korsgaard.

[6]Alasdair MacIntyre, *A Short History of Ethics: A History of Moral Philosophy from the Homeric Age to the Twentieth Century* (London: Routledge, 1966), 214.

[7]MacIntyre, "Replies," 203.

[8]Ibid., 207.

Liberalism's paradox is that it must *compel* people to accord with its ideal of universally *free* individuals. Institutionally isolated from the real goals and practices of those subject to their government, the most idealistic of politicians will find themselves faced with a choice between deceit and impotence. Liberal theory is therefore ideological, subtly legitimating rule by competing elites in the state, as it does in the economy, and thereby legitimating "the large inequality of access to and influence upon political decision-makers . . . rooted in gross inequalities of money and economic power."[9] MacIntyre concedes that this Aristotelian critique of modern political theory and practice is less well elaborated than is his critique of modern moral philosophy, whilst insisting that an Aristotelian politics ought to start from participative and unmanipulative practices and, therefore, from rejection of "the political institutions of the modern state-and-market."[10] It should learn from "all those movements of resistance to the imposition by the state and the market on local societies of measures destructive of their shared life and of the possibility of their achieving their common goods."[11]

MacIntyre's first principles and final ends are not abstract ideals but conceptions of the practice of human being, human dependence, and human flourishing. He defends both "Aristotle and Marx"—that is, a Marx shorn of his residual idealism and liberalism—in holding "that conceptions of what a human being is by nature and of what it is to flourish as a human being, at once animal and rational, are indispensable to our social and historical thinking" as "both plain persons and theorists." In turn, such social and historical thinking enables us not only "to spell out those conceptions more adequately" but also to actualize "in different circumstances" our conception of what it *is* to flourish.[12]

This paper compares aspects of MacIntyre's own historical thinking with that of liberalism. It does so in three stages. First, his thinking is compared with that of history as progress toward liberal ideals. It then narrows its focus in contrasting his thinking with that of Oxford's last great liberal idealist, R. G. Collingwood. Finally, it compares MacIntyre's account of modern intellectual history with that briefly but influentially proposed by John Rawls.

I.

Progress. History might enable liberalism to evade its paradox. If people are somehow compelled by history to become free individuals, then their freedom

---

[9]Alasdair MacIntyre, "What More Needs to Be Said? A Beginning, Although Only a Beginning, at Saying It," *Analyze and Kritik* 30, no. 1 (2008): 261–81, at 263; cf. 263–5, 268–9.

[10]MacIntyre, "Replies," 204. The concession is to Pierre Manent and, most especially, the late Emile Perreau-Saussine.

[11]Ibid., 211.

[12]Ibid, 218.

is not theoretically contradicted or practically contravened by coercion or manipulation exercised by any other individual. Liberal historiography, therefore, recounts the history of impersonal institutions. More specifically, it recounts the history of the development of the state and commerce: the state because the rule of its law allows individuals freedom from one another; commerce because it allows individuals to acquire what they want to live as they will. Such a history has standardly been taken to represent the achievement of human freedom and prosperity, and often to represent the actualization of humans' potential to control themselves, their society, and nature. Sometimes, it has even been taken to represent the moral progress of human relationships, human actions and human intentions.

Historically, a crucial source of liberal historiography was the Scottish Enlightenment. Whilst English contractarians justified sovereignty individualistically, with a market metaphor, Sir James Dalrymple of Stair, as MacIntyre records, took a more jurisprudential approach in *The Institutions of the Law of Scotland*, taking inspiration from Justinian's *Institutiones* of Roman civil law and, in turn, inspiring the *Philosophiae Moralis Institutio Compendiaria* of Francis Hutcheson.[13] With greater historical sensitivity, David Hume then recorded the creation, "progress," and "refinement" of *English* constitutional and other institutions,[14] whilst, within what he called this "historical Age and . . . historical Nation,"[15] his compatriots speculated about the stages through which history as a whole had advanced to its present level of production and civilization. As has been famously quipped of Adam Smith, his "immense design of . . . the origin and development of cultivation and law" described "how, from being a savage, man rose to be a Scotchman."[16]

The decisive turn to a distinctly modern and modernizing historiography occurred in Prussia, with Kant. One way of understanding this historiographical turn has been made famous by Karl Löwith: as that from an eschatological understanding of history as determined by the providential will of God to that of understanding it as determined by the wills of those humans who enact it.[17] There is another way, which makes Kant still more pivotal: as a turn from a

---

[13]Alasdair MacIntyre, *Whose Justice? Which Rationality?* (Notre Dame, IN: University of Notre Dame Press, 1988), 226–8.

[14]David Hume, *The History of England, from the Invasion of Julius Caesar to the Revolution in 1688*, ed. William B. Todd (Indianapolis, IN: Liberty Classics, 1983).

[15]David Hume, quoted in Mark G. Spencer, "Introduction," *David Hume: Historical Thinker, Historical Writer*, ed. Mark G. Spencer (University Park, PA: Pennsylvania State University Press, 2013), 1.

[16]Walter Bagehot, *Biographical Studies*, 2 ed., ed. Richard Holt Hutton (London: Longmans, Green, & Co., 1889), 255.

[17]Karl Löwith, *Meaning in History* (Chicago: University of Chicago Press, 1949).

teleological understanding of human beings, as individuals, to a teleological understanding of the human species as a temporal whole. This new understanding of that for which we may *hope* for humanity must, of course, on a Kantian account, be distinguished from that which we might *know* in terms of natural laws. It must even be distinguished from our understanding of what one *ought to do*, since one's moral freedom from nature's determination requires one's rational determination of universalizable laws of action matching nature's universal laws of motion, and such moral laws of free action must, on Kant's account, be unconditional and undetermined by any end. Even so, when Kant moves on to his second *Critique* and his writings on both theology and politics it seems clear that one should understand his "kingdom of ends" as a historical *goal*, and not just as an imperative for individuals here and now. More strikingly still, actualization of that goal depends less fundamentally on individuals' exercise of their rational wills than on nature's prior endowment of humans with the capacity to will and act rationally and purposively. Kant sounds more rigorously teleological than even Aristotle when proposing that nature compels humans to actualize their potentialities or powers. This he proposes most incisively in *Idea for a Universal History with a Cosmopolitan Purpose* and most elaborately in *Critique of the Power of Judgement*.

The two principal sources of Kant's historicism are Christian eschatology and the new social and historical thinking developed, above all, in Scotland. Smith's *The Wealth of Nations* had just been published and immediately translated (albeit not yet with the eloquence of Christian Garve) into German. Even if Kant's turn to history might have been inspired by Herder and his idea of "unsocial sociability" by Rousseau or Montaigne, it was Smith who best explained how selfish actions, when constrained by civil institutions of coercion and commerce, might have aggregatively beneficial consequences in a way that can be understood as systemically caused. Progress could now be explained in a way that allowed Kant to attribute the course of history to a "plan of nature," even if not to dignify such speculation with the status of determinate knowledge. Human progress could be understood as actualized through education and law, politics and commerce, competition and war. As individuals had had to submit to the state's institution of civil law through reason and need, in order to ensure their "negative" or "external freedom" from one another, so too would states have to form a league of nations as the condition of perpetual peace between them and, therefore, of security in the freedom of themselves and their citizens.

Kant's conception of institutional progress was elaborated by such compatriots as Fichte, Schelling and, most influentially, Hegel, who theorized the historical bifurcation of the premodern household economy into the modern family and the commercial "system of needs." This system of satisfying material needs, regulated by private and corporate law, Hegel called *bürgerliche gesellschaft* and separated from the coercive power and universal authority of the state, with which such "civil society" had traditionally been identified. In this way, contractarians' conceptual opposition of individual to state was understood to be mediated by familial and by civil or corporate institutions, so that individuals could be reconciled to the universality of the state and society through more particularistic identities and participatory activity.

After Hegel, historiography became central to efforts to defend the autonomy of the human, social, or moral sciences from those of nature. Protagonists of these sciences were seldom so keen as their Enlightenment forebears to understand history as progress, except when expressed in terms that were economic, institutional and imperial. Leopold von Ranke led those who opposed Hegel's philosophical universalizing of history. Even those who—in Germany and in Italy—went back to Kant returned more often to his express opposition of freedom to nature than to his cautiously naturalistic and optimistically institutional teleology. Alexander von Humboldt might have followed in the "humanistic eschatology" of "Kant, Schiller, or Herder" when proposing reason's "progress toward the achievement of human perfection," and Wilhelm Windelband might later have seen merit in teleology, but it was Dilthey who pointed the way in insisting that, even if trying to make sense of history "in terms of the accomplishment of certain values and goals" by humanity as a whole, it must be understood that "those goals and values are not inherent in individuals, nations or history itself."[18]

The other, causal and historiographically conflictual, side of the Kantian divide of empirical actuality from moral rationality was best elaborated by Marx and Marxists. Marx conceived history materially, and in a way sympathetic to the explanatory methods of natural and economic science. Nonetheless, his subject remained the history of humanity as a whole. His historical ideal remained that of Kant's kingdom of ends, redescribed as a community of individuals freed from the class conflict caused by material scarcity and by private ownership of that capital which represented labour's investment in history. Where he therefore broke from Kant and Hegel was in seeing progress only in production and the accumulation of capital, in renaming as "capitalism" civil society's system of needs, and in identifying commerce with alienation and exploitation rather than freedom. What history had so far been accumulating and actualizing, on Marx's account, was not the ethical ideal but only its necessary conditions.

During much of the twentieth century, it was Marxists who most confidently claimed that history was on their side. Even as a Marxist, MacIntyre was exceptional in refusing this boast. What has often been called his pessimism

---

[18]Frederick C. Beiser, *The German Historicist Tradition* (Oxford: Oxford University Press, 2011), 191, 390–2, 356.

was informed in part by Karl Popper's scepticism about their historical claims,[19] and in part by the far more radical scepticism of Nietzsche. Marxists, as much as liberals, were susceptible to the self-images of their own ideology. In moral theory, they failed to advance beyond either Kantianism or consequentialism. In power, they were often still keener than liberals to institutionalize manipulation. For MacIntyre, Eastern state capitalism often exceeded Western private capitalism's betrayal of Enlightenment ideals.

MacIntyre's practical break from institutional Marxism followed publication of the first of his histories of moral philosophy. *A Short History of Ethics* began neither from the pre-Socratic philosophers of nature nor from Socrates's questioning of justice. Instead, like Nietzsche, it identified its subject's genesis in what its subtitle called "the Homeric Age" and in what might be emulated "by a contemporary admirer of the Homeric ideal."[20] In this "prephilosophical" world there is no separation of "ought" from "is," and the lesson to be learned from the genealogy of morals that MacIntyre goes on to recount is historically relativist and virtually perspectivalist. As he was later to reflect, "*A Short History of Ethics* should perhaps have ended by giving Nietzsche the final word."[21]

After Virtue, the second of his histories of ethics, continued to do "poetic justice to Nietzsche" by taking its historical embarkation from Homer.[22] Unlike his earlier history, however, this second book was structured unchronologically. Famously, and effectively, the book's structure took a different and more rhetorical form in beginning with a dramatic but entirely imaginary disaster, to which an analogy was then drawn with the Enlightenment's disruption of moral reasoning. Even so, a more substantive difference of this book's account of history from that of the first is its cautious combination with a conception of human nature and flourishing and, more importantly as yet, with a bolder account of what it called "a sociology."[23] One expression of this boldness is its expansion of what MacIntyre continued to call "Homeric society"[24] into a broader category of "heroic society."[25] Genealogy is here replaced by historical sociology, as those virtues MacIntyre once attributed to the contingencies of post-Mycenaean, dark age Greece become virtues identifiable with roles and practices common to a

---

[19]For a critique of Popper inspired in large part by MacIntyre, and with which he might be expected to largely agree, see Peter Skagestad, *Making Sense of History: The Philosophies of Popper and Collingwood* (Oslo: Universitetsforlaget, 1975).

[20]MacIntyre, *Short History*, 6.

[21]Alasdair MacIntyre, "An Interview with Giovanna Borradori," *The MacIntyre Reader*, ed. Kelvin Knight (Cambridge: Polity Press, 1998), 261.

[22]Alasdair MacIntyre, *After Virtue: A Study in Moral Theory*, 3rd ed. (Notre Dame, IN: University of Notre Dame Press, 2007), 120.

[23]Ibid., 196.

[24]MacIntyre, *Short History*, 9. MacIntyre, *After Virtue*, 122.

[25]MacIntyre, *After Virtue*, chap. 10.

geographically diffuse kind of society, even if he does not go so far as to embrace the kind of stadial history that was pioneered in the Scottish Enlightenment, embraced by Hegel, and culminated in historical materialism.

MacIntyre's sociology is that of social "practices" and organizational "institutions"; of goods and goals internal to practices and common to their practitioners and, conversely, of such zero-sum goods as money, power, and status, which are objects of competition between individuals and are distributed by institutions. These concepts are designed to describe and evaluate capitalism's division of labour and its corporate, managerial, and bureaucratic structure. In *After Virtue* he famously supplemented discussion of social roles with a more novel and critical account of such contemporary, manipulative "characters" as "the bureaucratic manager,"[26] who personify modernity's institutionalized betrayal of liberal ideals. In such ways, he has modernized teleological understandings of human action and human relationships into a mode of radical social critique. On his account, not only "plants and animals, including human beings," but also "a range of types of human activity have ends in this [Aristotelian] sense." His argument is that "individual goods can only be achieved through . . . directing ourselves towards the achievement of some of our common goods," that this requires the well-resourced education of all and our shared participation in political deliberation, and that "it is hard, often impossible to satisfy these conditions in societies structured by those institutions that are indispensable to the modern state and to the globalizing market."[27]

Although MacIntyre's critique of capitalist modernity gains force from both Marx and Nietzsche, it concurs with Marx rather than Nietzsche in its refusal to repudiate the Enlightenment's social hopes. "The whole Nietzschean research program," MacIntyre tells us, is intended to answer "the question of what history is and achieves."[28] What history is, on the Nietzschean account, is a story of contingent revaluations, manipulative deceits, and virtuous self-assertion. Whereas *After Virtue* traced the history of modern philosophy's "moral fictions" of natural rights, utility, and "managerial effectiveness" back to the catastrophic fragmentation of a once-coherent scheme of thought and action, Nietzsche condemned the whole of moral theory, theology, and rationalist universalism as a colossal confidence trick. His genealogical research programme, continued by Heidegger and Foucault, was intended to unmask and deconstruct this post-Homeric moral project. On MacIntyre's account, this programme is misdirected in taking as its object moral reasoning as such. It succeeds against Kant because

---

[26]Ibid., 25–31, 73–8.
[27]MacIntyre, "What More Needs to Be Said?," 262–3.
[28]MacIntyre, *Three Rival Versions of Moral Enquiry* (Notre Dame, IN: University of Notre Dame Press, 1990), 49, 54.

the moral enquiry into which he was provoked by Descartes, Rousseau, and Hume addressed unnecessary questions, unrelated to the purposes and enquiries of ordinary practical reasoners. It also succeeds in unmasking claims of power to authority, as does Marxism in exposing capitalist ideology. It thereby helps us to understand modernity, even if it takes the manipulativeness it unmasks to be an ineliminable aspect of the human condition and, in this sense, ahistorical.

The Nietzschean research programme deconstructs modernity's self-images of historical achievement, both liberal and Marxist. On the Nietzschean view, it is as though the lives of individuals and societies remain as precarious and contingent now as they were at the time of Achilles and Odysseus, Helen and Penelope. With this, MacIntyre concurs in stressing humans' continuing vulnerability as embodied beings, whilst arguing against Nietzsche about the moral importance of mutual dependence. He differs also in *After Virtue*. Even though it begins by noting moral fragmentation, and even though he shares none of the confidence of Kant, Hegel, or Marx in the necessity of progress, its central contention is that coherence can be restored to moral theory only by making its central or first principle that of a teleology understood in terms of progress toward essential goods. For an individual to lead a fulfilled life is "to make progress . . . toward a given end."[29] Similarly, "a tradition is in good order . . . when progress is taking place."[30] If a tradition of reasoning fails to make intellectual progress, it will die. "What rendered Newtonian physics rationally superior to its Galilean and Aristotelian predecessors . . . was that it was able to transcend their limitations by solving problems in areas in which th[ey] . . . could by their own standards of scientific progress make no progress."[31] Conversely, Aristotelian ethics has been able to continue to make "progress in the development of the concept" of virtue,[32] and *After Virtue*'s greatest achievement was to further that progress by setting out non-naturalistic premises for the concept with regard to individuals' lives, to traditions, and to social practices. Such practices "find their point and purpose in a progress towards and beyond a variety of types and modes of excellence," and "it is in participation in the attempts to sustain progress" toward such goods internal to practices that individuals find their own good qua practitioners and, thereby, have their desires educated in a way that enables them to learn the point and purpose of the virtues.[33] An "essential function of the virtues," MacIntyre goes on to tell us, is to "resist the corrupting power of institutions."[34]

---

[29]MacIntyre, *After Virtue*, 34.
[30]Ibid., 146.
[31]Ibid., 268.
[32]Ibid., 187.
[33]Ibid., 189–90.
[34]Ibid., 194.

It is here that MacIntyre's social and historical thinking departs most radically from that of liberalism. His history is more that of the actualization of goods internal to practices than one of the establishment of institutions and of their successful imposition of rules. Such imposition of rules is a part of the point and purpose of institutions, but their more essential purpose, he suggests, is other than this. Social "practices cannot be sustained" "without . . . truthfulness, justice and courage," but nor can they be sustained "for any length of time" without institutions; without, that is, the authoritative imposition of rules and without institutions' authoritative distribution of resources.[35] Institutions, on his account, are both required for the progress of practices in pursuing their particular goods, such as the truths internal to physics, but also constantly threaten those practices with corruption.

II.

Civilization. In 1776—at the time of America's revolution, Hume's death, and Smith's *Wealth of Nations,* but five years before Kant's first *Critique* and eight before his *Idea for a Universal History*—Edward Gibbon published the first volume of his *History of the Decline and Fall of the Roman Empire.* This was "a *pre*history to 'the Enlightened narrative'" of progress. Pre-Christian Roman and Greek historians had conceived of history as moving not ever onward to an eventual *eschaton,* but in a series of cycles or "revolutions," in which the progress of civilizations reversed into processes of decline and barbarization. With the Renaissance, prior to the Enlightenment's narrative, this conception was revived as a warning against luxury, corruption and hubris, in a distinctly "moral historiography."[36]

Awareness of the danger of civilizational decline persisted even in Kant. Like many contemporaries, he thought that the degeneration of Roman "morals can still instruct us."[37] Unlike many of his successors, he warned that "the progress of the species . . . offers no guarantee against regression, with which it is always threatened by intervening revolutionary barbarism."[38] In *Idea for a Universal History,* he therefore raised the questions of "whether the discord that is so natural to our species will . . . perhaps annihilate again, through barbaric devastations, this

---

[35]Ibid., 192, 194.

[36]J. G. A. Pocock, *Barbarism and Religion,* vol. 3: *The First Decline and Fall* (Cambridge: Cambridge University Press, 2003), 11; emphasis added.

[37]Immanuel Kant, "On the Feeling of the Beautiful and Sublime," in *Immanuel Kant: Anthropology, History, and Education,* trans. Paul Guyer, ed. Günter Zöller and Robert B. Louden (Cambridge: Cambridge University Press, 2007), 61 (2:225).

[38]Immanuel Kant, *"Anthropology from a Pragmatic Point of View,"* in *Immanuel Kant: Anthropology, History, and Education,* trans. Robert B. Louden, ed. Günter Zöller and Robert B. Louden (Cambridge: Cambridge University Press, 2007), 421 (7:326).

[civilized] condition," and of whether we are too "civilized, perhaps to the point of being overburdened, by all sorts of social decorum and propriety," observing that "being civilized" involves only "the *use*" of the idea of being "moralized."[39] In this he represented the ethical worries expressed by Adam Ferguson, whose *Essay on the History of Civil Society* was famous in Germany,[40] and whose "sociology" it is that MacIntyre commends as "the empirical counterpart of the conceptual account of the virtues which" he gives in *After Virtue*; "a sociology which aspires to lay bare the empirical, causal connection between virtues, practices and institutions."[41] Kant's tentative answers to his own questions anticipated what has since been argued by many historians: that Roman "influence on the *barbarians*" informed "a regular course of improvement of state constitutions in our part of the world," revealing a "germ of enlightenment that developed further through each revolution and this prepared for a following stage of improvement." The morally "useful" consolation for present suffering that he therefore offered was that "the human species is . . . working itself upward toward the condition in which all germs nature has placed in it can be fully developed and its vocation here on earth can be fulfilled." In this way, "the treatment of history proper, that is written merely *empirically*," may be rendered consistent with his "philosophical history," and classical history may be understood in a way that addresses the cosmopolitan "interests" "with which one now writes the history of one's time."[42] Such optimism became endemic to the nineteenth century, when classicism's cautionary lesson was neglected amidst the celebration of intellectual, industrial, and imperial expansion.

Earlier, Gibbon and Kant had been anticipated in their concern with barbarism's threat to civilization by many Italian historians. The greatest of these was Giambattista Vico. He, MacIntyre says, was the first to emphasize "that the subject matters of moral philosophy . . . are nowhere to be found except as embodied in the historical lives of particular social groups"—in their "discourse" and "institutionalized practice."[43] On this account of ethics, Kant's answer to Ferguson's worries was inadequate since morality's meaning is inseparable from its discursive and institutional usage.

The historical line of historiographical influence from Vico to MacIntyre is traceable back through R. G. Collingwood and Benedetto Croce (and *not*,

---

[39]Immanuel Kant, "Idea for a Universal History with a Cosmopolitan Aim," in *Immanuel Kant: Anthropology, History, and Education*, trans. Allen W. Wood, ed. Günter Zöller and Robert B. Louden (Cambridge: Cambridge University Press, 2007), 115–6 (8:25–6); emphases altered.

[40]Fania Oz-Salzberger, *Translating the Enlightenment: Scottish Civic Discourse in Eighteenth-Century Germany* (Oxford: Oxford University Press, 1995).

[41]MacIntyre, *After Virtue*, 195–6.

[42]Kant, "Idea for a Universal History," 118–20 (8:29–31); Kant's emphasis.

[43]MacIntyre, *After Virtue*, 265.

as has sometimes been suggested, through Herder). The first philosophy book MacIntyre ever read was Collingwood's *Autobiography*,[44] which, in recounting the life of its author's mind, his questions and progressive elaboration of answers, his thoughts and their enactments, epitomizes Collingwood's famous historiographical-cum-philosophical methodology.

What initially interested MacIntyre, as schoolboy, was not Collingwood's status as Waynflete Professor of Metaphysical Philosophy at Oxford, but his hardly lesser status as practicing archaeologist and historian of Roman Britain. As an empirical historian, Collingwood was something of a second, but more parochial Gibbon. His practical concern in material remains was very specifically with Rome's civilization of Britain. Charged with writing the first volume of the *Oxford History of England*, he omitted England's pre-Roman history and commissioned another historian to recount Roman Britain's conquest by Germanic barbarians.[45] Himself the son of a scholar of such barbarian invaders,[46] it was nonetheless through Croce and Vico that he was to think of the philosophical significance of civilization's antagonists, of what they called "the transition . . . from the savage to the heroic or barbaric condition and from the latter to the civilised," and of the danger of what Vico dubbed a "barbarism of reflection or civilisation," "incomparably worse than the primitive noble barbarism," in which self-interest is pursued through manipulation.[47] It was also through the Italians that Collingwood was to think philosophically of his own practice of empirical history and archaeology. As an anti-empiricist historian of ideas, and as a philosopher of history as ideas' enactment, his concern was with the entirety of Western civilization.

For Collingwood, truth and rationality are one. To know the past is to understand our present, and our enquiries into the past are always guided by our own present questions, concerns, and presuppositions. We know history through the presence of past artefacts, both textual and non-textual, and through enquiring as to their function. In this way we can rethink people's past purposes and thereby explain both past "events"—or rather, as he makes clear

---

[44]R. G. Collingwood, *An Autobiography* (Oxford: Oxford University Press, 1939).

[45]R. G. Collingwood and J. N. L. Myres, *Roman Britain and the English Settlements*, 2nd ed. (Oxford: Oxford University Press, 1937), 120–60.

[46]Matthew Townend, *The Vikings and Victorian Lakeland: The Norse Medievalism of W. G. Collingwood and His Contemporaries* (Kendal, U.K.: Cumberland and Westmorland Antiquarian and Archaeological Society, 2009).

[47]Benedetto Croce, *The Philosophy of Giambattista Vico*, trans. R. G. Collingwood (London: Macmillan, 1913), 103, 213ff, 124. Cf. Giambattista Vico, *The New Science of Giambattista Vico: Unabridged Translation of the Third Edition (1744) with the Addition of "Practice of the New Science,"* trans. Thomas Goddard Bergin and Max Harold Fisch (Ithaca, NY: Cornell University Press, 1984), 424.

in his *Autobiography*, past *actions*[48]—and the provenance of present ideas. On this account, theory and practice are inseparable and, as Collingwood eventually concluded, metaphysics is the historical science exploring actors' shared premises or "absolute presuppositions."[49] His own self-consciously philosophical enquiries having begun when, at age eight, he happened upon his father's copy of Kant's *Groundwork of the Metaphysics of Morals*, it is unsurprising if his conclusion about "metaphysics" is redolent of Kant's use of the term there (and, we might add, appears like a historicization of what Kant says of the categories). Facts are the province of the natural sciences; human, historical sciences are concerned with ideas and their enactment, including even the ideas and enactments of natural science. His greatest difference from Kant, which he learned from continental neo-Kantians, is that metaphysics is itself, like all human enquiries, an essentially historical subject. What even this neo-Kantian insight took from Kant, on Collingwood's account—or, that is, on the account that he maintained for *almost* all of his life—was Kant's "analysis of human nature as essentially moral nature or freedom." This analysis shows "why there should be such a thing as history; it is, [Kant] shows, because man is a rational being, and the full development of his potentialities therefore requires an historical process."[50] This *process* is that which Kant had called enlightenment and Collingwood was to call civilization.

Classified by others "as an 'idealist,'" and indeed one of the last of the philosophically and politically important line of idealists in Oxford, Collingwood held an idealism that was much more that of the Italians whom he translated than of the city's famous "school of [T. H.] Green,"[51] with its distinctive revival of German idealizations of the progress of morality, freedom, and reason in an Aristotelian idiom of the common good.[52] If we say, with the MacIntyre of *After Virtue*, that "Vico and Hegel" were "to some greater or lesser degree Aristotelians,"[53] then we must say that, to a great degree, so too were Green and his followers. Even if they followed Hegel whilst Collingwood pursued Vico, they and he were at least allied in Oxford.

---

[48]Collingwood, *An Autobiography*, 127–8. The artefact that most interested MacIntyre, and had been explained most fully by Collingwood, was Hadrian's Wall: see Collingwood, *An Autobiography*, 128–30; R. G. Collingwood, "The Age of Conquest," in Collingwood and Myres, *Roman Britain and the English Settlements*, 120–60.

[49]R. G. Collingwood, *An Essay on Metaphysics* (Oxford: Oxford University Press, 1940).

[50]R. G. Collingwood, *The Idea of History*, ed. T. M. Knox (Oxford: Oxford University Press, 1946), 98.

[51]Collingwood, *An Autobiography*, 56.

[52]Ibid..

[53]MacIntyre, *After Virtue*, 277.

Collingwood's *Autobiography* takes issue with those Oxford intuitionists who had honed their metaethics in criticism of Oxford idealism, and whom he labelled *realist*.[54] He applauded the way in which Green's school had instructed its students "that some understanding of the nature of moral or political action, some attempt to formulate ideals and principles, was an indispensable condition of engaging creditably in these activities."[55] He therefore deplored the way in which such Oxford realists as H. A. Prichard were arguing that moral philosophy "was based on a mistake" and "denying the conception of a 'common good,' the fundamental idea of all social life, insisting instead that all 'goods' are private."[56] Such realists taught that we live "in a world of 'hard facts' to which 'thoughts' make no difference," against which Collingwood objected that thoughts and "theories" provide reasons for the actions which shape societies and their histories. What realist logicians posited as knowledge was an account of scientific methodology, which they supposed could be applied to any subject matter without making any difference to it. This methodology was attributed by the realists to Francis Bacon and credited with "the gigantic increase since about 1600 in [man's] power to control Nature."[57] They were wrong, according to Collingwood: not about that scientific "revolution" but about its empirical methodology. The method recommended by Bacon—like Socrates before him and Descartes soon after—was that of "question and answer," of identifying and solving problems and then proceeding to the next issue, and the next, in an ongoing process of enquiry. It was a method exemplified by Kant's sustained enquiries into what can be known, what should be done, and what can be hoped. It was exemplified also by empirical science's accumulation of knowledge, sometimes for its own sake and sometimes in answering questions of how to achieve other ends. "Bacon had promised that knowledge would be power, and power it was: power to destroy the bodies and souls of men more rapidly than had ever been done by human agency before [1914]." That the Great "War was an unprecedented triumph for natural science" was no criticism of science, or of its methodology. Instead, Collingwood urged it as the problem now confronting politicians, philosophers, and historians. "The War was an unprecedented disgrace to the human intellect," since "it seemed almost as if man's power to control 'Nature' had been increasing *pari passu* with a decrease in his power to control human affairs."[58] Writing with prescience in his *Autobiography*, in late 1938, he warned that "not only would any failure to control human affairs result in more and

---

[54]Collingwood, *An Autobiography*, especially 14–26, 44–52.
[55]Ibid., 47.
[56]Ibid., 49; see H. A. Prichard, "Does Moral Philosophy Rest on a Mistake," in H. A. Prichard, *Moral Writings*, ed. Jim McAdam (Oxford: Oxford University Press, 2002), 7–20.
[57]Collingwood, *An Autobiography*, 91.
[58]Ibid., 91.

more widespread destruction as natural science added triumph to triumph, but the consequences would tend more and more to the destruction of whatever was good and reasonable."[59] His urgent challenge was to find some good and reasonable solution. "We might very well be standing on the threshold of an age in which history would be as important for the world as natural science had been."[60] The understanding of history was in accelerating "progress,"[61] having already "passed through a Copernican revolution" since Kant and now being recognized as "the science of human affairs."[62] It had defeated the "sham science" of "psychology," as Hegel had defeated that of "'phrenology'" a century before,[63] and was now passing from the "pre-Baconian" stage of what he famously ridiculed as Rankean "scissors-and-paste" history through its own "Baconian revolution" to a veritably scientific or "Baconian history."[64] The realists were wrong in wanting to import what they supposed to be the methods of physics into the study of human affairs. Rather, historians should create their own method of scientific enquiry,[65] suited to the subject matter of human society, human purposiveness, and human conduct.

Three decades after Collingwood wrote his *Autobiography*, his Oxford opponents became MacIntyre's targets. Twice MacIntyre aimed at Prichard Collingwood's joke that equating Plato's *polis* with Hobbes's state, or Aristotle's *dei* with Kant's "ought," was akin to mistaking Greek descriptions of triremes for accounts of modern steamships.[66] Although the joke was at the expense of idealism's critics, it could not have been made by those Oxford idealists for whom Kantian morality could answer Aristotle's questions and the modern state should pursue the common good in the same way as did the ancient *polis*. Collingwood's point was that questions asked by classical philosophers did not yield the same answers as questions asked by moderns because their objects of enquiry differed, and so too did their presuppositions. MacIntyre's point was then similar: that the actions of ancient Athenians were informed by an entirely different ethic than were those of contemporary Oxonians and that, as he had learned from Collingwood, "morality is an essentially historical subject matter

---

[59]Ibid..

[60]Ibid., 88.

[61]Ibid., 79, 87.

[62]Ibid., 79, 115.

[63]Ibid., 116, 143, 95; cf. Alasdair MacIntyre, "Hegel on Faces and Skulls," in MacIntyre, *The Tasks of Philosophy: Selected Essays* vol. 1 (Cambridge: Cambridge University Press, 2006).

[64]Collingwood, *An Autobiography*, 133, 124–25. See also Collingwood, *The Idea of History*, 269–70.

[65]See especially Collingwood, *An Autobiography*, 77–9.

[66]MacIntyre, *A Short History of Ethic*, 254–5; MacIntyre, *Against the Self-Images of the Age* (London: Duckworth, 1971) 161; cf. Collingwood, *An Autobiography*, 59–64.

and . . . philosophical inquiry, in ethics as elsewhere, is defective insofar as it is not historical."[67] The "philosophical point[s]" that he fully expressed in *A Short History* were Collingwoodian ones: that history's purpose is not "that it should culminate with us," that "what is held to be right or good is not . . . universal," that "moral concepts are embodied in and are partially constitutive of forms of social life"[68] and, most radically, that "each form of life carries with it its own picture of human nature," and therefore that human nature cannot provide any factual or "neutral standard" of evaluation.[69] In crucial respects, MacIntyre has now moved on from such Collingwoodian claims, as we will see.

The final chapter of Collingwood's *Autobiography*, "Theory and Practice," moves from his attack on "the moral corruption propagated by . . . 'realist' dogma," through praise of Marx as "a fighting philosopher" who provided "a philosophy that should be a weapon,"[70] on through an explanation of fascism as defending capitalism and an intransigent attack on the British government's policy of appeasement, to the book's concluding attack on Oxford realists as "the propagandists of a coming Fascism" in Britain.[71] When war came, within a year, Collingwood's contribution to Britain's defence was *The New Leviathan*.[72] This book retained a militant tone but delivered a different message. Since his *Autobiography*, the USSR, which had dared to resist fascism in Spain, had allied itself abortively with Nazi Germany, and the weapon he now wielded in Britain's defence was western history, from which he dismissed not only Russia but also Germany and German philosophy. About Italy, he was virtually silent. In the book's fourth and final part, "Barbarism," he updated Gibbon's *Decline and Fall* by moving "The Germans" from the position of being the original barbarian invaders to that of the "Fourth" and final "Barbarism."[73] "Kant and his successors"[74] were implicated in this barbarism and, therefore, decried and dismissed. Unlike Hobbes, they had, allegedly, no idea of "society" as persons' freely willed association, since their "*Gesellschaft*" lacks the Western concept's

---

[67]MacIntyre, "An Interview with Giovanna Borradori," 261.

[68]MacIntyre, *A Short History of Ethics*, 1, 4.

[69]Ibid., 268. In its second, 1998 edition, MacIntyre discusses his later retraction of these last claims at xv–xvii. The original book might be regarded as Collingwoodian in form and range, as well as argument, insofar as it resembles far more closely Collingwood's *Idea of History* and *Idea of Nature* (see n90) than Sidgwick's *History of Ethics*.

[70]Collingwood, *An Autobiography*, 147, 152, 153.

[71]Ibid., 167.

[72]R. G. Collingwood, *The New Leviathan: Or Man, Society, Civilization and Barbarism* (Oxford: Oxford University Press, 1942),

[73]Ibid., chap. 45. Collingwood expressly follows Gibbon regarding the preceding barbarisms of "the Saracens," "The 'Albigensian heresy'" and "'The Turks."

[74]Ibid., 272.

heritage of Roman civil law.[75] "The Germans," Collingwood alleges, "could not understand" what he calls "the classical politics" of Hobbes and *his* successors, in part "because they lacked experience" of "free joint activity." He objects to what Hegel says of "'objective'" mind and Marx of the relation "of the economic order to the consciousness of those involved in it,"[76] in apparent disregard of what Smith had said after Hobbes and before them, and also to "Marx's monstrous lie that all States have always been organs for the oppression of one class by another"[77] and to Marx's socialism, which he now sees as based "on the traditional German hatred of freedom" and "the traditional German worship of the herd."[78]

The *Autobiography* had ranged against Oxford's realists the Crocean proposition "that one and the same action" can be "a 'moral' action . . . a 'political' action as action relative to a rule, and at the same time an 'economic' action as means to an end."[79] *The New Leviathan* historicized this proposition in combining it with Collingwood's account of science. "History," it declares, "is to [moral] duty what modern science is to right, and what Greco-Medieval science was to utility" or teleology.[80] This collapse of teleology into utilitarianism followed the recent, ahistorical categorizations of C. D. Broad and, even, by the recently deceased leader of mainstream British idealism, J. H. Muirhead.[81] On Collingwood's cautious account of progress, as the process of civilization, teleology is designated the most primitive of the three modes of thought and action. Nonetheless, it has not simply been left behind in the historical past. Unlike Thomas Kuhn, with whom he is often compared (and whom it is sometimes even suggested he may have inspired), what Collingwood intends here is not a stadial history punctuated by revolutions in which one paradigm is replaced by another. Rather, he proposes a "Law Of Primitive Survivals"[82] by which utility persists alongside the "*regularian principle* or *rule*"[83] of right. The teleology with which he identifies utility is strikingly exempted from such persistence when he traces the "regularian tradition" from "the early civilizations of the Near East" to "modern Europe . . . through the work of Roman law and Jewish religion." "The Greeks" are dismissed from this history, having "s[e]t light to

---

[75]Ibid., 137. Here it is interesting to note that Collingwood's point is silently contradicted by his most famous follower in Quentin Skinner, *Hobbes and Republican Liberty* (Cambridge: Cambridge University Press, 2008).

[76]Collingwood, *The New Leviathan*, 272–3.

[77]Ibid., 89.

[78]Ibid., 277.

[79]Collingwood, *An Autobiography*, 147.

[80]Collingwood, *The New Leviathan*, 128, 126.

[81]C. D. Broad, *Five Types of Ethical Theory* (London: Kegan Paul, Trench, Trubner, 1930); John H. Muirhead, *Rule and End in Ethics* (Oxford: Oxford University Press, 1932).

[82]Collingwood, *The New Leviathan*, 65; emphasis omitted.

[83]Ibid., 113; Collingwood's emphases.

this ancient tradition, which is why the social and political experiments of the Greeks perished for lack of root, while the Romans created a legal fabric that is still alive."[84] We can see why MacIntyre, although praising the *Autobiography*, disregards *The New Leviathan*.

MacIntyre now differs fundamentally from Collingwood in at least two respects: the first theoretical, the second political. Before drawing these contrasts, though, a more incidental and tentative contrast may be drawn between their methodologies of morals. In *The New Leviathan*, Collingwood, having discussed action under the headings of "utility" and of regularian "right," moves on to a third category of "duty," by which he denotes "the act which is both possible and necessary: the act which at that moment character and circumstance combine to make it inevitable, if [on]e has a free will, that [on]e should freely will to do."[85] A duty is something that one must do, here and now, which is not a means to an end and is not given by any rule. This might seem redolent of what MacIntyre has taken from Knud Ejler Løgstrup's account of "the ethical demand." Such a demand is made upon one immediately, because of the particularity both of one's own situation and of some other who is in need of one's assistance. What such cases reveal, MacIntyre proposes, is that "accounts of morality as a kind of rule-following, whether utilitarian or Kantian, are . . . not merely philosophically mistaken, they are morally distorting, in that they distract us from attention to and action in terms of the singularity of this or that particular situation."[86] A virtuously habituated actor is one who acts immediately, undeductively and uncalculatively when the situation demands. The great difference of the positions of Løgstrup and MacIntyre from that of Collingwood is that he, unlike they, historicizes such a demand. On Collingwood's wartime account, acknowledgement of such a demand is a mark of modern civilization. This true morality of duty emerged from a historical synthesis of the Roman principle of right and institutions of civil law with the experience of those wider and highly un-Prussian conditions of civil society, civility, and modern civilization that "produced Locke or Hobbes."[87] Here, Collingwood radically revised his recent historical judgement that modernity maintained "the constellation of absolute presuppositions originally sketched by Aristotle" and defined by "the 'Catholic Faith.'"[88] Now he pronounced that "the revival of Greek philosophy by the German romanticists was in one thing at least a disaster: it gave the Germans . . . what they mistakenly thought good authority for rejecting the classical politics"

[84]Ibid., 127
[85]Ibid., 124; emphases omitted.
[86]Alasdair MacIntyre, "Danish Ethical Demands and French Common Goods: Two Moral Philosophies," *European Journal of Philosophy* 18, no. 1 (2010): 1–16, at 5.
[87]Collingwood, *The New Leviathan*, 384.
[88]Collingwood, *An Essay on Metaphysics*, 227.

of Hobbes.[89] In contrast, MacIntyre would seem to regard the truth and immediacy of such demands to be an aspect of the human condition, irrespective of history and culture. Indeed, we might suppose from what he says of modern moral philosophies of rule-following that he might consider modernity peculiarly susceptible to disregard of such a non-nomological ethic.

If this understanding of MacIntyre's apprehension of Løgstrup is correct, then it exemplifies what he regards as his most important difference from Collingwood: his rejection of Collingwood's historically relativist reduction of truth to enquiry. MacIntyre agrees that all claims to truth are made from some historically particular standpoint, but denies that this necessarily detracts from their veracity. Rather, the claims made by an enquirer may be more or less adequate to their object. That is, they may be more or less true and correct. The inadequacy of Collingwood's own standpoint on truth is largely due to what remain the Kantian presuppositions of his enquiries. The sceptical limits of Kant's critical philosophy are marked by what he says of the unknowability of noumenal things-in-themselves, in a way reflected by Collingwood's claim that past events can be known only through present reenactment of their enactors' ideas. Whereas Collingwood attempts to disentangle Kant's idea of *noumena*,[90] MacIntyre follows C. S. Peirce in denying that minds are incapable of corresponding to that which reality presents or, better, signifies to them. Truth is not a construct of the mind but the adequacy of a mind to its object: an adequacy that advances historically through the discoveries of cooperative enquiry,[91] *and* through confrontation between rival traditions of enquiry to discover which is the more adequate and the more true. Such a conception of truth informs the good aimed at by every practice of theoretical enquiry. What MacIntyre has here added to Peirce is that enquiries as to the truth of an object are plural and rival, so that even science may advance through revolutions. What he adds to Collingwood is that truth is singular.

MacIntyre's political difference from Collingwood is also fundamental. What they share is an intransigent opposition to fascism. What divides them is their conception of political community. Collingwood, admirer of the Roman *imperium*, championed liberal democratic states against fascist states. MacIntyre, admirer of the Athenian *polis*, even whilst deploring the social exclusions it shared with Rome, champions participative local communities against the exclusions essential to *all* bureaucratic states. Whereas Quentin Skinner and David Boucher

---

[89]Collingwood, *The New Leviathan*, 272.

[90]R. G. Collingwood, *The Idea of Nature*, ed. T. M. Knox (Oxford: Oxford University Press, 1945), 116–20.

[91]See especially Charles Saunders Peirce, "Fraser's Edition of *The Works of George Berkeley*," *Collected Papers of Charles Sanders Peirce* vol. 8: *Reviews, Correspondence, and Bibliography*, ed. Arthur W. Burks (Cambridge MA: Harvard University Press, 1958), 13.

follow Collingwood in attempting to reconceptualize contemporary liberal politics, MacIntyre acknowledges and rejects the reality of liberalism's practice as incompatible with its ideals.

Collingwood had been determined to draw some parallel between the fall of Rome and what he perceived as the latest threat to Western civilization. At first, still mindful of Oxford realism and being no less concerned than had been Vico or Ferguson with the threat of internal corruption, he railed against Gibbon for supposedly fabricating "the fable that the Roman Empire fell not through its own religious decay but beneath the swords of the barbarians."[92] As yet, he blamed rationalistic secularism for having demoralized the modern individualism that had originated from Christianity. In *The New Leviathan*, as we have seen, he reversed his position, prioritizing the clear and present danger that was external and Germanic, and thereby anticipating André Piganiol's famous claim that "Roman civilization did not die a natural death; it was assassinated."[93] MacIntyre, in contrast, warned against drawing "precise parallels between . . . our own age . . . and the epoch in which the Roman empire declined into the Dark Ages," even whilst warning of the danger to "civility and the intellectual and moral life" posed by the emotivist culture of "the new dark ages which are already upon us," in which capitalist and managerial "barbarians . . . have already been governing us for quite some time."[94] The institutions through which they rule are sometimes as capable of morally barbarous acts as was Rome, and MacIntyre has recently recounted his early conviction that the wartime "firebombings of Dresden and Tokyo . . . are prime examples of actions that should never be done."[95] As with Løgstrup's ethical demands, the standards by which these historical crimes ought to be judged may be inferred from aspects of the human condition that are ahistorical. These include our potentialities for reason and purposiveness, morality and freedom, but they also include our physical embodiedness, needs, and mutual dependencies. To presuppose the separation of freedom from nature, *noumena* from *phenomena*, is a philosophical error from which other errors cannot but follow.

III.

Liberalism. Such contemporary societies as those of the USA, UK, and Germany are characterized by MacIntyre as liberal. Historically, these are

---

[92]R. G. Collingwood, "Fascism and Nazism," *Philosophy* 15, no. 58 (1940): 168–76, at 170.

[93]Quoted (with revision) from Ian Wood, *The Modern Origins of the Early Middle Ages* (Oxford: Oxford University Press, 2013), 292.

[94]MacIntyre, *After Virtue*, 263.

[95]Alasdair MacIntyre, "The Illusion of Self-sufficiency," in *Conversations on Ethics*, ed. Alex Voorhoeve (Oxford: Oxford University Press, 2009), 115.

societies in which the power of ancient monarchical regimes, legitimated by a hierarchical church, has been overthrown or reformed away. To characterize them as liberal—rather than as, say, capitalist, secular, or simply modern—is to imply that their institutional structure should be attributed, primarily, to the enactment of those liberal ideals in terms of which they are often legitimated. Liberalism is not simply an ideological mask worn by economic forces or a will to power. Even so, MacIntyre objects, its ideals of liberty, equality and social justice have been betrayed. For example, "in such societies as the United Kingdom and the United States significant progress towards educational and social equality in the last forty years, let alone income equality, has been nonexistent."[96] Such progress, he implies, would have been achieved had politics been enlivened by a teleological understanding of human action and human relationships.

The kind of teleology to which MacIntyre refers when he speaks of human action and human relationships is that which he introduced in *After Virtue*. As we have noted, this is primarily an account of shared practices within which practitioners' desires are socialized and educated as they learn to act for the sake of goods internal to the practice, helping them to understand themselves teleologically, as progressing in enacting their understanding of their own good. As yet, though, what he said of actions and relationships might still have been described in terms of that "utility" with which Collingwood identified Greek teleology. The good life for man might as yet, MacIntyre happily conceded, amount to no more than a quixotic quest for the good life for man.[97]

MacIntyre's questions and answers took him deeper into Aristotelianism, and into *Thomistic* Aristotelianism, as an increasingly distinctive and histori-cally definable tradition of enquiry into the human good. One line of enquiry brought him into disagreement with not only Nietzsche but also many Greeks about the impotence of reason in the face of tragedy. According to some, Sophocles represented "the liberal temper in Greek politics" and his *Antigone* expressed the familiar liberal conception of "history as progress."[98] Accordingly, against the Sophoclean claim that duties of kinship and household might clash irreconcilably with those of citizenship and political community, MacIntyre argued for the unity of the virtues and the architectonic ordering of goods. *Whose Justice? Which Rationality?*, the third of his histories of ethics, therefore recounts "the division of the post-Homeric inheritance" between two rival re-valuations of norms and acts, and how Athens was "put to the question" as to

[96]MacIntyre, "Replies," 203.
[97]MacIntyre, *After Virtue*, 219.
[98]Eric A. Havelock, *The Liberal Temper in Greek Politics* (London: Jonathan Cape, 1957), 66–70.

which of these two budding traditions to accept and institutionalize.[99] In this, even before passing on through the Middle Ages to the Scotland of Hutcheson and Hume, the book sets out Aristotelianism's anti-utilitarian premises. Against utilitarianism, MacIntyre insists on the rationality of ends as well as of means, and on differentiating "goods of excellence" from instrumental "goods of effectiveness." Although the latter distinction is of those virtues which practitioners characteristically learn from powers to acquire the money and status which are institutions' characteristic currencies, its referents are internal to human beings and not just to their shared activities. In such ways, *Whose Justice? Which Rationality?* progresses a teleological understanding of past and present actions, relationships and selves.

A teleological understanding of human action and human relationships has occasionally been present even amongst those MacIntyre calls political elites. It was, for example, evident in some of those New Liberal politicians active around the beginning of the twentieth century who had been taught in Oxford's school of Green, and under whom some progress towards educational, social, and even income equality *was* made.[100] In their self-image, they were actualizing the progress of reason and freedom toward a socially inclusive kingdom of ends. Even so, such episodes are now long ago and contemporary liberalism is expressly and emphatically anti-teleological.

This is not to imply that contemporary liberalism is anti-teleological in *every* sense. One might well suspect that many liberals retain the kind of belief in progress toward their ideals that was suggested by Kant and most powerfully expressed by Hegel, and which was long ago expressed in terms of a process of civilization. When, in 1989, Francis Fukuyama first revived the Hegelian idea of the end of history, and when, in 1993, Samuel Huntington first warned of the clash of civilizations, they were disowned so shrilly by fellow liberals that one might suspect disingenuousness. Much had changed since Collingwood. Fascism had been defeated, Western Europe's empires had been dismantled and so too had that of the USSR, shortly followed by the dismantling of the USSR itself. Two decades before that there had occurred the greatest act of theory: the publication of John Rawls's *A Theory of Justice*.[101] It was this, and not idealism, which dealt utilitarianism a disabling blow. Such had been the impact of this *magnum opus* that MacIntyre could not afford to ignore it in *After Virtue*, which, in turn, was widely assimilated to a so-called "communitarian critique of liberalism," whereby "liberalism" denoted *A Theory of Justice*.

[99]Alasdair MacIntyre, *Whose Justice? Which Rationality?* (London: Duckworth, 1988), chaps. 3–4.

[100]See, for example, Michael Freeden, *The New Liberalism: An Ideology of Social Reform* (Oxford: Oxford University Press, 1978).

[101]John Rawls, *A Theory of Justice* (Cambridge, MA: Harvard University Press, 1971).

After Virtue was not intended as a critique of Rawls. Its express target was what it famously characterized as "the Enlightenment project" in moral theory. However, the Enlightenment project has since receded from MacIntyre's view, re-glimpsed only as a plurality of "some Enlightenment projects reconsidered,"[102] and the book's fifteenth chapter already glances at the "histories of a number of traditions."[103] In place of its metanarrative, *Whose Justice? Which Rationality?* in 1988 and then, in 1990, *Three Rival Versions of Moral Enquiry* went on to recount plural narratives of rival traditions of moral theory and institutionalized action and order. Noting the past and present fact of this plurality of traditions, each of which is committed to an idea of truth, MacIntyre argues for the theoretical and practical superiority of Thomistic Aristotelianism's commitment to human and common goods as actions' final ends and theory's first principles.

That *A Theory of Justice* was composed in the ahistorical mode of analytic philosophy Rawls emphasized in concluding it, claiming "the perspective of eternity" from which one can "regard the human situation . . . from all temporal points of view."[104] This Anglo-American mode of philosophizing is that of which MacIntyre had learned from Collingwood to be most critical.

Rawls, to the dismay of many of his followers, learned something of the same lesson. In part, he learned it from reflecting upon the history of liberalism.[105] He had attempted to theorize institutional justice as the "congruence" of liberalism's rules and "right" with a Kantian concept of the human "good," as rational participation in interpersonal justice. In short, *Theory* claimed the perspective of eternity because it attempted to theorize (as "a well-ordered society") the institutional principles of Kant's kingdom of ends. It could ignore history because it aimed to express the aim and end of history.

Hobbes's *Leviathan* had taught that stability is the precondition of justice, and if justice is to be a virtue of institutions their *first* virtues must be stability and legitimacy. This is a lesson that Kant had acknowledged in *Toward Perpetual Peace* and "The Doctrine of Right." It is a lesson that Rawls hoped he had adequately accounted for by making safe for analytic philosophy liberalism's original theoretical device of the social contract. He had not. Kant had never succeeded in rendering congruent natural necessity and moral freedom, experience and reason, theory and practice; nor had Rawls. In search of congruence, Kant had turned to history. So too did Rawls. What he had to render congruent were the

---

[102]Alasdair MacIntyre, "Some Enlightenment Projects Reconsidered," in *Ethics and Politics: Selected Essays*, vol. 2 (Cambridge: Cambridge University Press, 2006).

[103]MacIntyre, *After Virtue*, 222.

[104]Rawls, *A Theory of Justice*, 587.

[105]John Rawls, *Lectures on the History of Moral Philosophy*, ed. Barbara Herman (Cambridge, MA: Harvard University Press, 2000); John Rawls, *Lectures on the History of Political Philosophy*, ed. Samuel Freeman (Cambridge, MA: Harvard University Press, 2007).

idea of justice and the experiential and historically-given fact of a plurality of "reasonable" traditions or "comprehensive doctrines."

Rawls's turn to history is brief but significant. He had never intended to theorize the justice of particular acts or individual actors but only the constitutive principles of those institutions constituting society's "basic structure." That structure must include a sovereign and constitutional state but he supposed himself to have left open whether its economic institutions should be capitalist or socialist. Even so, he accepted that the presuppositions of *Theory* were too comprehensive and that liberalism needed to limit its first principles to ones still more specifically "political."

When first introducing his shift to a specifically political liberalism, Rawls re-characterized *Theory* as having addressed "classical problems that had been at the center of the historical debates concerning the moral and political structure of the modern democratic state."[106] Now, "for orientation," he began afresh by renouncing the "ambitions" of "the so-called Enlightenment project of finding a philosophical secular doctrine, one founded on reason and yet comprehensive."[107] Instead of beginning within the Enlightenment's bounds of reason alone, he located the genesis of his own newly identified tradition of a specifically political liberalism in the Reformation, which was itself a contingent historical fact that he now acknowledged to be in need of explanation by reference to a genealogy traceable back to the time of "a polis in which the Homeric epics . . . play a central part."[108] Ignoring, like MacIntyre, the interlude of Rome's imperial civilization, Rawls thence jumped to the very different period of "Medieval Christianity" in order to explain "the different problems of political philosophy in the modern as compared with the ancient world."[109] In place of the disaster posited in the opening chapter of *After Virtue*, he recalled the Reformation's "division of Christendom as a disaster," because the cause of gross instability and inter-religious war, and as "the historical origin of political liberalism (and of liberalism more generally)."[110] Hobbes offered the social contract as a solution to the urgent problem of political obligation, after which the contingent emergence "of liberal constitutionalism came as a discovery of a new social possibility: the possibility of a reasonably harmonious and stable pluralist society." Like its causal condition, "this is a phenomenon new to historical experience,

---

[106]John Rawls, *Political Liberalism*, 3 ed. (Cambridge, MA: Harvard University Press, 2005), xxviii.

[107]Ibid., xviii. Rawls outlines his own understanding of the Enlightenment's moral project at xxvi–xxvii.

[108]Ibid., xxii.

[109]Ibid., xxiii, xxi.

[110]Ibid., xxiv.

a possibility realized by the Reformation"[111] even if unforeseen by Enlightenment *philosophes*.[112]

In continuing to offer liberalism as a solution to the political problem of pluralism, Rawls effectively acknowledged that political philosophy is inseparable from its past. In effect, he indicated an alternative narrative of liberalism's history to that introduced in *After Virtue* and elaborated in *Whose Justice?* His synoptic *Justice as Fairness: A Restatement* adds to that narrative in posing "four roles of political philosophy." Each of these roles aims at overcoming the problem of pluralism. The first role was that begun by "Hobbes's *Leviathan* (1652)—surely the greatest work of political philosophy in English," and continued by Locke. It is the role of identifying pluralism as a problem to be solved and, to that end, attempting to find some small ground on which there could be an overlapping consensus.[113] Political philosophy's second role, which Rawls designates with Kant's term "orientation," is that of contributing to how people think of their participation in a "civilized" "society with a history." Its "third role, stressed by Hegel in his *Philosophy of Right* (1821), is that of reconciliation." This is the task of helping people to understand their society's institutions as having "developed over time as they did to attain their present, rational form."[114] As he elaborated in his *Lectures on the History of Moral Philosophy*, this "role of political philosophy . . . is to grasp the social world in thought and to express it in a form in which it can be seen by us to be *rational*" or, better, "'reasonable,'" most profoundly because "it shows us our freedom of will" as something "that we have . . . through institutions." In this way it improves on Kant, insofar as Kant theorized freedom in disregard of "all the contingencies of our society and its history."[115] Indeed, Rawls endorses all that Hegel says in elaborating his "liberalism of freedom"[116] and, even, repeatedly commends Hegel's historicism when noting how Luther and Calvin prepared the way for a liberalism that can have been no part of their intention.[117] His only hesitation appears at the very end of the *Lectures*, when he identifies as Aristotelian the perfectionist logic of Hegel's argument that "we need . . . a philosophical conception of the world as

---

[111]Ibid., xxiv–xxvi.

[112]John Rawls, "Constitutional Liberty and the Concept of Justice," in John Rawls, *Collected Papers*, ed. Samuel Freeman (Cambridge, MA: Harvard University Press, 1999), 91–2.

[113]John Rawls, *Justice as Fairness: A Restatement*, ed. Erin Kelly (Cambridge, MA: Harvard University Press, 2001), 1–2. See also Rawls, *Lectures on the History of Moral Philosophy*, 10. Rawls expresses this first role in other, vaguer terms.

[114]Rawls, *Justice as Fairness*, 3.

[115]Rawls, *Justice as Fairness*. Conversely, Rawls defends Kantian contractarianism from Hegel's criticism in *Political Liberalism*, 285–8.

[116]Rawls, *Lectures on the History of Moral Philosophy*, 330, 349, 365–6.

[117]Rawls, *Political Liberalism*, xxiv; Rawls, *Lectures on the History of Moral Philosophy*, 5; Rawls, *Justice as Fairness*, 34.

a whole, including a philosophy of history."[118] In this, he apparently neglects the prior role played by Kant.

The final task that Rawls attributes to political philosophy "is a variation of the" third, in reconciling historicism to pluralism. "Eventually we want to ask whether the fact of reasonable pluralism is a historical fate we should lament," and the task is "to show that it is not." Liberalism should be "realistically utopian," limiting its ambitions to "historical conditions" under which affirmation of "one comprehensive conception" is impossible.[119] The dismay felt by many of his erstwhile followers might have been shared by Collingwood and Kant, since civility is replaced by public reasonableness and a limit is placed on progress, both domestically and, as Rawls made clear in *The Law of Peoples*, internationally.

Liberals should not be dismayed if they recall that their history is that also of the institutions of state and commerce. Their previous caution against triumphalism after the fall of the USSR has been vindicated by the failure of any *Pax Americana* to match Rome's achievement. Even so, what could not be disseminated hegemonically by force of arms has spread by imitation. The institutions of Rawls's "basic structure" and MacIntyre's "state-and-market" have been copied, even whilst the Enlightenment's social hopes have diminished. Ruling elites have almost everywhere appreciated the efficacy of urging their subjects to enrich themselves, progressing consumer civilization along with the rule of law and developing "free joint activity" along with the rule of joint-stock corporate capital. Those elites, constituting our present *ancien regimes*, may not be barbaric, but they nonetheless remain institutionally alien to those they rule.

London Metropolitan University
London, United Kingdom

---

[118]Rawls, *Lectures on the History of Moral Philosophy*, 371; cf. 334.

[119]Rawls, *Justice as Fairness*, 4–5. See also Rawls, *Lectures on the History of Political Philosophy*, 10–1.

MacIntyre on the Practice of Philosophy and the University

Bryan R. Cross

Abstract. Especially since his "Reconceiving the University as an Institution and the Lecture as a Genre," Alasdair MacIntyre has repeatedly returned to the subject of reconceiving university education, proposing a vision of what a university is and what a university education should be that differs widely from contemporary institutions and practices, and offering strong criticisms of the contemporary research university. He has argued provocatively that in its present form, the contemporary research university is not a university at all because it does not carry out the purpose of a university. MacIntyre has also argued that philosophical practice always takes place within some tradition or other, and has identified as his own the broader Aristotelian-Thomistic tradition in which philosophy is to be understood as a craft. In this essay I examine and develop the relationship between MacIntyre's critique of the contemporary research university, and his conception of philosophy as a craft practiced within a tradition.

I.

*I**ntroduction.** Especially since his "Reconceiving the University as an Institution and the Lecture as a Genre," published as the last chapter of *Three Rival Versions of Moral Enquiry*, Alasdair MacIntyre has repeatedly returned to the subject of reconceiving university education, proposing a vision of what a university is and what a university education should be that differs widely from contemporary institutions and practices, and offering strong criticisms of the contemporary research university. He has argued provocatively that in its present form, the contemporary research university is not a university at all because it does not carry out the purpose of a university. According to MacIntyre, between the Ninth (1875–1889) and Eleventh (1910–1911) editions of the *Encyclopaedia Britannica*, educational institutions in general, and universities in particular, ceased to carry out the purpose of education when they abandoned a unified vision of the world and thus when "moral and theological truth ceased to be recognized as objects of substantive enquiry and instead were relegated to

©2014, *American Catholic Philosophical Quarterly*, Vol. 88, No. 4
doi: 10.5840/acpq201492233

the realm of privatized belief."[1] At the same time, in view of the intractability of moral and more general philosophical disagreements in contemporary philosophy, MacIntyre has also argued that philosophical practice always takes place within some tradition or other, and has identified as his own the broader Aristotelian-Thomistic tradition in which, according to MacIntyre, philosophy is to be understood as a craft.

Here I set out to examine two areas of MacIntyre's thought and develop the relationship between them: his critique of the contemporary research university, and his conception of philosophy as a craft practiced within a tradition. My purpose is to answer the following question: How is MacIntyre's conception of philosophy as a craft practiced within a tradition related to his critique of the contemporary research university; and what are the implications of that relationship?

II.

MacIntyre's Critique of Contemporary Philosophy: A Discipline in Crisis. In order to investigate this question, it is worth examining briefly MacIntyre's critique of contemporary philosophy, before turning to his conception of philosophy understood as a craft. For many years MacIntyre has been pointing to a fundamental problem in contemporary philosophy. In 1982, in an article titled "Philosophy, the 'Other' Disciplines, and their Histories: A Rejoinder to Richard Rorty," MacIntyre expressed agreement with Rorty's claim in *Philosophy and the Mirror of Nature* that philosophy as practiced professionally today lacks *any* systematic unity. MacIntyre writes, "If philosophy as practiced professionally today lacks *any* systematic unity—and on this, at least, Rorty and I do agree—this is itself now a central philosophical problem."[2] Contemporary philosophy, claimed MacIntyre, "has finally lost any serious intellectual unity."[3] There are now, he said, "as many paradigms as there are major philosophy departments."[4] Philosophy presently retains the appearance of unity not by its answers to any philosophical questions, but only by the questions themselves and an historical continuity with a unified philosophical practice inherited from Plato and preserved in its unity during the Enlightenment era, where Rorty's narrative begins.

---

[1]Alasdair MacIntyre, *Three Rival Versions of Moral Enquiry: Encyclopedia, Genealogy, and Tradition* (Notre Dame, IN: University of Notre Dame Press, 1990), 217.

[2]Alasdair MacIntyre, "Philosophy, the 'Other' Disciplines, and Their Histories: A Rejoinder to Richard Rorty," *Soundings* 65, no. 2 (Summer 1982): 127–45, at 134, emphasis in original.

[3]Ibid., 120.

[4]Ibid., 139.

In MacIntyre's 1984 article titled "The Relationship of Philosophy to Its Past,"[5] he notes that the severe disagreements among philosophers have contributed to the general disregard for the discipline of philosophy because it is no longer seen as a truth-discovering practice by those in other areas of academia and by the general public. Today university administrators with the power to make funding decisions are beginning to view philosophy with the same suspicion. The substantive and intractable disagreements among philosophers have led to the marginalization of philosophy as an integrating science in the university and in society, and to its de facto replacement by physics, biochemistry, neurophysiology, psychology, and other similar sciences. MacIntyre has described this marginalization as not only the "relegation of philosophy in the vast majority of colleges and universities to a subordinate position in the curriculum, an inessential elective for those who happen to like that sort of thing," but also one reflected in the culture as a whole, which invites us to ignore or dismiss difficult philosophical questions.[6] The chronic and irresolvable character of philosophical disagreements has contributed over time to a shift in the conception of philosophy, even the self-conception of philosophy by academic philosophers, from a truth-discovering practice to an activity or set of activities unified by a much less clearly defined nature and end.[7]

Also in 1984, in his postscript to the second edition of *After Virtue*, MacIntyre described this same consequence:

> For what the progress of analytic philosophy has succeeded in establishing is that there are *no* grounds for belief in universal necessary principles—outside purely formal enquiries—except relative to some set of assumptions. Cartesian first principles, Kantian *a priori* truths and even the ghosts of these notions that haunted empiricism for so long have all been expelled from philosophy. The consequence is that analytic philosophy has become a discipline—or a subdiscipline?—whose competence has been restricted to the study of inferences. Rorty puts this by saying that

---

[5]Alasdair MacIntyre, "The Relationship of Philosophy to Its Past," in *Philosophy in History: Essays on the Historigraphy of Philosophy*, ed. Richard Rorty, J. B. Schneewind, and Quentin Skinner (Cambridge: Cambridge University Press, 1984), 31–48.

[6]Alasdair MacIntyre, "Philosophy Recalled to Its Tasks: A Thomistic reading of *Fides et Ratio*," in MacIntyre, *The Tasks of Philosophy: Selected Essays*, vol. 1 (Cambridge: Cambridge University Press, 2006), 181–2.

[7]MacIntyre writes, "For it was in part, at least, the discovery of rival theological modes of enquiry embedded in rival forms of religious practice similarly unable, and for similar reason, to defeat each other's claims at a fundamental level by rational argument that led to the Enlightenment and post-Enlightenment discrediting of theology as a mode of rational enquiry. So the question necessarily arises: why should philosophy not suffer the same discredit?" MacIntyre, "The Relationship of Philosophy to Its Past," 35.

"the ideal of philosophical ability is to see the entire universe of possible assertions in all their inferential relationships to one another, and thus to be able to construct, or criticize, any argument."[8]

MacIntyre laments that "analytic philosophy has become a discipline . . . whose competence has been restricted to the study of inferences," that analytic philosophy has largely been reduced to formal logic. But the problem he diagnoses extends rather broadly to academic philosophy as it is now commonly practiced, especially in North America and the United Kingdom.

Three years later, in 1987, in an article titled "Philosophy: Past Conflicts and Future Direction," MacIntyre wrote:

> [I]n modern academic philosophy no issue, or almost no issue, is ever conclusively settled. The striking ability of the members of our profession to keep problems unresolved is bound up with the fact that the criticism of any philosophical theory characteristically consists in an elucidation of the logical and conceptual commitments involved in holding it, in the light of which we can evaluate what the costs of continuing to hold it are. Only there are no accepted standards of evaluation by which to measure such costs, that is to say, no shared understanding of what philosophical rationality consists in, of what costs are too high to pay.[9]

Because there is no "accepted standard of evaluation," this activity of elucidating the various logical possibilities and the costs of holding each can reach no decisive conclusion regarding which position is correct. Each individual inquirer is left to decide for him or herself which of the costs is least, and which of the benefits is best.

The following year, in his opening chapter of *Whose Justice? Which Rationality?*, MacIntyre returned again to the fragmented and unhelpful condition of contemporary academic philosophy, writing:

> Modern academic philosophy turns out by and large to provide means for a more accurate and informed definition of disagreement rather than for progress toward its resolution. Professors of philosophy who concern themselves with questions of justice and of practical rationality turn out to disagree with each other as sharply, as variously, and, so it seems, as irremediably upon how such questions are to be answered as anyone else. They do indeed succeed in articulating the rival standpoints with

---

[8]Alasdair MacIntyre, *After Virtue*, 2nd ed. (Notre Dame, IN: University of Notre Dame Press, 1984), 266–7, emphasis in original.

[9]Alasdair MacIntyre, "Philosophy: Past Conflicts and Future Direction," *Proceedings and Addresses of the American Philosophical Association*, supplement to vol. 61 (September, 1987): 81.

greater clarity, greater fluency, and a wider range of arguments than do most others, but apparently little more than this.[10]

And in many other places throughout his corpus MacIntyre offers this sort of critique of contemporary philosophy.[11]

For MacIntyre, the result of assuming that substantive first principles are universally accessible to all rational persons, and of disregarding the essential role of embeddedness within a tradition in the dialectical discovery of first principles, is that philosophy becomes entirely a matter of personal opinion. That is because the only first principles that are universally accessible are those of formal logic and the most general moral principles, which are incapable of adjudicating particular moral questions. So by limiting itself to these most general first principles, philosophy is left only with working out the logical implications and relations of the variously proposed moral concepts and systems. As a result, according to MacIntyre philosophy is now viewed as "a harmless, decorative activity," and those who teach it as comparable to those who teach dance.[12] Such philosophy has no way of "providing grounds for conviction on matters of any substance."[13]

---

[10]Alasdair MacIntyre, *Whose Justice? Which Rationality?* (Notre Dame, IN: University of Notre Dame Press, 1988), 3.

[11]See, for example: Alasdair MacIntyre, "Moral Philosophy: What Next?," in *Revisions: Changing Perspectives in Moral Philosophy*, ed. Stanley Hauerwas and Alasdair MacIntyre (Notre Dame, IN: University of Notre Dame Press, 1983), 1; MacIntyre, "A Perspective on Philosophy," *Social Research* 51, no. 2 (Summer 1984): 477–92; MacIntyre, *Whose Justice? Which Rationality?*, 335; Alasdair MacIntyre, *God, Philosophy, Universities* (Lanham, MD: Rowman & Littlefield, 2009), 11, 176.

[12]MacIntyre writes,

> Philosophy thus conceived is neither the support for the established political order for which the adherents of that order had once hoped nor the threat to it which they had once feared. It does not engender conflict either with or on behalf of government. It is, in the main a harmless, decorative activity, education in which is widely believed to benefit by exercising and extending capacities for orderly argument, so qualifying those who study it to join the line of lemmings entering law school or business school The professor of philosophy, on this view, stands to the contemporary bourgeoisie much as the dancing master stood to the nobility of the ancient regime. The dancing master taught the eighteenth-century expensively brought up young how to have supple limbs, the philosophy professor teaches their twentieth-century successors how to have supple minds.
>
> This is an image not indeed of how we are, but of how we are widely regarded, an image which we generally take some trouble not to admit beyond the fringes of consciousness. Were we to face it squarely, we would have to face the question of whether it is worth going on doing philosophy, as it is now generally done. (MacIntyre, "Philosophy: Past Conflicts and Future Direction," 85)

[13]MacIntyre, *Whose Justice? Which Rationality?*, 335.

These are strong terms and severe criticisms. They would be no criticism at all if MacIntyre believed that this is how philosophy rightly practiced should be understood, as its natural or ordinary condition. For MacIntyre, however, this condition of modern philosophy corresponds to the imaginary post-catastrophic society he describes in the opening chapter of *After Virtue*. It is a symptom of a flaw so deeply accepted in contemporary academic philosophy that it is not recognized as a flaw, and for this reason it is accepted as indicating the limits of philosophy rather than as indicating that in some significant way academic philosophy has deviated from certain internal standards of philosophical practice and from the resources of the tradition in which that practice has been developed.

III.

MacIntyre on Philosophy as a Craft. MacIntyre's conception of philosophy as presented in *Three Rival Versions* is informed by the long philosophical tradition extending from Plato and Aristotle up to the present. According to this ancient philosophical tradition, philosophy is a craft, a *techne*, and to learn philosophy the enquirer must become a certain kind of person with particular virtues and training. MacIntyre writes:

> From the standpoint of the *Gorgias* and the *Republic* the enquirer has to learn how to make him or herself into a particular kind of person if he or she is to move towards a knowledge of the truth about his or her good and about *the* human good. What kind of a transformation is required? It is that which is involved in making oneself into an apprentice to a craft, the craft in this case of philosophical enquiry. . . . What then is it about the structure of a craft and of a craft guild which is important for philosophy? What is it that philosophy as a craft shares with other crafts, such as furniture making or fishing, which it may well not share with philosophy conceived in rival modes, such as those of Descartes or of Nietzsche?[14]

In the same chapter MacIntyre uses different but related terms to refer to the craft of philosophy, referring to it as the "philosophy of craft-tradition,"[15] "tradition-

---

[14]MacIntyre, *Three Rival Versions*, 60–1, emphasis in original. One might object that in chapters three and four of Book VI of his *Nicomachean Ethics* Aristotle uses the term *techne* to refer only to that by which something is made, whereas philosophy is concerned not with making, but with acquiring wisdom and acting according to practical wisdom. One might thus conclude that MacIntyre's use of the term "craft" in reference to philosophy is not that of Aristotle and the Aristotelian tradition. But it is important to note that the usage of this term, especially in its Latin form, developed such that by analogy it could be used of the results of inquiry in areas of theoretical knowledge.

[15]Ibid., 69.

constituted, craft-constituted enquiry,"[16] and "the master-craft of master-crafts."[17] He attributes to St. Thomas Aquinas the notion that philosophical activity is a craft, even "the chief of crafts."[18]

The conception of philosophy as craft, albeit one in which the goods discovered are internal to its practice, is essential to MacIntyre's *After Virtue* project, because it distinguishes his position both from that of sophistry, represented by Nietzche, and that of the Enlightenment, represented in *Three Rival Versions* by way of the encyclopaedist tradition. According to this tradition of philosophy as craft, the philosopher is opposed to the sophistry that denies that there is any philosophical truth or wisdom to be acquired in philosophy. In the sophistical tradition the philosophical teacher or "master-craftsman" is viewed as exerting power and domination under the false guise of illumination and instruction.[19] Against the sophists, the philosophical tradition stemming from Plato and Aristotle maintains that philosophical truth can be and has been discovered, and that its teachers are passing on those discovered truths, not engaged in exerting power over their students under an illusion of pedagogy.

Philosophy according to this same tradition is also opposed to the Enlightenment notion that philosophical truth "can be discovered or confirmed by any adequately intelligent person, no matter what his point of view."[20] The Enlightenment figure affirms that philosophical truth and wisdom can be acquired without entering into any practice, craft, or tradition, and without submitting to the rational authority of a craftsman. For the encyclopaedists, according to MacIntyre,

> to be rational is to think for oneself, to emancipate oneself from the tutelage of authority. Any notion that I can only think adequately by and for myself insofar as I do so in the company of others, to some of whom authority must be accorded, is quite alien to the encylopaedist.[21]

This description of the encyclopaedist's conception of philosophy shows precisely why it is incompatible with the notion of philosophy as a craft. For MacIntyre, just as understanding of substantive first principles can be acquired only through a dialectical process within a tradition, so philosophical truth and wisdom can be acquired only by entering into the craft of philosophy and the community constituted by practitioners of this craft, in which and by which the craft is sustained and developed.

---

[16]Ibid., 81.
[17]Ibid., 68.
[18]Ibid., 127.
[19]Ibid., 66.
[20]Ibid., 60.
[21]Ibid., 64.

Entering into the craft of philosophy involves submitting oneself to a philosophical master who has expertise in the craft, in order to learn by observation and discipline habits and insights necessary to become a practitioner of the craft and thereby discover the goods internal to this craft. MacIntyre writes,

> [T]he apprentice has to learn, at first from his or her teachers and then in his or her continuing self-education, how to identify mistakes made by him or herself in applying the acknowledged standards, the standards recognized to be the best available so far in the history of that particular craft. . . . [T]he apprentice has to learn to distinguish between the kind of excellence which both others and he or she can expect of him or herself here and now and that ultimate excellence which furnishes both apprentices and mastercraftsmen with their *telos*. . . . [U]nless we already have within ourselves the potentiality for moving towards and achieving the relevant theoretical and practical conclusions we shall be unable to learn. But we also need a teacher to enable us to actualize that potentiality, and we shall have to learn from that teacher and initially accept on the basis of his or her authority within the community of a craft precisely what intellectual and moral habits it is which we must cultivate and acquire if we are to become effective self-moved participants in such enquiry. Hence there emerges a conception of rational teaching authority internal to the practice of the craft of moral enquiry, as indeed such conceptions emerge in such other crafts as furniture making and fishing, where, just as in moral enquiry, they partially define the relationship of master-craftsman to apprentice.[22]

What the apprentice needs to learn in order to enter into the practice of philosophy is not reducible to information intelligible to her in her initial condition. She must first come to see that she does not, and in her present condition cannot, see certain things, and thereby identify in herself her "defects and limitations . . . with respect to the achievement of [the *telos* of the craft]."[23] The initial self-knowledge required is a coming to see that on her own, apart from a craft and apart from the guidance provided by a master of the craft, she cannot learn certain things she does not know. The philosophical apprentice must then attain certain virtues, moral and intellectual, in order to begin to see and appreciate the goods (e.g., truths, wisdom, and beauty) internal to the practice in which these goods are pursued and contemplated.

One important implication of MacIntyre's conception of philosophy as a craft or practice concerns its relation to history. In *After Virtue* MacIntyre wrote,

---

[22]Ibid., 62–3.
[23]Ibid., 62.

> To enter into a practice is to enter into a relationship not only with its contemporary practitioners, but also with those who preceded us in this practice, particularly those whose achievements extended the reach of the practice to its present point.[24]

The standards of excellence internal to the craft in relation to its *telos* and the rationality of its rules are not necessarily knowable outside the craft. In this way the craft can be opaque to the outsider. A craft's standards of excellence and the rules of the craft are shaped and developed within the craft in the course of the development and life of the craft over time. Fully understanding and entering into the craft, therefore, requires understanding the historical development of its standards and rules, insofar as they sometimes failed and were subsequently modified or further specified or clarified.

This is why, according to MacIntyre, the presupposition of the encyclopaedists that "all reasoning must be such as would be compelling to any fully rational person whatsoever" entails "an exclusion of tradition as a guide to truth."[25] The notion that "all reasoning must be such as would be compelling to any fully rational person whatsoever" fails to recognize the possibility of historical development within a social practice of rules and standards of excellence through encounters with obstacles and failures. Such a notion "flattens" and diminishes rationality by conceptually removing from it the dimension made possible by the conjunction of extended temporality and community.[26] This notion implicitly presupposes that reality as approached philosophically is no richer or more profound in its intelligibility and etiology than can be discerned by each rational person synchronically and individualistically, without the benefit of advances in understanding attained by previous members of one's community of enquirers. In this respect this Enlightenment notion oversimplifies reality.

The historical aspect internal to the very concept of a craft implies that philosophy is neither ahistorical nor reducible to the history of philosophy. When Quine joked that there are two sorts of people interested in philosophy, "those interested in philosophy and those interested in the history of philosophy," MacIntyre noted in response, "The counter-joke is: the people interested in philosophy now are doomed to become those whom only those interested in the history of philosophy are going to be interested in in a hundred years time."[27] Approaching philosophical questions and problems in a traditionless manner relegates the ideas and theories worked out by its proponent to the status of recent history upon his or her death. Only within a tradition of philosophical

---

[24]MacIntyre, *After Virtue*, 194.
[25]MacIntyre, *Three Rival Versions*, 65.
[26]This dimension is what MacIntyre means by "tradition-constituted rationality."
[27]MacIntyre, "The Relationship of Philosophy to Its Past," 40.

practice do the philosopher's contributions to the practice transcend the merely historical. Hence the paradox of MacIntyre's reply to Quine, according to which one truly transcends the history of philosophy not by ignoring its history but by entering into the philosophical craft in which its history is preserved and presently advanced teleologically toward a communally shared, though only partially understood, goal. Philosophy in the future, for MacIntyre, will overcome the contemporary reduction of philosophy to elucidating the various logical possibilities.

For this reason, according to MacIntyre, a "piecemeal" approach to philosophy that seeks to solve particular problems in contemporary or historical philosophical systems, while attempting to disassociate itself from any particular tradition and speak to all rational persons by constructing arguments intended to be accessible to all rational persons, is a traditionless approach to philosophy that does not recognize philosophy as a craft, has no internal teleology, and thus lacks the unity such a teleology supplies. Merely utilizing historical figures and works that developed within the craft of philosophy does not constitute entering into that craft because the encyclopaedist, as such, can do the same.

So the key difference between the craft of philosophy and the encyclopaedists' utilization of and engagement with figures within the history of philosophy is not merely historical awareness. Both the practitioner of the craft of philosophy and the historically informed encyclopaedist can set down some sort of history of philosophy. The encyclopaedist sees the various philosophical positions and arguments provided by all the same figures in the history of philosophy, but by failing to recognize the "tradition-constituted, craft-constituted" character of philosophical practice, he or she sees no continually developing philosophical rules, discovered truths, and developed standards of excellence to which one must be subject in order to enter into and practice the craft. The craft dimension of philosophy's history, and therefore the perception of the craft's tradition as normative for philosophical practice, remains hidden to him or her. Instead, he or she retains the working assumption of the encyclopaedist tradition that philosophical truth can be discovered or confirmed by any adequately intelligent person, no matter what his point of view, and that philosophical argumentation can be rightly understood and evaluated by any rational person regardless of his background or tradition. The practitioner of the craft, by contrast, sees in philosophy's history a narrative of discovery, organic development and social recognition of philosophical truths, rules and standards of excellence disclosed by the practice of a singular craft to which each generation of those who enter into this craft is subject, including the present practitioner him or herself.

Concerning the encyclopaedist's form of philosophy, MacIntyre writes the following:

There is consequently no progress in this type of academic philosophy, whether medieval or modern, except in skill, method, and technique in the formulation of problems. Beyond this, philosophical positions merely replace and displace one another without any overall directedness appearing. Hence not even retrospectively is it possible to give a teleological account of its history, for no *telos* emerges. And thus although the concerns and detailed findings of this philosophy are of the highest relevance to a number of types of tradition of rational enquiry, it is not itself such a tradition and is indeed institutionalized in such a way as to exclude the type of claim and argument characteristic of such traditions from its professionalized discourse.[28]

There can be no substantive progress in this type of academic philosophy, according to MacIntyre, for the same reason that there can be no progress in the moral disagreements of our time. The first principles to which all persons have direct access and share in common are not sufficiently substantive to provide the means of adjudicating the disagreements. By way of the encyclopaedic approach, even one with a comprehensive awareness of the history of philosophy, philosophical disagreements remain intractable and progress is impossible because the substantive resources by which such disagreements can be resolved and progress achieved are available only in and through the body of tradition the encyclopaedist fails to perceive as normative for the practice of the craft of philosophy.

IV.

MacIntyre's Critique of the Contemporary Research University. What, then, is MacIntyre's critique of the contemporary research university? For MacIntyre, following John Henry Newman, the purpose of a university is to cultivate and form educated persons. To be educated, however, is not merely to have acquired skills or competency in some area of specialization or expertise. To be "educated" is to have undergone a perfection of the intellect,[29] the "true enlargement of mind which is the power of viewing many things as one whole, of referring them severally to their place in the universal system, of understanding their respective values, and determining their mutual dependence."[30] According to MacIntyre, the educated human being knows how to think like and with mathematicians, historians,

---

[28]MacIntyre, *Three Rival Versions*, 160.

[29]By "perfection of the intellect" MacIntyre does not mean absolute perfection, as though no room for further perfection remains. Rather, he means that the intellect has fulfilled its function, which is to grasp the universal, and thus gain a comprehension of the whole and of the parts in relation to that whole.

[30]Alasdair MacIntyre, "The Very Idea of a University: Aristotle, Newman and Us," *British Journal of Educational Studies* 57, no. 4 (December 2009): 353.

physicists, etc. Such a person is capable of bringing his or her understanding of these various disciplines to bear in particular situations, and in this way he or she possesses the habit of good judgment. Moreover, the educated person is capable of integrating knowledge of the various disciplines into the broader philosophical questions concerning the whole of reality, of integrating the various domains of knowledge into a comprehensive understanding of the order of things.[31]

MacIntyre maintains that the contemporary research university does not provide this to its students. Instead, it aims fundamentally at training them thoroughly in a specific discipline for marketability in that field upon graduation or for further specialization in that discipline in graduate school, while at the same time giving them a superficial exposure to a few disciplines. And, for MacIntyre, the research university's focus on specialized training, coupled with its abandonment of the very notion of any integrated understanding of the full range of human and scientific disciplines, not only deprives students of the perfection of the intellect that is education, but may well prevent students from attaining true education.[32] Thus, insofar as the contemporary research university, by its very internal curricular structure, fails to educate its students, it is not properly a university.

So why, according to MacIntyre, did universities cease to be universities? In his chapter titled "Reconceiving the University as an Institution and the Lecture as a Genre," MacIntyre draws a connection between the change found in the Ninth Edition of the *Encyclopaedia Britannica* and the change in university education. That change was the loss of "a unified secular vision of the world and of the place of knowledge and of enquiry within it":[33] what MacIntyre calls "the demise of encyclopaedia." According to MacIntyre, three changes eliminated the "unified secular vision of the world" from encyclopedias, and thus from universities. These include:

(1) the fragmentation of enquiry into independent, specialized professional activities

(2) the loss of an educated public,

(3) the cessation of the recognition of moral and theological truth as objects of substantive enquiry in academia.[34]

---

[31]These criteria of an educated person are drawn from Alasdair MacIntyre, "Comments," Colloquium on *God, Philosophy, Universities*, Notre Dame Center for Ethics and Culture, Notre Dame, IN, April 22, 2010.

[32]MacIntyre writes, "To develop highly specialised knowledge only in one particular sphere, to focus one's mind on only one subject-matter, may certainly be valuable, but it will not enable the mind to achieve its specific perfection and is apt to prevent the mind from doing so." MacIntyre, "The Very Idea of a University," 353.

[33]MacIntyre, *Three Rival Versions*, 216.

[34]Ibid., 216–7.

What explains the "demise of the encyclopaedia"? Why was there a fragmentation of enquiry into independent specialized activities, the loss of an educated public, and why did moral and theological truths cease to be recognized in academia?

MacIntyre's answer to that question involves the development of the philosophical position known as modern liberal individualism, not to be confused with "liberal" or "conservative" political ideologies in contemporary American political discourse. Modern liberal individualism sought to remove itself from the restraints of tradition and appeal instead to "genuinely universal, tradition-independent norms" rooted in a universally shared rationality.[35] According to MacIntyre, the historical and philosophical shift within universities from functioning self-consciously within the shared values and ideas of traditions to functioning instead according to universal norms and standards of reason entirely independent of tradition depended in part on false premises, among which was

> the thesis that human rationality is such and the methods and procedures which it has devised and in which it has embodied itself are such that, if freed from external constraints and most notably from the constraints imposed by religious and moral tests, it will produce not only progress in enquiry but also agreement among all rational persons as to what the rationally justified conclusions of such enquiry are. From this liberal standpoint the enforcement of prior agreement as a precondition of enquiry was simply an error, an error resulting in arbitrary constraints upon liberty of judgment.[36]

The essence of modern liberal individualism is its presupposition that human rationality arrives at a consensus among rational persons when the influences of moral and religious tradition are stripped away. Hence, modern liberal individualism views the influences of moral and religious traditions as interfering with the formation of that rational consensus.

So we can trace MacIntyre's explanatory sequence as follows. The embrace of modern liberal individualism brought about three changes: the fragmentation of enquiry, the loss of an educated public, and the collapse of academic recognition of moral and theological truths. Those three changes eliminated the "unified secular vision of the world." And the collapse of a unified vision of the world undermined the possibility of a unified university curriculum and thus removed the very heart of what makes universities to be authentic universities.

The importance to education of a unified vision of the world reveals the necessary relation between MacIntyre's conception of philosophy as a craft within a tradition and his critique of the contemporary research university.

---

[35]MacIntyre, *Whose Justice? Which Rationality?*, 335.
[36]MacIntyre, *Three Rival Versions*, 225.

For MacIntyre the "craft-constituted" character of philosophy explains why the embrace of modern liberal individualism entails the fragmentation of philosophy both into a multiplicity of isolated specializations and into the multiplication of intractable, radical disagreements concerning answers to philosophy's fundamental questions. Liberal individualism's failure to recognize that philosophy flourishes essentially as a craft embedded within a tradition leads inevitably to this twofold fragmentation of philosophy. A necessary consequence of this fragmentation of philosophy is the loss of its capacity to provide publicly a unified understanding of reality as a whole. With the loss of that capacity philosophy can no longer perform the integrative function by which a university is and remains a university. In this way, MacIntyre's understanding of philosophy as a craft is *essentially* related to his critique of the contemporary research university.

Here I want to forestall one immediate objection to my thesis. One might object that what makes MacIntyre's conception of philosophy inimical to the contemporary research university is not his notion that philosophy is a craft, but rather his view of the necessary role of tradition in the practice of philosophy. In short, the objection is that it is not his conception of philosophy as craft, but his claim that philosophy is dependent upon tradition that is doing the work.

In response to this objection we can recognize that for MacIntyre there is a close relationship and overlap between crafts and traditions. Crafts are supported by traditions, sustain traditions, and can be understood themselves as a kind of tradition. MacIntyre uses the term 'tradition' in different senses, but provides a key definition in *Whose Justice?* where he writes, "A tradition is an argument extended through time in which certain fundamental agreements are defined and redefined in terms of two kinds of conflict."[37] MacIntyre's notion of tradition is living and dynamic, not static. He explicitly distances himself from Edmund Burke, Michael Polanyi, and Thomas Kuhn for their conception of tradition as rigid.[38] A craft or practice relies on tradition but is more than a tradition so defined because it has both a *telos*, in relation to which standards of excellence internal to that craft are determined, and a teaching authority internal to the craft involving persons who know, maintain, protect, and hand down the craft. Tradition may be opaque to the outsider, but the notion of craft, especially as that within which and by which tradition is sustained, explicitly denotes *opacity* to the outsider, by way of dependence upon master-craftsmen in order to gain the view-from-within. This opacity of the craft explains why philosophy cannot flourish even under a liberal individualism fully aware of the history of philosophy.

---

[37]MacIntyre, *Whose Justice? Which Rationality?*, 12.
[38]See MacIntyre, "Epistemological Crises, Dramatic Narrative and the Philosophy of Science," *The Monist* 60, no. 4 (1977): 453–72.

It also explains why MacIntyre's critique of the contemporary research university is essentially related to his understanding of philosophy as *craft*.

V.

Implications. I want to consider briefly two implications of this essential relation between philosophy conceived as a craft and MacIntyre's critique of the contemporary research university. First is the recognition not only that one entails the other, but also that the denial of one entails the denial of the other. An approach to philosophy that denies its craft-constituted character entails that the accompanying educational curriculum lacks the unity without which its students cannot achieve a perfected intellect and the sustaining institution exist as an authentic university. Likewise, the contemporary research university with its fragmented and specialized programs of education contains implicitly and communicates pedagogically both the denial of philosophy's craft-character and the denial of philosophy's capacity to flourish as a craft that advances toward its *telos* of providing an integrated and unified understanding of reality. The disunity of the curricular structure is not neutral regarding philosophy's capabilities: it both presupposes and implicitly teaches that philosophy is incapable of providing this unified picture or approaching such a provision. MacIntyre affirms this in *God, Philosophy, Universities*, when he writes:

> [T]he conception of the university presupposed by and embodied in the institutional forms and activities of contemporary research universities . . . suggests strongly that there is no such thing as the universe, no whole of which the subject matters studied by the various disciplines are all parts or aspects, but instead just a multifarious set of assorted subject matters.[39]

By failing to provide students with a unified understanding of reality and the relation of the disciplines to each other and to the whole order of things, the contemporary research university communicates implicitly not only that there is no such thing as the universe, but that even if there were such a thing, there is no craft capable of discovering it.

A second implication of this essential relation between MacIntyre's critique of the contemporary research university and his conception of philosophy as a craft is that the remedy is at least two-fold. Quite obviously, this remedy must include the presence within the university of faculty who recognize the craft-constituted character of philosophy, faculty who have entered the craft as apprentices and become mastercraftsmen. But this remedy also requires nothing less than what MacIntyre refers to as "a different kind of curricular ordering of the

---

[39]MacIntyre, *God, Philosophy, Universities*, 174.

disciplines from that divisive and fragmenting partitioning which contemporary academia imposes."[40] The institution cannot become an authentic university without revising the curriculum from its "divisive and fragmenting partitioning" to one that reflects and communicates both the unity of the disciplines and the unity of the order of things.

In sum, MacIntyre's critique of the contemporary research university can be seen as a recognition of what follows from conceiving of philosophy as a craft, a conception that flows not only from an insight into our inherent limitations and dependence as human beings on one another, not only our social dependence on past generations and present peers, but also from an insight into the sapiential nature of philosophy as the pursuit of wisdom and what follows practically from an intellectual humility before the greatness of the object pursued by this craft.

Mount Mercy University
Cedar Rapids, Iowa

---

[40]MacIntyre, *Three Rival Versions*, 220.

Beyond the Naked Square:
The Idea of an Agonistic Public Sphere

Sante Maletta

Abstract. The major aim of this paper is to present some reflections about the political domain and the common good that may be helpful in answering the following issue: How can religions contribute to the common good? The problematic background of this paper can be summarized by the so-called Dilemma of Böckenförde ("The free secular state lives according to presuppositions that it cannot itself guarantee"), which presents the difficulties secular states have in creating social capital, and by the Habermasian notion of a "post-secular society," an expression used by the German philosopher to summarize the curious situations of Western secularized states, where religions continue to play important public roles.[1] I will first discuss the notion of "neutralization" with the support of Carl Schmitt. Then I will present Chantal Mouffe's doctrine of "agonistic pluralism" and her partial legitimization of the presence of religions in the political domain. Finally, I will criticize Mouffe's approach with the help of Alasdair MacIntyre's phenomenology of social practices in order to stress the importance of public religions in contemporary liberal societies.

I.

"Sovereign is he who decides on the exception."[2] I hold that Schmitt's emphasis on the category of decision does not imply a sort of irrational "decisionism," but it is a reaction to the formalistic and positivistic approaches prevailing in the philosophy of law at the beginning of

---

[1]See Ernst-Wolfgang Böckenförde, "The Rise of the State as a Process of Secularization," in Böckenförde, *State, Society and Liberty: Studies in Political Theory and Constitutional Law* (New York: Berg, 1991), 45; Jurgen Habermas, "On the Relations between, the Secular Liberal State and Religion," in *Political Theologies: Public Religions in Post-Secular World*, ed. Hent de Vries and Lawrence E. Sullivan (New York: Fordham University Press, 2006), 251–60. I want to thank Maria Bond for her language revision of this paper.

[2]Carl Schmitt, *Political Theology: Four Chapters on the Concept of Sovereignty* (Cambridge, MA: MIT Press, 1985), 5.

©2014, *American Catholic Philosophical Quarterly*, Vol. 88, No. 4   pp. 767–777
doi: 10.5840/acpq201492231

the twentieth century.[3] Schmitt stresses the fact that, beyond any norms or rules, there is always the will of a subject. He means decision as the *representation* of a transcendent principle—an idea—by a personal authority. Decision is supposed to mediate between the idea and the social reality that needs ordering.

Decisions open up the possibility of conflicts, and conflict is the essence of the political domain. According to Schmitt, what characterizes the political is "the distinction of friend and enemy [which] denotes the utmost degree of intensity of a union or separation, of an association or dissociation."[4] This dissociation is at its utmost when it includes the possibility of a bloody conflict that cannot be turned either into a conflict of interest or into an ideal or normative conflict:

The political enemy need not be morally evil or aesthetically ugly; he need not appear as an economic competitor, and it may even be advantageous to engage with him in business transactions. But he is, nevertheless, the other, the stranger; and it is sufficient for his nature that he is, in a special intense way, existentially something different and alien, so that in the extreme case conflicts with him are possible. These can neither be decided by a previously determined general norm nor by the judgment of a disinterested and therefore neutral third party.[5]

The enemy is not private (*inimicus*) but public (*hostis*). One is ready to risk her life to fight back when something essential is in danger, something without which her life, as a member of a group, would no longer have meaning. The political community characterizes individuals as a whole when they share the same opinions about the *non-negotiable* issues identifying their political existence. This means that the political authority, i.e., the decision-maker, is what produces the sense of the political community. An important outcome of such an approach is that, in its neutralization of conflicts, the state—as the sense-maker—cannot use repressive means only.

This is what happened with the end of civil religious wars and the rise of the modern state. The sovereign took the chance to occupy the theological sphere—i.e., the conflictual "central domain" (*Zentralgebiet*) in the sixteenth century—and to neutralize it. This is part of the *secularization* process. The sovereign does this by wisely "pouring" persuasion and coercion. Through this *Sinngebung*, the state keeps control over the definition of the political identity of the community—i.e., what constitutes friend and enemy—as it is the only power authorized to define the non-negotiable issues. This neutralization is always unstable and precarious and aims to turn any radical antagonism *outward*.

---

[3]For such an approach see M. Nicoletti, *Trascendenza e potere: La teologia politica di Carl Schmitt* (Brescia: Morcelliana, 1990); M. Maraviglia, *La penultima guerra: Il "katéchon" nella dottrina dell'ordine politico di Carl Schmitt* (Milan: Led, 2006).

[4]Carl Schmitt, *The Concept of the Political* (Chicago, IL: University of Chicago Press, 2007), 26.

[5]Ibid., 27.

It is a kind of *active* neutralization as it is based on a decision that produces community. This means that that kind of disorder, which the decision intends to overcome, is not absolute; rather, there is an *ethical* prerequisite to the political decision. Decision *restores order* instead of creating a new one. Moreover, as neutralization is an occurrence of decision, i.e., a mediation between an ideal and a social reality, the neutralization and secularization embodied by the modern state are also possible as long as there is something to neutralize and secularize: i.e., an idea, a truth.

But during the modern era, the *Zentralgebieten* changed—"from the theological to the metaphysical domain, and from there to the humanitarian-moral and finally to the economic domain"[6]—and this affected the nature of neutralization. Schmitt considers the first stage of this process—the shift from the theological to the metaphysical domain—as "the strongest and most consequential of all" as it "has determined the direction of all further development."[7] Theology was abandoned because it was controversial (it was *neutralized*: "Concepts elaborated over many centuries of theological reflection now became uninteresting and merely private matters"[8]) in favor of another domain, taken as *neutral*, where Europeans "hoped to find minimum agreement and common premises allowing for the possibility of security, clarity, prudence, and peace."[9] But this is an illusion: "Europeans always have wandered from a conflictual to a neutral domain, and always the newly won neutral domain has become immediately another arena of struggle, once again necessitating the search for a neutral domain."[10]

The present widespread "belief in technology" is founded on the opinion that we have found "the absolute and ultimate neutral ground," and that "technology appeared to be a domain of peace, understanding, and reconciliation."[11] But there is something new in technology; its neutrality is different from the neutrality of the other domains. As it is "always only an instrument and weapon," technology cannot produce any single decision, "least of all for neutrality," as it is "culturally blind."[12] This means that, in the domain of technology, people live as if conflicts could be overcome not through personal decisions representing some kind of truth, but through a mere automatic process: that is, through technology itself.

---

[6]Schmitt, "The Age of Neutralizations and Depoliticizations," in *The Concept of the Political*, 82.
[7]Ibid., 89.
[8]Ibid., 90.
[9]Ibid., 89.
[10]Ibid., 90.
[11]Ibid., 91.
[12]Ibid., 91–2.

Schmitt goes back to this question in one of his last relevant works, *Political Theology II*.[13] Here he no longer stresses the unsuccessful neutralizing action of technology but rather he holds that behind this there is a "spirit," i.e., a *decision* about non-negotiable issues. This kind of neutralization is dangerous because those who are subject to it are unaware of it. There is an *ideological* dynamic at play: technology claims to be neutral, but it is actually subject to some social interests. Behind its mask of apparent neutrality, technology imposes a social sense (a "super-sense") that removes any differences and proclaims the end of any divisions. On the contrary, this deceitful neutralization increases antagonism, as it delegitimizes the enemy, who is treated at best as a "positive" fact (in the Hegelian sense of the expression), as someone whose existence is no longer justified.

A good example of this ideological neutralization is given by Chantal Mouffe. Those scholars who, nowadays, aim to overcome any antagonistic model of the political in the direction of a discursive democracy tend to use an ideological strategy that goes like this: conflicts are foreclosed through the rhetorical usage of the category of modernization, "whose effect is to discriminate between those who are in tune with the new conditions of the modern, post-traditional world and those who still cling desperately to the past."[14] These scholars are therefore allowed to "draw a political frontier between 'the moderns' and 'the traditionalists or fundamentalists,' while at the same time denying the political character of their move."[15] In other words, the ideological aspect of this move is that this friend/enemy discrimination is hidden by presenting this frontier as sociological evidence. The conclusion, which seems plausible, is that "the political in its antagonistic dimension has not disappeared, but . . . manifests itself under a different guise, as a mechanism of exclusion justified on pseudo-scientific grounds."[16] There are two possible consequences of this ideological move: either the excluded stay away from the public domain (apathy) or they go back to it in an intolerant way (fanaticism).

II.

Since the 1990s, Chantal Mouffe has used Schmitt's category of the political to explain the origins of what she calls "post-political society," characterized by the two aforementioned phenomena, seemingly contradictory, but actually symbiotic: apathy and fanaticism. From her viewpoint, the post-political society

---

[13]Carl Schmitt, *Political Theology II: The Myth of the Closure of Any Political Theology* (Cambridge: Polity, 2008).

[14]Chantal Mouffe, *On the Political* (London: Routledge, 2005), 54.

[15]Ibid., 55.

[16]Ibid.

is the outcome of the liberalist strategy to expel conflicts from the political domain either through negotiation among interests or through rational discussion and deliberation. Mouffe's Schmittian move is to recall that the principle of the political is the friend/enemy distinction, and that there is no political domain without the exclusion of some "other," without a "constitutive outside."[17] What makes the citizens of a political community equal is at the same time what makes them different from those who are outside the community. A political body is such only when it has its own political identity—and identities always entail differences.

But Mouffe's aim is to go beyond Schmitt's approach, which has as its main weakness its failure to legitimate pluralism in a political body. Pluralism actually exists only in the international domain, where—according to the Westphalian system of international relations—sovereign states face each other under the unwritten rules of the *jus publicum aeropeum*. Schmitt explicitly rejects the idea of a pluralist state and holds that democracy is incompatible with liberalism, as pluralism makes decision impossible.

Mouffe faces the following question: "How can we envisage a form of commonality strong enough to institute a 'demos' but nevertheless compatible with certain forms of pluralism: religious, moral, and cultural pluralism as well as pluralism of political parties?"[18] This is possible if we recall that a political identity is never natural or spontaneous; it is a linguistic production and "must be seen as the *result* of the political process of hegemonic articulation."[19] However such an identity is never "fully constituted" and it can exist only "through multiple and competing forms of *identifications*."[20] If it is true that "there is no hegemonic articulation without the determination of a frontier, the definition of a 'them,' in the case of liberal democratic politics this frontier is an internal one and the 'them' is not a permanent outsider."[21]

A theoretical move is presupposed: the difference between the political, "the dimension of antagonism that is inherent in human relations," and politics, the ensemble of practices, discourses, and institutions that seek to domesticate hostility and weaken potential antagonism.[22] This difference is the core of what Mouffe calls *agonistic pluralism*:

---

[17]For the notion of "constitutive outside" see Derrida, *On Grammatology* (Baltimore, MD: John Hopkins University Press, 1976), 33–65.

[18]Chantal Mouffe, "Carl Schmitt and the Paradox of Liberal Democracy," *The Canadian Journal of Law and Jurisprudence* (January 1997): 21–33, at 32.

[19]Ibid.

[20]Ibid.

[21]Ibid., 33.

[22]Chantal Mouffe, *Deliberative Democracy or Agonistic Pluralism* (Vienna: Institute for Advanced Studies, 2000), 15.

the aim of democratic politics is to construct the 'them' in such a way that it is no longer perceived as an enemy to be destroyed, but an 'adversary' i.e. somebody whose ideas we combat but whose right to defend those ideas we do not put into question.[23]

An adversary is no longer an enemy in the Schmittian sense, since she acknowledges a common ground, the principles of liberal democracy (i.e., liberty and equality for all). In other words, the major aim of democratic politics is to transform antagonism into agonism and "this requires providing channels through which collective passions will be given ways to express themselves over issues, which, while allowing enough possibility for identification, will not construct the opponent as an enemy but as an adversary."[24] Sharing the same principles does not prevent conflict, as principles can affect politics only through different interpretations, and this produces a "conflictual consensus." On one hand, conflict circumvents apathy and disaffection with political participation because it enables processes of polemical identification; on the other hand, the consensus on the basic principles of liberal democracy prevents "the crystallization of collective passions around issues, which cannot be managed by the democratic process."[25]

A relevant outcome of Mouffe's perspective is that pluralism involves the end of any substantive idea of the good life as the core of the identity of a political body. No Schmittian active neutralization of the political is possible anymore. Not a total one, at least. Liberal democracy, in fact, cannot hold a relativistic conception of the world:

a liberal democratic state must be agnostic in matters of religion and morality [but] it cannot be agnostic concerning political values, since by definition it postulates certain ethico-political values that constitute its principles of legitimacy.[26]

This is a logical consequence of the Wittgensteinian doctrine of the primacy of *Lebensformen* over rules and procedures: "procedures only exist as a complex ensemble of practices. Those practices constitute specific forms of individuality, which make possible the allegiance to the procedures."[27] Therefore, "what is really at stake in the allegiance to democratic institutions is the constitution of an ensemble of practices that make the constitution of democratic citizens possible. This is not a matter of *rational justification* but of *availability* of democratic

---

[23]Ibid.
[24]Ibid., 16.
[25]Ibid., 16–7.
[26]Mouffe, "Religion, Democracy, and Citizenship," in *Political Theologies*, 321.
[27]Mouffe, "Deliberative Democracy or Agonistic Pluralism," 12.

forms of individuality and subjectivity."[28] In summary, democratic politics requires "a democratic *Sittlichkeit*,"[29] i.e., a democratic form of life.

It is now possible to conceive of a notion of citizenship as allegiance to the ethico-political values of liberal democracy, which is able to "reconcile the strong meaning it had in the civic republican tradition with the pluralism constitutive of modern democracy."[30] Therefore, it is not possible for democratic politics "to do without an idea of political community and a reference to the common good."[31] This is a delicate point, since Mouffe's aim is to go beyond the liberals/communitarians divide by making a sort of Hegelian synthesis. To be compatible with pluralism, the notions of political community and of common good need particular definitions. Political community is to be imagined "as a surface for inscribing demands where a 'we' is constituted."[32] The common good is seen as a "vanishing point," a "horizon of meaning." It functions as a *social imaginary*, "that is, as that on which its very impossibility of achieving full representation bestows the role of a horizon that is the condition of possibility of any representation within the space that it delimits."[33] As already seen above, consensus on principles does not prevent the rise of political fights and divisions because these principles work through conflicting interpretations—each producing its own conception of citizenship—in order to define the common sense and establish hegemony.

Can religions contribute to the common good, then? And how?

For Mouffe, there is no reason to keep religions outside the political realm, as they produce important forms of identification which motivate people to political participation. The unique requirement for religions is to respect the constitutional limits of liberal democratic regimes. As the ethico-political principles which legitimize these regimes are subject to different possible interpretations, the constitutional limits can also change in time and space. So there is of course no space for theocratic or fundamentalist approaches in the political domain. Moreover (but this is controversial: see below), there does not seem to be space for any kind of civil religion à la Rousseau, intended as an "appropriation of religion by politics for its own purposes."[34] In summary, religious groups can

---

[28]Ibid., 10.

[29]Chantal Mouffe, "Wittgenstein and the Ethos of Democracy," in *The Legacy of Wittgenstein: Pragmatism or Deconstruction*, ed. Ludwig Nagl and Chantal Mouffe (Frankfurt: Peter Lang, 2001), 136.

[30]Mouffe, "Religion, Democracy, and Citizenship," 322.

[31]Ibid.

[32]Ibid.

[33]Ibid.

[34]Ronald Beiner, *Civil Religion: A Dialogue in the History of Political Philosophy* (Cambridge, UK: Cambridge University Press, 2011), 1. "Civil religion is the empowerment of religion, not for the sake of religion, but for the sake of enhanced citizenship—of making members of the

play a public role either in the political society (through the creation of single-issues movements, or institutional lobbying, or electoral mobilization), or in the civil society (through the participation in open public debates about public affairs and the common good).[35] In all of these cases, religious identities can be powerful sources for political and civil participation, when they do not exceed constitutional limits.

III.

Mouffe's perspective is interesting but not completely persuasive. The most controversial point in her approach is when she holds that what is at stake in the allegiance to democratic institutions is not consent but the *practices* that make the constitution of democratic citizens possible. These practices—according to the approach particular to the second Wittgenstein espoused by Mouffe—are an essential prerequisite for democratic politics, and as such, they seem to go beyond any rational justification. The same is true for the common good defined in terms of a social imaginary, i.e., as a quasi-transcendental condition of possibility for the existence of social sense. In summary, Mouffe's *vis polemica* against the models of discursive democracy defended by Rawls and Habermas brings her to hold that the question of the different forms of practical rationality is *not relevant* for the issue of the allegiance to the democratic institutions. This view is dangerous as it opens the possibility of *non-rational* developments in the radical democratic approach to the problems of post-political societies. It is not by chance that Mouffe legitimizes the presence of passions in the public domain and their support of political participation and justifies any "attempt to mobilize those passions toward democratic designs."[36] In such an approach, there is a danger present in any form of political radicalism from Rousseau on: the illusory temptation to justify and perform (for good purposes, of course) an instrumental approach to the modern social imaginary and its emotional potentialities—what Charles Taylor calls "the dark side of our modern Western social imaginary."[37] The possibility of such a development is strengthened by the fact that, in Mouffe's perspective, the main goal of any political fight is hegemony, i.e., the construction of a *new common sense*, something that necessarily involves

---

political community better citizens, in accordance with whatever conception one holds of what constitutes being a good citizen" (2).

[35]José Casanova, *What is a Public Religion?*, in *Religion Returns to the Public Space: Faith and Policy in America*, ed. H. Heclo and W. M. McClay (Baltimore, MD: The John Hopkins University Press, 2003).

[36]Mouffe, *Religion, Democracy, and Citizenship*, 324.

[37]Charles Taylor, *Modern Social Imaginaries* (Durham, NC: Duke University Press, 2004), 182.

also the non-rational aspects of human life. If this is true, in this perspective, one could eventually justify some kind of civil religion able to gain the hegemonic position in the society if it works to mobilize individuals in the good direction.

I believe that this danger can be avoided if we look for a phenomenology of social practices that is more accurate than the one provided by Mouffe through her interpretation of the second Wittgenstein. This can be found in the works of Alasdair MacIntyre. Here I summarize this approach.[38]

The prerequisite to understanding the MacIntyrian approach to social practices is to take the "first person viewpoint," that is, the viewpoint of the acting person. To non-participants, in fact, a practice may appear to be constituted only by rule-following behavior; to participants, on the contrary, rules are first of all means to a good internal to the practice. In other words, a practice is not only a rule-conforming behavior, but, above all, a *goal-oriented action* where goals are goods that give point and purpose to the rules.

MacIntyre's phenomenology of practices cannot be understood without highlighting the strong interdependence between practices and institutions: they belong to the same single causal order. Institutions support practices first by enforcing the rules and second by acquiring and distributing goods external to practices such as money, power, or social status—therefore, institutions may corrupt practices by diverting actors' intentions from internal to external goods. To resist this corrupting power, practices need both intellectual and moral virtues. The first teach us which goods are internal to a practice and which deserve to be achieved in our lives. The second—such as courage, truthfulness, justice—help us in this intellectual activity. When an individual constantly raises questions about the goods of the practices she is engaged in and what place they should have in her own life, in fact, what she realizes sooner or later is that she cannot do that without involving those who take part in the practices, that is, without a *common* reasoning and a *common* deliberation about action.

This approach does not deny the existence of conflicts in common practical reasoning. On the contrary, it takes into account the fact that, when an individual raises questions about the good and the goods of her life, she can do this only from *within* a certain tradition of moral enquiry—better still, from within a particular *interpretation* of this tradition. Traditions of moral enquiry live on the competition with other traditions and with conflicting interpretations within the same tradition.

A very relevant point that Mouffe misses is that practice, when it is in good order—i.e., when it is a goal-oriented activity ordered by virtues and rules and

---

[38]See Kelvin Knight, "Practices: The Aristotelian Concept," *Analyse and Kritik* 30 (2008): 317–29; Kelvin Knight, "Rules, Powers, and Goods," in *Powers and Capacities in Philosophy: The New Aristotelianism*, ed. John Greco and Ruth Groff (London: Routledge, 2012), 319–34.

not corrupted by institutions—requires the *educations of desires* and their redirection to internal goods. In other words, desires can be considered neither as positive data nor as something non-rational that can be changed only through rhetorical means. This is the strongest and most unaware form of contemporary reification: when human beings relate to their own desires as if they were "objective things" (as it happens for instance when they turn to a marriage bureau), they are alienated from themselves.

Here we may find a model of political community that relies on a bond which is not cultural, ethic, or linguistic, but rather *rational*. What generates the social bond is, in fact, *the question of the order of the goods*, because it is impossible to tackle this problem without involving the others with whom one is engaged in the activities of practices. It is practical rationality itself, therefore, that has a political dimension. From this viewpoint, politics is to be considered the activity of answering questions about the ordering of practices in ordinary life.[39] Politics is a second-order practice that, in summary, embodies the common good itself.

This approach opens up the possibility of a new assessment of the public role of religions. In general, religions enforce the moral virtues that strengthen our resistance to the corruptive power of institutions. Moreover, religions—especially those that have always been effective in the Western societies (Judaism, Christianity, Islam)—are to be considered also as intellectual bodies. Therefore, they develop, in their own educational and research institutions, traditions of inquiry into the human good which are still effective in post-secular societies and which cannot legitimately be excluded from the political debate without taking the risk of weakening the moral and intellectual virtues of the people. But the most relevant beneficial effect of religions can be understood when we consider one major trait of liberal societies, what MacIntyre calls the "compartmentalization of roles." Such compartmentalisation occurs when "each distinct sphere of social activity comes to have its own role structure governed by its own specific norms in relative independence of other such spheres."[40] The precepts of the virtues are understood as prescriptions for the development of habits that make an individual more efficient in her role-playing. Virtues lose their subjective dimension. They no longer support the development of awareness of the goals included in one's social role and therefore the possibility of criticising them. The outcome of the compartmentalisation of roles is a divided self, which lacks the two virtues basic to the exercise of its moral responsibility—*integrity*, which sets limits to one's adaptability to social roles, and *constancy*, which sets

---

[39]Cf. Mark C. Murphy, "MacIntyre's Political Philosophy," in *Alasdair MacIntyre*, ed. Mark C. Murphy (Cambridge, UK: Cambridge University Press, 2003), 163.

[40]Alasdair MacIntyre, "Social Structures and Their Threat to Moral Agency," in *Ethics and Politics: Selected Essays*, vol. 2 (Cambridge, UK: Cambridge University Press, 2006), 167.

limits to one's flexibility of character. In summary, the compartmentalisation of roles produces an uncritical and therefore irresponsible moral agent.

To avoid this outcome, we do not need a positive religious faith: the mere posing of the religious problem—what is the sense of my life? what is my good? how should I live? *unde malum?*—allows the subject to gain a unitary perspective on her own existence, to take a position from which it is easier for her to resist and criticize the immoral demands of the social roles and the corrupting power of institutions. The more one practises the moral and intellectual virtues, the more one is able to do this. But this can be done only within communities, which, in Western societies, have generally been and still are *religious* communities.

Religions can and do play a decisive role within contemporary liberal societies: they make possible the constitution of subjects who are able to partially detach from their own social roles and to have a critical stance over them. This is a necessary prerequisite for the existence of different social identities in competition about the definition of the common good.

In other words, religions can and do play an important public role as they belong to the small group of social agencies that are still able to educate moral conscience. Conscience brings into the public space what liberals usually try to keep in the private forum, i.e., non-negotiable issues. But when everything is negotiable, it is very difficult to resist the corrupting power of the institutions.[41] Without non-negotiable issues, pace Mouffe, the political domain loses its agonistic spirit and degenerates into apathy and fanaticism. The political domain in a liberal democratic regime lives thanks to a tension between its constitutional limits and the challenges represented by the non-negotiable issues.

University of Calabria
Cosenza, Italy

---

[41]In *Toleration and the Goods of Conflict*, MacIntyre holds that toleration is not a virtue per se, but "just in so far as it serves the purposes of a certain kind of rational enquiry and discussion, in which the expression of conflicting points of view enables us through constructive conflict to achieve certain individual and communal goods." (See MacIntyre, "Toleration and the Goods of Conflict," in *Ethics and Politics: Selected Essays*, vol. 2, 223.) From this perspective, intolerance can sometimes be justified. But MacIntyre emphasizes that "to draw the line between those points of view concerning the human good whose expression is to be tolerated and those points of views whose expression is not to be tolerated" (214) should not be among the powers of the government. It is a rational activity peculiar to each particular community. Though we know that the modern liberal state has never been neutral, its neutrality is "an important fiction" (vi).

Catholic Social Teaching and the Firm.
Crowding in Virtue: A MacIntyrean Approach to Business Ethics

Geoff Moore, Ron Beadle, and Anna Rowlands

Abstract. Catholic Social Teaching (CST) aspires to an economy that serves needs, upholds justice, and inculcates subsidiarity. But it suffers from a significant omission—it fails to look "inside" the business organisations that comprise the fundamental building blocks of the economic system. It is therefore ill-equipped to suggest how businesses could be reformed to meet these aspirations. MacIntyre's Thomistic Aristotelian account of the relationships between goods, virtues, practices and institutions provides resources that could enable CST to overcome this lacuna. This paper describes the MacIntyrean account and compares it with CST's existing categories. It then analyses the case of the Lloyds Banking Group. This allows not only diagnosis, but potentially a prescriptive account of how virtue may be "crowded-in" to business organisations. The paper concludes by suggesting that this approach might make a distinctive contribution to CST, and hence enable CST to make an even more significant contribution to business ethics.

I.

Introduction. Set within the context of Catholic Social Teaching (CST), the papers delivered at Cambridge University in the 2012 Margaret Beaufort lecture series on "The crisis of capitalism and the common good" offered an eclectic mix of perspectives on the subject matter to hand. But they were consistent in one respect: their collective failure to look "inside" the business organisation that forms the basic building block of the economic system.[1] In a similar vein, a product of the American Catholic "True wealth of

---

[1]Stefano Zamagni, "Imagining a Civil Economy" (The Crisis of Capitalism and the Common Good, Margaret Beaufort lecture series, Cambridge University, 2012) did make mention of the organisation of work and of employment and labour issues; and, more specifically, Daniel Finn, "On the Moral Ecology of Markets," ibid., did discuss briefly issues of corporate culture and of the standards of morality of both individuals and organisations. The papers are, as yet, unpublished.

©2014, *American Catholic Philosophical Quarterly*, Vol. 88, No. 4   pp. 779–805
doi: 10.5840/acpq201491830

nations" project,[2] from which the Margaret Beaufort lectures drew, makes specific reference to "the corporation" on just 6 pages in a 350-page volume,[3] and even here the emphasis is on the corporation-as-institution rather than "opening up" the corporation to scrutiny on the inside.

Pope Benedict XVI's papal encyclical *Caritas in Veritate*,[4] on the other hand, does offer a stakeholder view of the firm, which has the merits of considering the role of business not only in relation to its shareholders, but also to its various stakeholder groups such as workers, suppliers, customers, wider society and the natural environment. To that extent it provides some, though brief, consideration of the internal workings of the firm though, as Breen notes, it "does not specifically suggest how to adjust the corporate form to internalize values other than profit maximization."[5]

There appears, therefore, to be a significant lacuna in CST in relation to the "inside" of business organisations and hence to business ethics broadly defined. This paper seeks to show how a virtues-based approach, drawing on MacIntyre's framework of goods, virtues, practices, and institutions, might contribute to CST in this regard. The paper proceeds as follows. First, MacIntyre's Thomistic Aristotelian account is provided. Second, we summarise CST and outline the compatibilities and incompatibilities of the MacIntyrean approach to that of CST. In the third section we then consider a particular case study in order to ground the discussion. Lloyds Bank in the UK has recently been fined by the Financial Conduct Authority for the mis-selling of financial products. It provides a salutary example of how virtue was crowded out from the internal workings of the firm. This then leads to a consideration of how virtue might be "crowded in" to business organisations. We conclude by suggesting that CST might be developed along these lines to overcome the observed deficiency, and hence how it might make an even more significant contribution to business ethics than has hitherto been possible.

II.

Goods, Virtues, Practices, Institutions. If businesses are to be places in which common goods are to be achieved, as CST maintains they should, then we

---

[2]Daniel Finn, ed., *The True Wealth of Nations: Catholic Social Thought and Economic Life* (New York: Oxford University Press, 2010).

[3]Jon Gunnerman, "Capitalism, Spirit and Common Wealth," in *The True Wealth of Nations*, 289–317.

[4]Pope Benedict XVI, *Caritas in veritate*, Encyclical letter on integral human development in charity and truth, Vatican Website, June 2009, http://www.vatican.va/holy_father/benedict_xvi/encyclicals/documents/hf_ben-xvi_enc_20090629_caritas-in-veritate_en.html, sec. 40.

[5]John M. Breen, "Love, Truth and the Economy: A Reflection on Benedict XVI's *Caritas in Veritate*," *Harvard Journal of Law and Public Policy* 33, no. 3 (2010): 987–1029, at 1015.

need to know what might enable and what might frustrate this. MacIntyre's conceptual framework of goods, virtues, practices and institutions, presented in his seminal *After Virtue*[6] and applied in his work thereafter, provides guidance not just for business organisations but for organisations of all kinds and, indeed, for any and all human associations in which work is undertaken and goods produced.

The breadth of MacIntyre's framework not only suggests its explanatory scope but also the extent to which business organisations share with other forms of productive association (e.g., churches) both the potential for the achievement of genuine human goods and for their corruption. His substantive comments on business have been overwhelmingly critical[7] and would be of little interest if they were unaccompanied by an explanation of the particular vulnerabilities of business organisations to certain types of corruption. This is, however, just what he provides—a conceptual framework that establishes the conditions for the achievement of common goods and how these conditions are undermined. What is this framework?

The goods achieved and enjoyed within human associations, including in organisations of different kinds, are here defined as goods "internal to" the practices whose work comprises the activity of the association. So, for example, appropriate diagnosis stands to medicine and composition to music as goods internal to practices. Such goods include both the excellence of products and the perfection of the individual *qua* practitioner.[8] In turn, the practices of which they are partially definitive comprise

> [a]ny coherent and complex form of socially established cooperative human activity through which goods internal to that form of activity are realized in the course of trying to achieve those standards of excellence which are appropriate to, and partially definitive of, that form of activity.[9]

Whilst practices differ significantly, not least between those whose focus is material and in which technical rationality is likely to predominate, and those whose focus is human action and interaction and in which wisdom predominates,[10] the achievement of goods internal to every practice requires the

---

[6]Alasdair MacIntyre, *After Virtue*, 3 ed. (London: Duckworth, 1981/2007).

[7]John Dobson, "Alasdair MacIntyre's Aristotelian Business Ethics: A Critique," *Journal of Business Ethics* 86, no. 1 (2009): 43–50.

[8]Alasdair MacIntyre, "A Partial Response to My Critics," in *After MacIntyre*, ed. John Horton and Susan Mendus (Cambridge: Polity Press, 1994), 283–304. See also MacIntyre, *After Virtue*, 189–90.

[9]MacIntyre, *After Virtue*, 187.

[10]Joseph Dunne, "An Intricate Fabric: Understanding the Rationality of Practice," *Pedagogy, Culture and Society* 13, no. 3 (2005): 367–89.

exercise of the virtues, and this for three distinct reasons. First, without temperance, fortitude, patience, diligence, and the like we cannot develop the practical knowledge and technical skills which enable us to succeed in the tasks of practice, tasks which require more of us as we progress.[11] Practices are ordered hierarchically so we cannot become architects without learning about the properties of different materials, we cannot become engineers without an understanding of calculus, and so on. But technical skills alone do not enable us to achieve and enjoy the goods internal to practices; we also need to understand the purposes of practices and our accountabilities in relation to them. Our work as practitioners requires us to recognise good reasons for engagement, not for this or that practitioner, but good reasons as such within the practice, to learn about the factors that must be taken into account in our practice and those that must not:

> Particular physicians and teachers may be motivated by a wide range of desires: for money, for prestige, for power, but it is only insofar as they pursue the end of the medical art or the end of the school that they are good physicians or good teachers.[12]

Decisions around, for example, the appropriate use of tools, the precision of calculations *and* decisions around the ingredients in a dish and the colours in a portrait are to be judged by standards of excellence that have emerged over time from deliberations between practitioners:

> The standards of achievement within any craft are justified historically. They have emerged from the criticism of their predecessors and they are justified because and insofar as they have remedied the defects and transcended the limitations of those predecessors as guides to excellent achievement within that particular craft.[13]

We come to learn about such standards and about their justification through on-going deliberative enquiry, and to treat ourselves and our fellow practitioners as rational agents pursuing common enquiries into the tasks that confront us requires us to enjoy a particular quality of relationship. This provides a second set of dependencies upon the virtues; for in order to become practitioners we must order our relationships with those from whom we initially learn, those with whom we will subsequently work, those who will be subject to our work, and

---

[11]Ibid.

[12]Alasdair MacIntyre, "Intractable Moral Disagreements," in *Intractable Disputes about the Natural Law—Alasdair MacIntyre and Critics*, ed. L. Cunningham (Notre Dame, IN: University of Notre Dame Press, 2009), 47.

[13]Alasdair MacIntyre, *Three Rival Versions of Moral Enquiry* (London: Duckworth, 1990), 64. In MacIntyre's terminology, crafts are examples of practices.

those whom we will ultimately teach, in adherence to the precepts of natural law. To begin we need a teacher and:

> we shall have to learn from that teacher and initially accept on the basis of his or her authority within the community of a craft precisely what intellectual and moral habits it is which we must cultivate and acquire if we are to become effective self-moved participants in such enquiry. Hence there emerges a conception of rational teaching authority internal to the practice of the craft of moral enquiry, as indeed such conceptions emerge in such other crafts as furniture making and fishing, where, just as in moral enquiry, they partially define the relationship of master-craftsman to apprentice.[14]

As we progress within the practice we learn to deliberate well about the achievement of goods internal to practices, for to judge rightly in concrete and particular cases requires us to listen appropriately, to correct others (whatever their status) when they err and to gratefully receive such correction ourselves. In other words we learn about justice, courage and wisdom.[15]

The third role of the virtues requires us to understand the relationship between practices and the institutions within which they are housed. For, inasmuch as practices are ordered to the achievement of internal goods, so institutions must be ordered to the achievement of external goods.[16]

MacIntyre provides a number of illustrations, "Chess, physics and medicine are practices; chess clubs, laboratories, universities and hospitals are institutions."[17] Business organisations, it has been argued, can be considered in the same vein, and hence can be regarded as a particular type of institution which houses one or more practices and whose products or services it provides for customers.[18] Selling products and services to customers is the defining characteristic of business, the process through which it generates sufficient external goods to maintain itself as an institution. But this process creates particular temptations and vulnerabilities which are characteristic of but not unique to business: "it is . . . always possible for a particular individual or social group *systematically to subordinate goods of the one kind to goods of the other*,"[19] and we can infer from this that it is internal goods

---

[14]Ibid., 63

[15]Ibid., 201.

[16]MacIntyre, *After Virtue*, 194.

[17]Ibid. See Geoff Moore, "Churches as Organisations: Towards a Virtue Ecclesiology for Today," *International Journal for the Study of the Christian Church* 11, no. 1 (2011): 45–65 for an application of MacIntyre's framework discussed here to churches.

[18]Ron Beadle, "Why Business is not a Practice," *Analyse und Kritik* 30, no. 1 (2008): 227–41.

[19]Alasdair MacIntyre, *Whose Justice, Which Rationality?* (London: Duckworth, 1988), 35, emphasis added.

which will normally be subordinated to external goods. Thus, each and every process through which institutions receive the resources they need is potentially corrupting, whether this is the need to acquire appropriate patrons for the arts and sciences of fifteenth century Europe; the need for state support for the circus artists of the Soviet Union; or the need for companies to generate revenue from customers, extract labour from employees, or secure capital from investors. In each case, sponsors and others must be persuaded, but may be manipulated or coerced, into providing the necessary resources.

In negotiating such relationships the legitimate, if subordinate, institutional objective may be all too easily transformed into an illegitimate and superordinate objective. Investors may be promised too much, customers mis-sold, labour exploited, costs reduced, and quality eroded in order to meet financial targets and so on.[20] In short, the pursuit of external goods may come to dominate decision making and in some cases to degenerate into avarice.[21] The third role of the virtues, then, is to so order institutions that they serve rather than corrupt practices. It is here that we find the tension central to MacIntyre's sociology of practices and institutions, that between the generation and prioritisation of internal and external goods.[22] Empirical work using MacIntyre's framework has illustrated cases in which virtue requires courageous resistance to vicious purposes,[23] withdrawal from institutions in order to found alternatives,[24] the reestablishment of professional values and commitments,[25] and whistle-blowing.[26] In each case:

> The virtues which we need in order to achieve both our own goods and the goods of others . . . only function as genuine virtues when their exercise is informed by an awareness of how power is distributed and of the

---

[20]James Hine, "The Shadow of MacIntyre's Manager in the Kingdom of Conscience Constrained," *Business Ethics: A European Review* 16, no. 4 (2007): 358–71.

[21]Alasdair MacIntyre, *Marxism and Christianity*, 2 ed. (London: Duckworth, 1995), xiii.

[22]Geoff Moore and Ron Beadle, "In Search of Organisational Virtue in Business: Agents, Goods, Practices, Institutions and Environments," *Organisation Studies* 27, no. 3 (2006): 369–89; Keith Breen, "Production and Productive Reason," *New Political Economy* 17, no. 5 (2012): 611–32.

[23]Mervyn Conroy, *An Ethical Approach to Leading Change: An Alternative and Sustainable Application* (Basingstoke: Palgrave Macmillan, 2010); Tracy Wilcox, "Human Resource Management in a Compartmentalized World: Whither Moral Agency?," *Journal of Business Ethics* 111 (2012): 85–96.

[24]Georg Von Krogh, Stefan Haefliger, Sebastian Spaeth, and Martin W Wallin, "Carrots and Rainbows: Motivational and Social Practice in Open Source Software Development," *MIS Quarterly* 36 (2012): 649–76.

[25]Bert van de Ven, "Banking After the Crisis: Towards an Understanding of Banking as a Professional Practice," *Ethical Perspectives* 18, no. 4 (2011): 541–68.

[26]Ron Beadle and Geoff Moore, "MacIntyre: Neo-Aristotelianism and Organization Theory," *Research in the Sociology of Organizations* 32 (2011): 85–121.

corruptions to which its use is liable. Here as elsewhere in our lives we have to learn how to live both with and against the realities of power.[27]

Figure 1 below presents this framework of goods, virtues, practices and institutions diagrammatically.[28]

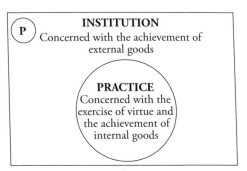

Figure 1. The practice-institution combination

There is, however, one further aspect of this diagram that we have not so far considered. In addition to what we might helpfully refer to as the core practice at the heart of the institution, there is also the practice of the making and sustaining of the institution—shown in Figure 1 by the "P" within the circle in the top left hand corner. As MacIntyre argues:

> the making and sustaining of forms of human community—*and therefore of institutions*—itself has all the characteristics of a practice, and moreover of a practice which stands in a peculiarly close relationship to the exercise of the virtues.[29]

This, then, also requires virtuous agents at the institutional level if the institution is to serve its proper but subordinate function. But this also implies that those who manage the institution, regardless of the extent of their engagement with the core practice, have the opportunity to gain the internal goods available from this rather different practice of institution-making. Management may, on this understanding, be re-described as a domain-relative practice.[30]

---

[27]Alasdair MacIntyre, *Dependent Rational Animals: Why Human Beings Need the Virtues* (London: Duckworth, 1999), 102.

[28]See Beadle and Moore, "MacIntyre: Neo-Aristotelianism and Organization Theory"; Geoff Moore, "Re-Imagining the Morality of Management: A Modern Virtue Ethics Approach," *Business Ethics Quarterly* 18, no. 4 (2008): 483–511.

[29]MacIntyre, *After Virtue*, 194–5, emphasis added.

[30]Gregory Beabout, "Management as a Domain-Relative Practice that Requires and Develops Practical Wisdom," *Business Ethics Quarterly* 22, no. 2 (2012): 405–32.

On this account, then, organisations as practice-institution combinations are "*essentially* moral spaces."[31] In other words, individuals, whether involved in the core practice (whatever that may be), or in the secondary practice of making and sustaining the institution, have the opportunity to exercise and, indeed, to develop the virtues. But, as will be clear by now, what this framework also offers is a way of looking "inside" business organisations, at the practices which form their core, and relating these practices to the institutional form that houses them. And, as we noted above, the inherent tension that exists between the practice and the institution, between internal and external goods, becomes readily apparent, and the vulnerabilities of "the ideals and the creativity of the practice . . . to the acquisitiveness of the institution, [and of] the cooperative care for common goods of the practice to the competitiveness of the institution"[32] becomes clear. In other words, the "black box" of the business organisation is open for inspection and analysis, and even for prescription as to how common goods might more effectively be achieved.

III.

The Virtuous Business Organisation. Following MacIntyre, therefore, we can describe properly ordered business organisations as practice-institution combinations. However, for such entities to be virtuous five pre-requisites can be identified.[33]

The first is a teleological pre-requisite—that the particular organisation has a good purpose. And, as Beabout and Kempster et al. have recently argued,[34] institutional leaders are pivotal to the practice-institution relationship not only in their decision-making processes and criteria, but also in the institution's own sense-making around purpose.

In relation to the purpose of the organisation, we can make a helpful comparison with purpose at the individual level. MacIntyre draws on Aristotle's notion of *eudaimonia* ("blessedness, happiness, prosperity. It is the state of being well and doing well, of a man's [*sic*] being well-favoured himself and in relation to the divine"[35]) to argue, in his terms, that *the* good for an individual will

---

[31]Beadle and Moore, "MacIntyre: Neo-Aristotelianism and Organization Theory," 103, emphasis in original.

[32]MacIntyre, *After Virtue*, 194.

[33]See Geoff Moore, "Virtue in Business: Alliance Boots and an Empirical Exploration of MacIntyre's Conceptual Framework," *Organisation Studies* 33, no. 3 (2012): 363–87, at 366–7; Moore and Beadle, "In Search of Organisational Virtue in Business," 375–80.

[34]Beabout, *Management as Practice*; Steve Kempster, Brad Jackson, and Mervyn Conroy, "Leadership as Purpose: Exploring the Role of Purpose in Leadership Practice," *Leadership* 7, no. 3 (2011): 317–34.

[35]MacIntyre, *After Virtue*, 148.

arise from some combination of the internal goods achieved from the various practices in which the individual engages. But he extends this to the notion of the common good, the "goods of those types of communities in and through which the goods of individual lives are characteristically achieved."[36] Thus, and according to McCann and Brownsberger:

> the normative character of MacIntyre's definition of a social practice . . . is secured within a larger account of the moral life as a whole. There must be some *telos* to human life, a vision anticipating the moral unity of life, given in the form of a narrative history that has meaning within a particular community's traditions; otherwise the various internal goods generated by the range of social practices will remain disordered and potentially subversive of one another. Without a community's shared sense of *telos*, there will be no way of signifying "the overriding good" by which various internal goods may be ranked and evaluated.[37]

If we now apply this at the level of the organisation, the same line of argument follows. The internal goods of the practice are, in the case of a business organisation, "the excellence of the product or service and the perfection of the practitioners in the process."[38] The common good, however, is not the simple combining of internal goods from all practices, but will involve an evaluation and ranking of such goods. Given that, "the ordering of goods within the activities of individual lives, so that the good of each life may be achieved, is found to be inseparable from the ordering of those goods in achieving the common good,"[39] so there will need to be a similar process by which the internal goods of various practices are ordered to achieve the common good: "In contemporary societies our common goods can only be determined in concrete and particular terms through widespread, grassroots, shared, rational deliberation."[40] The implication for a business organisation, as with any productive association, is that virtue requires an engagement in discussion, both internally and with appropriate communities, as to what its internal goods offer in contribution to the common good of those communities.

---

[36]MacIntyre, "A Partial Response," 288.

[37]Dennis McCann and M. L. Brownsberger, "Management as a Social Practice: Rethinking Business Ethics after MacIntyre," *The Annual of the Society of Christian Ethics* (1990): 223–45.

[38]Moore, "Virtue in Business," 366. See also MacIntyre, "A Partial Response," 284; and MacIntyre, *After Virtue*, 189–90.

[39]MacIntyre, "A Partial Response," 288.

[40]Alasdair MacIntyre, "Intolerance, Censorship and Other Requirements of Rationality" (lecture, London Metropolitan University, October 28, 2010), accessed February 18, 2014, www.londonmet.ac.uk/research-units/hrsj/events/public-events/.

The second pre-requisite is that the institution's primary task is to nurture the particular core practice that is at its heart and to sustain the pursuit of excellence within that practice. In this context the impact of the mode of institutionalization on the relative priority afforded to the pursuit of the external and internal goods is critical.[41] Thus, for example, financial services are provided by shareholder-owned and stock-market listed banks and by mutually owned societies (building societies in the UK). We might anticipate that such difference in institutional form would lead to a variance in the extent to which the core practice is nurtured—a point to which we will return in considering the Lloyds case below. However, it is also the case that the external goods that institutions generate serve a necessary function (they are *goods*). As such, the virtuous organisation must ensure that it secures sufficient external goods to sustain itself and to provide the resources necessary for the maintenance and development of the practice. This, of course, may well be some distance from the profit-maximising position of many businesses.

This, however, leads to a further consideration of internal and external goods and how they interact. While it is clear that internal goods are goods that are valued for their own sake, and should therefore be prioritized, it is also clear that it is impossible to attain them without access to external goods. And, indeed, it is also impossible to attain external goods without internal goods. There is, thus, an "essential but complex circularity between internal and external goods" including a recognition that "this can occur both within and outside of particular practice-institution combinations, through the use of external goods derived from one . . . combination to engage in another practice in order to obtain the internal goods therein."[42] The third pre-requisite which follows from this, again for both business organisations and any other productive association, is that virtue requires an "appropriate balancing in the pursuit of internal and external goods."[43] And this, of course, will require judgment to be exercised, such judgment also being something that practitioners have to learn.[44]

The fourth pre-requisite follows logically from the first three: the virtuous business organisation will require a sufficient number of virtuous agents in both the core practice and its institutional embodiment to ensure the determination and pursuit of a good purpose, the nurturing of the core practice, and, as above, the necessary balanced judgment in the pursuit of internal and external goods.[45]

---

[41]MacIntyre, "A Partial Response," in *After MacIntyre*, 289. Moore and Beadle, "In Search of Organisational Virtue in Business," 377–8.

[42]Moore, "Virtue in Business," 380.

[43]Ibid., 367.

[44]Dunne, "An Intricate Fabric"; John Halliday and Mary Johnsson, "A MacIntyrean Perspective on Organizational Learning," *Management Learning* 41, no. 1 (2009): 37–51.

[45]See Moore and Beadle, "In Search of Organisational Virtue in Business," 376.

The fifth and final pre-requisite for a virtuous business organisation is a conducive environment.[46] Just as there is a need within both the core practice and the institution for virtuous agents, there is also a need without the organisation for an environment that allows, or perhaps even nurtures, virtue in the organisational forms that it supports. A starting point here might be to ask whether the environment (regulatory, market, labour, and capital) discriminates between organisations in ways related to their exercise of the virtues and protection of practices.[47] However, it is also of note that the environment is not simply a "given," but something that business organisations "may, to some extent, be able to create or choose . . . and that exercising this discretion is a feature that we might expect to find in the virtuous corporation."[48]

Having described the conceptual framework that MacIntyre offers and considered the pre-requisites for virtue in such practice-institution combinations, we turn now to CST to consider the extent to which MacIntyre's framework is consistent with, and might make a contribution to, this body of work.

IV.

Comparisons with Catholic Social Teaching. Catholic Social Teaching is a body of theological ethics, emerging in its contemporary form from a series of global social letters issued by the papacy from 1891 to the present day. During the twentieth century this corpus of socio-economic reflection was augmented at a subsidiary level by documents produced by national and regional bishops' conferences and specialist Vatican departments.[49] Whilst these teaching documents have engaged with a wide range of social matters, the predominant emphasis has been upon the conditions of economic life, particularly the relations of labour and capital.

The key economic commitments proposed by CST tend to be summarised as: a call for living wages and just prices, a right to private property, but based on the principle of universal access, profit sharing, co-management and co-ownership of the means of production, a principled commitment to full

---

[46]Ibid., 378–80.

[47]For a somewhat similar account see Finn's consideration of the rules that define markets, the provision of essential goods and services, the morality of individuals and organisations, and civil society: Finn, *Moral ecology of markets.*

[48]Moore and Beadle, "In Search of Organisational Virtue in Business," 385.

[49]Of particular relevance to our considerations here, see David O'Brien and Thomas Shannon, eds., *Catholic Social Thought* (Maryknoll, NY: Orbis Books, 2010) for a comprehensive collection of the key social encyclicals from 1891–2009. See also Pontifical Council for Justice and Peace, *Compendium of the Social Doctrine of the Catholic Church* (London: Burns and Oates, 2005), 255–376, and Pontifical Council for Justice and Peace, "The Vocation of the Business Leader: A Reflection," 2012, http://www.uniapac.org/iso_album/j&p_eng.pdf.

employment, and a commitment to basic welfare provision based on need rather than productivity. Despite the unsystematic and heterogeneous exposition of economic ethics in the social encyclicals, reflection on economic life emerges from three structural foci within the official documents: core guiding principles, foundational theological anthropology, and a teleological account of the purposes of economic life.[50] First, CST proposes a set of permanent social principles, which it sees as rooted in both revealed theological sources and accessible to all through the exercise of human reason. Rooted in a biblical, ontological, and teleological account of human dignity and the common good, these principles function as a kind of complex ecological web of social ideas, each reliant upon the other for a comprehensive, immanent, and transcendent vision of socio-economic life. Nonetheless, the most explicitly economic of these principles are the teachings on "the universal destination of all goods" and the "preferential option for the poor."[51]

Second, CST is an explicitly theological form of ethics rooted in a normative account of the human condition. An account of the nature and purpose of human work has become a distinct centrepiece of the economic anthropology proposed by CST. Most relevant to our concerns here, work itself is considered to be part of the order of goodness. It is a co-creative and virtuous activity, essential to the social, relational, and material nature of our being, and a participation in the work of creation and redemption. Work has both objective and subjective elements, which are hierarchically ordered in moral terms towards the subjective value of work. The objective dimension of work refers to "the sum of activities, resources, instruments and technologies used by men and women to produce things."[52] The subjective dimension of work refers to the activity or process of production and creation undertaken as action by the human person.[53] Man is viewed as the subject and not the object of work, and therefore correspondingly CST affirms the primacy of labour over capital. A series of detailed exhortations

---

[50]This summary relates solely to the official tradition of Catholic Social Teaching, not to the wide, plural, and more contradictory body of Catholic Social Thought, which is a term used to refer to the informal reflections by Catholic theologians, ethicists, and philosophers beyond the official teaching documents of the popes, Church councils, pontifical councils, and regional and national bishops' conferences.

[51]For a more comprehensive summary of the economic teachings of the social encyclical tradition see Albino Barrera, *Modern Catholic Social Documents and Political Economy* (Washington, DC: Georgetown University Press, 2001). For a consideration of the economic teaching of the encyclicals in the light of concepts of the good see Patrick Riordan, *The Grammar of the Common Good*, (London: Continuum, 2008),118–50.

[52]Pontifical Council for Justice and Peace, *Compendium of the Social Doctrine of the Church*, 270.

[53]Ibid., 255–322

towards just prices, living wages, co-management, unionisation, and the nurture of skills-based vocational groupings follow from this wider anthropology.

Third, in the context of its teleological reflection on the key areas of social life, giving expression and form to the human vocation, CST offers an account of the broader moral purpose of economic life per se. Such teaching focuses particularly on discussion of the nature of economic goods, wealth, and poverty. All things perform a service of excellence within the social order particular to their nature, and under the fuller order of a divine life. This leads to an account of economic activity as an intrinsic form of moral activity. The proper purpose of economic activity is the production, distribution and consumption of material goods and services. This is an intrinsic but partial good directed towards a wider extrinsic good—peaceful and fulfilling human co-existence.

Business, as a particular form of economic activity, participates in service to this wider economic enterprise and social good in specific ways. It achieves service to the common good through engaging with excellence in the intrinsic activity appropriate to itself: production of useful goods and services, guided by the principle of justice. CST suggests that this activity be understood in relation to a dual economic and social function. The economic function lies in the generation of wealth through production of goods and services generated to meet real needs and interests. We should note that the human good served by business includes activities that extend well beyond the narrowly functional goals of subsistence, serving all aspects of the human good. Correspondingly, the social function of business lies in facilitating co-operative and co-creative relationships that give concrete expression to the social nature of the human person. Businesses are institutional vehicles for fostering skill and excellence, feeding concrete practices of virtue into both the subjective and objective goods of disciplined and creative human work. In this context, CST affirms in particular the contribution of SMEs, craft-based enterprises and family-based agricultural businesses.

CST has also offered reflection on the particular role of business owners and managers. Here, engagement with the virtue tradition per se remains fairly superficial, and tends towards a list of the particular virtues necessary to the exercise of leadership in business. CST highlights diligence, industriousness, prudence in engaging responsible risk, reliability and fidelity in interpersonal relationships, and courage in meeting difficult challenges and in taking difficult decisions.

CST has also increasingly affirmed the importance of the agency exercised by business managers in a social context in which business has become the operational heart of networks of technical, commercial, financial, and cultural bonds. Thus, responding to the shift in the kind of cultural power represented by business elites, the social task of the manager (as a contribution to the wider, extrinsic common good) is to exercise a duty of care for both the economic objectives of the company, and to exercise a further duty of care for wider economic efficiency and "care of capital," as the sum of the means of production. Such duty of care includes respect for the concrete human dignity of workers within the company, including those engaged in the enterprise through indirect employment (although without supplanting the necessary role of direct employers); and a commitment to the structuring of work to promote the goods of family life.[54] This social duty also encompasses oversight of the use of finite resources in a responsible way, with a stress on intergenerational and ecological justice. Here the vision of a wider stakeholder rather than shareholder theory is clear.

Such detailed commentary sits within the context of a wider teaching on the value and limits of a free market.[55] CST views a truly competitive market as an effective instrument for attaining important objectives of justice. However, the free market is not a fully realised good in itself, but always to be judged against the ends that it seeks to accomplish and in the context of the concrete practices and values that it inculcates on a societal level. An increased concern for the culture of the current market system has led to calls within CST for the creation of both an alternative metaphysics of markets rooted in the logic of gift and reciprocal exchange, as well as new subsidiary structures of governance at all levels of business enterprise: within each business to foster new forms of co-management, through local, national, and regional forms of association and government. The goal of governance at all levels is to maximise just distribution and meaningful economic participation for all. Just distribution is judged in relation to just prices (consumer), just wages (producer), just returns (owner), and just taxation (community). This treatment of exchange value represents the three facets of justice: commutative, contributive, and distributive.

Piecemeal and unsystematic as this teaching is, CST aims to remain as comprehensive as possible in its account of the human good, and thus whilst it lacks precision in its account of the good, it also retains some virtues of breadth and scope. It does so, firstly, in so far as it proposes a vision of economic life caught up not only in the search for a temporal common good but also as a pattern of theonomous participation. Secondly, it retains a primary commitment to including all aspects of the human good in analysis of economic life, and makes a priority for a historical foregrounding of the dimension of the human good we seem most at risk of excluding. This is the hermeneutic visible in each social encyclical, written as a dialogue with its immediate context. Arguably, this leaves a body of theory capable of challenging the direction of a culture

---

[54]Ibid., 336–45.
[55]Ibid., 347–50.

at macro and micro levels, but often missing an ability to speak to the more intermediate and internal life of business operations.

Three hermeneutic problems beset any attempt to integrate or compare the economic reflections provided by CST and those latent within MacIntyre's account of virtue. Firstly, CST does not claim to be a systematic form of theory. It defines itself as a pastoral theology oriented towards evangelising the social order. A consequence of its pastoral evolution over time is that CST quickly reveals itself as correspondingly inconsistent. For some, this will be grounds to dismiss CST. For others, this inconsistency represents less a fundamental logical incoherence and more the consequences of an inevitable historical complexity stemming from its multiple authorship, shifting historical influences, and the necessarily pastoral orientation of the tradition. Secondly, CST remains an explicitly theological form of ethics, rooting its social theory in a normative and analogical account of divine life. MacIntyre's account operates with a systematic, temporal, and primarily philosophical account of the good. Therefore, in constructing some level of comparison between CST and MacIntyre we are comparing two related but non-identical forms of social thought. Thirdly, MacIntyre's continuing use of Marx's account of capitalism's systematic injustices,[56] and his rejection of modern markets highlights that he maintains a more fundamental hostility than that found within CST.

All this being said, whilst MacIntyre's revisionist concept of the common good acts as both a direct critique and corrective to CST, arguably the distance between the two sources can be overstated. The fundamentally Thomist account of the good with which both sources operate provides for a degree of commonality. Our contention here is that there may be significant potential for scholars to offer constructive attempts to reconnect the two systems of thought. Therefore, whilst the estrangement between MacIntyre and CST is real, we argue that it might not be viewed as intractable. Our core interest in pursuing such a conversation remains the development of modes of ethical thought most suited to informing business practice. We offer some basic observations below, all of which doubtless deserve further unpacking.

The most well documented point of connection between the two concerns the notion of the common good. MacIntyre transforms the heuristic and analogical account of the common good rooted loosely in intrinsic and extrinsic goods into a fundamental, systematic distinction between internal and external goods: the good in which the aggregation and ordering of the internal goods of practices is seen to constitute the heart of the common good. MacIntyre's usage

---

[56]See Cornwell's discussion of MacIntyre's 2010 lecture, "The Irrelevance of Ethics": John Cornwell, "Alasdair MacIntyre and the 'Irrelevance of Ethics,'" *Rustat Conferences*, 2011, accessed February 21, 2014, http://www.rustat.org/media/documents/MacIntyre2010.pdf.

is consistent with the distinction drawn in CST between the common good and the total good (the sum of all individual goods).[57] However, it is worth noting two aspects of MacIntyre's notion of goods that appear to differ from CST. First, in his typology of goods as internal and external, and with a primary emphasis on the role of internal goods in the generation of the common good, MacIntyre would seem to add a distinction that CST draws only implicitly and inconsistently. Here MacIntyre's work should act at the very least as a stimulus towards a clarification of the terms of the good with which CST operates.

Second, we should note that MacIntyre typically uses the phrase "common goods," in the plural rather than the singular. This draws attention to the internal/external goods typology, but also acknowledges the sheer variety of goods and the infinite number of ways in which individuals and communities might amalgamate these towards their own good. It may also be a means of drawing attention to the difficulty (perhaps the impossibility) of defining such a thing as *the* common good which might apply to all societies at all times, or to pluralistic societies in our own. Whilst the language may differ subtly between the two sources, the commitment to shared, rational deliberation as the basis for the search for the common good remains in common: "In contemporary societies our common goods can only be determined in concrete and particular terms through widespread, grassroots, shared, rational deliberation."[58] MacIntyre's work invites CST to sharpen its account of the ways in which the temporal common good can be sought in a pluralist context.

Third, a similar pattern of critical dialogue can be proposed with regards the principle of subsidiarity. Subsidiarity is evident in MacIntyre's distinction between practices and institutions, and the prioritisation of the former over the latter. Indeed, as with MacIntyre's insightful analysis of goods, it may be that here he makes a further contribution to CST by identifying precisely how the principle might operate inside organisations. Similarly, in relation to the principles of distributism and social justice, the prioritisation of practices over institutions and of internal over external goods, and the attention that is given to the mode of institutionalisation, would seem to offer concrete ways in which these principles might be realised in practice.

As a form of explicit theological ethics, CST is necessarily more heuristic and open-ended in its account of the common good. This heuristic emphasis makes most sense in the context of what might be referred to as the "double realism" inherent in CST. Whilst MacIntyre's account of the good is grounded

---

[57]Stefano Zamagni, "Catholic Social Thought, Civil Economy, and the Spirit of Capitalism," in *The True Wealth of Nations*, 63–93, at 71.

[58]MacIntyre, "Intolerance, Censorship and Other Requirements of Rationality"; see n40 above.

in philosophical realism, CST is rooted in both theological and philosophical realism. After Augustine and Aquinas, CST posits in ontological and teleological terms that the true common good is God. As God cannot be fully known, CST's first contribution is, therefore, to delineate the common good as a theological horizon of possibility, but a possibility that can only be partially known. The ultimate horizon for human dignity and the common good is communion with God as the goal and fulfilment of human desires. By use of analogical reasoning this then leads to a realist account of the common good, focused on the social and fraternal nature of human persons, expressed in the concrete practices that structure human community. It is at this level that MacIntyre's account operates and where he finds the imprecision of CST wanting. The challenge remains for CST to find ways to engage with the need for greater precision whilst retaining the necessary open-endedness of a truly theological account.

To date CST has made no real attempt to engage with—or (less appropriately) to arbitrate between—the differing systematic theories of the good that have emerged from contemporary Catholic philosophers. John Haldane, Charles Taylor, and Alasdair MacIntyre have all offered differing accounts of the human and common good, developed in critical dialogue with CST.[59] CST rightly leaves open a space for more systematic improvisations on the tradition, but it finds itself potentially impoverished if it does not re-engage with those offerings once they are developed. Engagement with MacIntyre's virtue ethics as the grounds for a deeper pastoral engagement with economic life is but one clear case in point.

V.

The Case of Mis-selling at Lloyds Bank. Having now laid out the MacIntyrean framework and compared and contrasted it with CST as it stands, it is worth exploring this further by reference to a particular case. This will allow us to ground the discussion of the MacIntyrean concepts, and also allow a subsequent discussion of how applied virtue ethics founded on MacIntyre's work may lead not only to helpful diagnosis, but even to prescription as to how business organisations may be reformed. This will also enable a further point of reflection in relation to the development of CST.

On 10 December 2013, the UK's Financial Conduct Authority (FCA—the successor organisation to the Financial Services Authority [(FSA]) fined the Lloyds Banking Group plc £28,038,800 (reduced from £35,048,500 due to an agreement to settle at an early stage) "due to serious failings in the systems and controls governing the financial incentives that they gave to sales staff . . . [who]

[59]See dialogue between MacIntyre and Charles Taylor on the interpretation of the good: Charles Taylor, "Justice After Virtue," in *After MacIntyre*, 16–43; and MacIntyre, "A Partial Response," 283–304.

sold protection and investment products to customers on an advised basis."[60] This, however, was a mere drop in the ocean compared with the £6.325 billion that the Group had set aside as at the third quarter of 2013 as a provision for compensating customers who were mis-sold Payment Protection Insurance (PPI).[61] What had gone wrong?

Lloyds Banking Group plc consists of Lloyds TSB Bank plc (LTSB) and Bank of Scotland plc (BOS), the latter also including the former Halifax Building Society. As a result of the financial crisis in 2008, the UK Government holds a sizeable stake in the Group of around 33 percent. The firms within the Group are significant players in the provision of protection and investment products in the UK selling, during the "Relevant Period" related to the fine of 1 January 2010 to 31 March 2012, over 1,094,000 products to over 692,000 customers.[62] Although there were differences in the incentive schemes for sales staff (advisers) for the three parts of the Group, the deficiencies in these incentive schemes and the governance arrangements were similar. These schemes:

> included a number of higher risk features, such as variable salaries, bonus thresholds which involved disproportionate rewards for marginal sales, and an advanced payment option that could lead to bonus deficits if sales targets were not met. As a result, advisers who met sales targets qualified for substantial salary rises and bonus payments, while advisers who did not faced salary reductions. There was also a significant bias towards sales of protection products, which was a strategic area of focus for the Firms.[63]

Because of this, and the ability of advisers to assess their performance on a daily basis:

> There was a significant risk that, if not adequately controlled, advisers would sell products to customers that they did not need or want in an attempt to reach salary and bonus incentive thresholds.[64]

---

[60]Financial Conduct Authority (FCA), "Final Notice 2013," (FSA Reference Numbers: 119278, 191240, and 169628; London; 2013), accessed January 3, 2014, http://www.fca.org .uk/your-fca/documents/final-notices/2013/fsa-final-notice-2013-lloyds-tsb-bank-plc-lloyds-tsb -scotland-plc-and-bank-of-scotland-plc-together-lloyds-banking-group.

[61]FCA, "Final Notice," 30; Lloyds Banking Group, "Q3 2013 Interim Management Statement,"2013, accessed January 6, 2014, http://www.lloydsbankinggroup.com/investors/ financial_performance/company_results.asp. Since then, it has set aside a further £1.8 billion: see Sean Farrell, "Lloyds PPI Compensation Bill now Close to £10bn," *The Guardian*, Feb. 2, 2014, accessed Feb. 18, 2014, http://www.theguardian.com/business/2014/feb/03/lloyds-ppi -compensation-bill-10-billion-pounds.

[62]FCA, "Final Notice," 3.

[63]FCA, "Final Notice," 2.

[64]Ibid.

However, the FCA concluded that the systems and controls that were in place were inadequate and, moreover, that the "competency standards" which the firms used to "oversee adviser behaviour and mitigate the risk of unfair customer outcomes" were "flawed."[65] Thus, during the Relevant Period:

> 71% of LTSB advisers, 32% of Halifax advisers and 39% of BOS advisers received a monthly bonus on at least one occasion even though a high proportion of the sales reviewed had been found by the Firms to be unsuitable or potentially unsuitable.[66]

In addition to the formal monitoring systems, advisers were supervised by local sales managers. However, the bonuses of these sales managers were determined by the performance of the advisers in their teams. Hence, there was a direct conflict of interest leading to inadequate supervision.[67] This situation was exacerbated by the lack of management information, which might have enabled patterns in individual advisers' activities to be monitored.[68]

Finally, the governance systems which the firms had in place to oversee this area of activity suffered from "serious deficiencies":

> The root cause of these deficiencies was the collective failure of the Firms' senior management to identify sufficiently remuneration and incentives given to advisers as a key area of risk. This led to a failure to recognise that it was an area that required specific and robust oversight.[69]

All in all, this is a sorry tale, which is easily re-told in MacIntyrean terms. Before doing so, however, we need first to address the question as to whether the provision of financial services might be considered to be a practice in the MacIntyrean sense.[70] The argument against, stemming from the mediaeval understanding of the sterility of money,[71] would be that there are no goods internal to the practice, as banking, and the provision of financial services in general, is all about the achievement of external goods. The argument in favour would run along the lines that the wise investment of financial resources is of benefit to those who have the capital, giving them the opportunity not only to protect but also potentially to increase these external goods thereby enabling subsequent

---

[65]Ibid., 20.
[66]Ibid., 2.
[67]Ibid., 2, 23.
[68]Ibid., 2, 25.
[69]Ibid., 3, see also 23–6.
[70]See van de Ven, "Banking after the Crisis."
[71]See, for example, Odd Langholm, *The Aristotelian Analysis of Usury* (New York: Columbia University Press, 1984). Money was understood to be a concrete substance, such as coins, and for use in exchange. It was not in the nature of money to breed money.

engagement, for themselves or possibly for those who will inherit from them, in various practices which might lead to the achievement of a variety of internal goods. In addition, those who will then have access to the investments of others, for example by way of loans, will also have the opportunity to use these external goods to engage in other practices potentially gaining the internal goods thereby available. For example, one of the first co-operatives created by Don Arizmendiarrieta in Mondragon in the 1950s was a bank, which "was to become not just the financier of the co-operatives, but the major force in driving forward and shaping their development."[72] Clearly, questions relating to the purpose of investments and whether they would lead to an increase in the common good arise in any consideration of loan finance, but on the basis of this analysis there would appear to be a prima facie case for allowing the possibility of the provision of financial services as a practice.[73]

What, then, of the Lloyds Banking Group? Here it seems clear that the firms had lost sight of the purpose to which the practice of providing financial services might have been put,[74] had systematically subordinated internal to external goods, and so had prioritised the institution over the practice. The incentive schemes directed the advisers away from considering customers' needs, and the good for them, and towards their own pecuniary interests.

Each of the five pre-requisites for organisational virtue were therefore either deliberately ignored or put at risk. The need to ensure that the organisation had a good purpose related to its contribution to the common good of customers and the community more generally was effectively ignored or replaced by erroneous considerations of the achievement of market share, profitability and so forth—the common conflation in business organisations of purpose with success and external goods.[75] This may have something to do with the mode of institutionalisation of the Group—as a stock-market listed firm, and despite the British Government's

---

[72]Race Matthews, *Jobs of our Own: Building a Stake-Holder Society: Alternatives to the Market and the State* (Annandale: Pluto Press Australia, 1999).

[73]The case of a friend of one of the authors who faced the choice of he and his family leaving their tenanted farm or purchasing it when the landlord decided to sell up, may be instructive. The farmer approached a number of banks, each of which turned him down based on the business plan he submitted. Finally, one bank manager took the trouble to visit him, to talk about his plans and to walk around the farm with him. This bank manager, perhaps in the old style of banking, knew that he was investing in the farmer, not the numbers on the spreadsheet; he provided the loan and the farm is, more than five years later, still solvent.

[74]The closest that Lloyds comes to this currently is to state: "Our business is focused on retail and commercial financial services . . . it is our role to help businesses and individuals thrive, while making a positive contribution to the communities in which we operate." Lloyds Banking Group, "About Us," *Lloyds Banking Group*, accessed January 10, 2014, http://www.lloydsbankinggroup .com/about_us.asp.

[75]Moore, "Virtue in Business," 377.

current stockholding, the Group would inevitably have faced pressure from the financial markets to maximise returns. Clearly, however, there was a lack of attention to the core practice of providing financial services, one prime consideration being the benefit that customers or clients receive from the products or services provided.[76]

The balance between internal and external goods was clearly under threat, to the extent that the firms may have risked their own survival in the long term (it will be clear from the above that without nurturing the core practice, an organisation may, in effect, "kill itself from the inside").[77] The FCA report does not comment specifically on individual agents within the firms, though it seems, in effect, to place the blame with the senior management rather than with the advisers themselves. However, it would appear to be uncontroversial to suggest that the advisers, their direct managers, and the senior management of the firms all demonstrated a lack of virtue in both the design of the incentive and control systems, and in continuing to allow their operation even as evidence mounted of the effect on customers. The firms might claim that in a highly competitive market such practices were necessary for survival; however, part of the environment within which the firms operated was the regulation provided by the FCA and its predecessor, the FSA. The FCA report noted that:

> it has for many years been warning firms of the need to manage and control risks to customers arising from financial incentives given to sales staff, in particular in publications relating to the Authority's work on Treating Customers Fairly and payment protection insurance.[78]

Thus, while the business environment may not have been conducive to virtue, there were strong elements within it that should have alerted the firms to the fact that they were treading on dangerous ground.

The MacIntyrean framework, then, provides a means of organisational analysis and diagnosis of actual or potential problems within business organisations that have already or might subsequently lead to a deficit of organisational virtue and a failure to contribute to the common good.

Such diagnosis may be as far as CST would wish to go, since it serves the purpose of identifying at a broad level of analysis the kinds of issues that might need to be dealt with and provides a vocabulary for doing so. However, the body of work encompassing the application of MacIntyrean virtue ethics to business

---

[76]Ibid., 380.

[77]Geoff Moore, "On the Implications of the Practice-Institution Distinction: MacIntyre and the Application of Modern Virtue Ethics to Business," *Business Ethics Quarterly* 12, no. 1 (2002): 19–32, at 28.

[78]FCA, "Final Notice," at 3.

organisations has gone further to identify a more prescriptive approach.[79] It is to this that we now turn, leaving a consideration of whether CST would wish to similarly draw on this approach to the conclusions that follow.

VI.

Crowding-in Virtue to Business Organisations. One way of understanding the Lloyds case is from the perspective of the way in which virtue became "crowded-out" of the organisation and, by contrast, to identify ways in which virtue might be "crowded-in" both to Lloyds and to business organisations in general. This takes us into the general area of governance. Governance, of course, is a means of control, and it is often thought that endeavouring to control behaviour will crowd out virtue. If extrinsic incentives are offered (for example, when children were told they could retain some of the money they collected as charitable donations, the collection went down as a result),[80] individuals "no longer consider the question from the moral point of view, but rather examine it from the standpoint of their self-interest."[81]

However, organisations clearly need governance systems to operate, so the question that then arises is whether these systems can be designed in such a way that they crowd in, rather than crowd out, virtue. Space here precludes a detailed consideration of the theoretical and empirical studies (mostly from social dilemma games) that offer insights here.[82] But emerging from these a number of mechanisms have been identified,[83] and it will be informative to discuss these and others in relation to the pre-requisites for organisational virtue identified above.

First, and as discussed above both in general and in relation to Lloyds, there needs to be a consideration of the purpose of the organisation, and an attempt to define this in a way that leads to internal goods (both the excellence of the product or service and the perfection of the practitioners in the process) that contribute to the common good. That this will require discussion with relevant communities, or community representatives, has already been noted. However, this will also require discussion, not only at the highest levels in the organisation, but also throughout the organisation. Even if the purpose is largely formulated by the Board, it will need to be shared and thoroughly debated by all members

---

[79]Beadle and Moore, "MacIntyre: Neo-Aristotelianism and Organization Theory"; Geoff Moore, "The Virtue of Governance, the Governance of Virtue," *Business Ethics Quarterly* 22, no. 2 (2012): 293–318.

[80]Ernst Fehr and Armin Falk, "Psychological Foundations of Incentives," *European Economic Review* 46, nos. 4–5 (2002): 687–724, at 709–10.

[81]Joseph Heath, "The Uses and Abuses of Agency Theory," *Business Ethics Quarterly* 19, no. 4 (2009): 497–528.

[82]See Moore, "The Virtue of Governance," 307–9.

[83]Ibid, 309–11.

of the organisation in an attempt both to get "buy-in" and also to allow reflection and development over time. That this might require changes to the activities of the organisation should not be ruled out. Hence, this is not a one-off process, but a continual one, and one which all members of the organisation have to be assured derives from a serious commitment to define and live out an organisational purpose that is genuinely for the common good.

In relation to the institution's primary task of focusing on the practice at the core, various mechanisms can be identified which would help to crowd in virtue. First, it might be helpful for practitioners engaged in the core practice to think of themselves as engaged in a craft. While this is not necessarily an unproblematic concept, the key point is that, in its mediaeval conception, "craftsmen would always hold to the principles of their craft";[84] they would seek, in other words, to protect the practice against institutional corruption. To do so, they would need to establish a strong group identity, and this has also been identified as a means of crowding in virtue. Social dilemma games provide evidence of the benefits that accrue from enabling individuals to identify as part of a group, so enhancing co-operation.[85] Transparency is a further mechanism for encouraging this; internally, it reduces the "social distance"[86] between different groups of employees, which is then likely to help in enhancing group identity.

There are potential concerns here, however, if such identification is achieved by means of "in-group" versus "out-group" behaviour. In the Lloyds case, it may have been that the advisers were managed in such a way that, while forming an "in-group" themselves, they were seen to be potentially expendable, at least individually, creating an "out-group" as far as the organisation was concerned. This, again, may suggest that the institution and a concern for external goods, rather than the practice and a concern for internal goods, held precedence at Lloyds, and so provides a salutary lesson in ensuring the all members of an organisation feel part of the "in-group."

Further, to reinforce the sense of an organisation focused on the practice at its core, decision-making processes need to be designed in such a way as to enhance participation and self-governance by the organisation's membership.[87]

---

[84]Geoff Moore, "Humanizing Business: A Modern Virtue Ethics Approach," *Business Ethics Quarterly* 15, no. 2 (2005): 237–55, at 248 and see 247–52 for a broader discussion of craftsmanship.

[85]Margaret Blair and Lynn Stout, "Trust, Trustworthiness, and the Behavioural Foundations of Corporate Law," *University of Pennsylvania Law Review* 149, no. 6 (2001): 1735–810.

[86]Bruno Frey and Margit Osterloh, "Yes, Managers Should be Paid like Bureaucrats," *Journal of Management Inquiry* 14, no. 1 (2005): 96–111, at 105.

[87]Margit Osterloh and Bruno Frey, "Corporate Governance for Crooks? The Case for Corporate Virtue," in *Corporate Governance and Firm Organization: Microfoundations and Structural Forms*, ed. Anna Grandori (Oxford: Oxford University Press, 2004): 191–211, at 206–7.

Similarly, it has been suggested[88] that virtues need to be embodied in power-balanced structures that take account of the views of different constituencies within the organisation. With regard to the Lloyds case, the advisers seem to have found themselves on the end of a highly-geared salary and incentive system which they might have been unlikely to have agreed to had there been consultation about what the selling of financial products in the interests of customers genuinely involved. This also links to the need to design jobs in such a way that intrinsic motivation (the desire to do the job for its own sake), rather than extrinsic motivation (doing the job only for its material rewards), takes precedence. Again, job design at Lloyds clearly emphasised extrinsic motivation promoting both the lure of financial reward and the fear of financial failure.

A further mechanism for enhancing the priority of the core practice is particularly interesting in the context of the Lloyds case. It has been suggested that in order to crowd in virtue, employees need to be trusted to undertake their work rather than have onerous performance monitoring;[89] as Osterloh and Frey observe, "low levels of legal contract enforcement crowd in trustworthiness."[90] Clearly, this was far from the case in Lloyds. For employees to respond to and not take advantage of this, however, requires managers who are themselves trustworthy, for example who support employees through periods of illness or if redundancies are threatened.[91] One way of effecting this may be by an organisation going "out of its way to downplay its hierarchical structure";[92] another mechanism by which the priority of the practice might be enhanced.

We have paid considerable attention to the first two pre-requisites of organisational virtue, deliberately so given their importance and their implications for the three further pre-requisites. Ensuring a balance between the pursuit of internal and external goods may largely be achieved through the mechanisms already identified for ensuring the priority of the practice. However, one further mechanism relates to the issue of executive pay. There is a well-documented concern that those at the top of organisations that pay very high multiples (in the order of hundreds of times) of the pay of average workers, thereby lose the willingness of employees to co-operate.[93] In other words, if employees perceive that the senior management is there mainly to line their own nests, any sense

---

[88]Geoff Moore, "Corporate Character: Modern Virtue Ethics and The Virtuous Corporation," *Business Ethics Quarterly* 15, no. 4 (2005): 659–85, at 673–4.

[89]Ian Maitland, "Virtue or Control in the Governance of the Firm," presented at the annual meeting of the Society for Business Ethics, Anaheim CA, 2008.

[90]Osterloh and Frey, "Corporate Governance for Crooks?," 203.

[91]Dan Ariely, *Predictably Irrational: The Hidden Forces that Shape Our Decisions* (New York: Harper Collins, 2008), 80–4.

[92]Heath, "Agency Theory," 516.

[93]Frey and Osterloh, "Managers Should be Paid like Bureaucrats," 104.

that the organisation is pursuing a good purpose, or that the practice is being prioritised over the institution, will be difficult to maintain.

In the Lloyds case, the salary of the highest paid director in the year 2011–2012 (the end of the relevant period) was £3,379,000 of which the performance-related element was 44%.[94] Exact comparisons with the salaries of advisors are difficult precisely because of the performance-related element. However, the minimum salary for LTSB advisers during the Relevant Period was £18,189[95]—a ratio with the highest paid director of 1:186. While any critique of such a comparison is inevitably subjective, it may be reasonable to suggest that limiting executive pay well below this level might result in an increased legitimacy to manage employees,[96] and that the organisation and its senior managers would not then be open to the charge of being inappropriately focussed on external goods.

In relation to the need for virtuous agents at both the practice and institutional levels, the key mechanism is to ensure that employees with pro-social intrinsic preferences are selected[97] and nurtured. This recognises that this needs to be realised not only in recruitment and selection processes but also in the continuing development of individuals within the organisation, and relates to the internal good of the perfection of practitioners in the process of engaging in the organisational practices. It may have been that the incentive schemes that Lloyds offered attracted and then nurtured individuals with self-seeking rather than pro-social attributes, leading to a vicious cycle which it might have been difficult to break.

Finally, in relation to the pre-requisite of a conducive environment, we noted above that this was not entirely a "given" and that particularly those in senior positions in the organisation should see this as something they themselves could help create and influence. Clearly, employing and nurturing managers with pro-social interests would help here. In addition, external transparency—ensuring that key constituencies outside of the organisation are kept appropriately informed—is a mechanism for enhancing the legitimacy of the organisation and so encouraging a more conducive environment within which organisational virtue might flourish.

Perhaps unsurprisingly, there are links between many of these mechanisms; it would not be difficult to imagine a situation in which external transparency and a good purpose attracts pro-social individuals who are intrinsically motivated towards the work they do, work co-operatively and need little supervision.

---

[94]Lloyds Banking Group, "Annual Report and Accounts," 2012, , accessed January 6, 2014, http://www.lloydsbankinggroup.com/investors/financial_performance/company_results.asp, 107.

[95]FCA, "Final Notice," 8.

[96]Frey and Osterloh, "Managers Should be Paid like Bureaucrats," 105.

[97]Osterloh and Frey, "Corporate Governance for Crooks?," 204–5.

Obviously, external motivation is still important and organisations cannot assume that virtuous individuals will work for a pittance, nor that they would not be motivated by some appropriate level of performance-related pay. As with many of these mechanisms, it will be a matter of judgment in reaching a balanced position.

As already noted, in some cases, these mechanisms are consistent with the MacIntyrean framework which we described earlier. There should, as a result of implementing these, be a consistent focus on the core practice and the excellence of the product or service and, potentially at least, the moral development of the individual practitioners involved in it. Extrinsic motivation (pay, status and so forth at the individual level, profit at the organisational level) are not ignored, and external goods are accepted for what they are, but without getting the balance between internal and external goods out of kilter. The organisation thereby has the potential, through the provision of its internal goods, to contribute to the common good of the community. Together, these mechanisms might assist in making the implications of the diagnosis that a MacIntyrean analysis offers a reality in business organisations.

VII.

Conclusion. Having considered the lacuna within CST in relation to the "inside" of business organisations, we have offered a MacIntyrean framework of goods, virtues, practices, and institutions as a potential solution to this. In providing a summary of CST and then comparing and contrasting this with MacIntyre's approach, we have noted how CST may benefit in a number of specific areas; there would seem to be a good "fit," even if further work is required to explore and expand on this and, indeed, to bring the work of others into this conversation.

However, we have then gone further, first by providing a detailed case study in order to ground the MacIntyrean concepts, and then by discussing how governance systems may be designed which would enable virtue to be crowded in. We noted above that this may be further than CST would wish to go, since it begins to encroach on the area of policy prescription rather than (simply) seeking to make potentially abstract theological principles concrete. CST may be more comfortable with the "middle axiom"[98] approach to Christian social ethics, located between statements of general principle and prescriptive programmes of action.

---

[98]See, for example, Malcolm Brown, *Tensions in Christian Ethics: An Introduction.* (London: SPCK, 2010), 91–2.

Even if this were the case, however, MacIntyre provides resources for understanding the opportunities that work organisations provide for both the realization of common goods and for their frustration. It provides a warning for what people in business should guard against and how the virtues enable such resistance. We thus wish to suggest that MacIntyrean virtue ethics offers a distinctive contribution to CST and one which, if integrated within CST, would enable it to make an even more significant contribution to business ethics than has hitherto been the case.

Durham University
Durham, UK

Northumbria University
Newcastle, UK

Durham University
Durham, UK

Ends and Endings

Alasdair MacIntyre

Abstract. The question posed in this paper is: Is there an end to some type of activity which is the end of any rational agent? It approaches an answer by a critical examination of one view of human beings that excludes this possibility, that advanced by Harry Frankfurt. It is argued that once we have distinguished, as Frankfurt does not, that which we have good reason to care about from that which we do not have good reason to care about, we are able to identify a conception of a final end for human activity, one that we put to work when we consider the ways in which a life may have gone wrong and one that we find indispensable for our understanding of narrative.

I.

I begin with ends and will end with endings. Many types of thing have endings: lives, leases, eras, journeys, stories. It is with the endings of stories that I am concerned. So, although I begin from the arguments of a philosopher, I end with the tale of a novelist. About ends we need to note at once that the concept of an end has a range of very different applications and that, just because of the heterogeneous ways in which we ascribe ends, the concept itself may well seem problematic. Robert Sokolowski has distinguished three such ways,[1] among them the ascription of ends to nonhuman living beings, which have whatever ends they do because of the nature of the species to which they belong. A frog achieves its end when it has become perfectly what it had it in it to become by reason of being a frog of that particular species. It will have developed through stages towards that end, provided that, first, its habitat afforded it what it needed and, secondly, that it had not been the victim of parasites, disease, fungi, or predators. As with frogs, so also with—Sokolowski's examples—trees, spiders, zebras. (So also, I am disposed to remark, with plants.)

---

[1] Robert Sokolowski, "What is Natural Law? Human Purposes and Natural Ends," *The Thomist* 68, no. 4 (October 2004): 511.

©2014, *American Catholic Philosophical Quarterly*, Vol. 88, No. 4
doi: 10.5840/acpq201491528

We also ascribe ends to types of activity, to types of practice in which human agents engage, activities as different as those of physicians, furniture-makers, musicians. The end of the activities of a physician is to heal, that of a furniture-maker to make excellent furniture, that of a musician to perform excellently for an audience. Sokolowski's principal concern is to distinguish and contrast such ends with what may happen to be the purposes of this or that physician, furniture-maker, or musician on particular occasions, purposes that may be indefinitely various—to make money or acquire reputation, to please teachers or spouses, to pass time on a boring day, or indeed to achieve the ends of the practice in which they are engaged. What the purpose of any particular physician or furniture-maker or musician is is up to her or him. But the ends of each practice are what they are independently of the purposes of those individuals who happen to engage in it. It is of course true that no practice will be sustained whose practitioners do not by and large make the achievement of its ends a principal object of their purposes. But, as Sokolowski emphasizes, ends are one thing, purposes another.

The criteria in virtue of which we ascribe ends to trees, spiders, frogs, and zebras obviously differ from those in virtue of which we ascribe ends to the practices of physicians, furniture-makers, and musicians. Why then do we use the same expression? What makes this double use more than a pun? It is to the point that we treat both nonhuman animals and human practices as having determinate natures and that identify the end of either animal or practice, so as to make it intelligible that the activities characteristic of each species of animal or of each type of practitioner are what they are, and so as to distinguish that in living beings or in practitioners which is characteristic of movement towards their ends from that which is accident or aberration.

There is, that is to say, in both cases a story to be told about individuals, whether animals or practitioners, a story that has as its plot the actions and passions that lead to success or failure by that particular individual to achieve its, her, or his relevant end. What counts as the ending of such a story is determined therefore in part by the nature of that end. Note however that there are differences between the two cases in respect of the kind of story to be told. So far as nonhuman living beings are concerned, what purposes they have is something determined by their nature and in exercising those powers that enable them to be successful in the pursuit of just those purposes—to hunt for food, to escape from predators, to mate, to nurture their young—they move towards the achievement of their end. But for the human practitioner the relationship of her or his purposes to her or his end is quite other.

To achieve her or his end *qua* physician or furniture-maker or musician the practitioner has to find in the achievement of that end an overriding reason for having some purposes rather than others. Individuals who do not acknowledge such an overriding reason will always be apt to have purposes at odds with the end of the practice in which they are engaged. What is required by commitment to a practice is that the individual has the purposes that she or he has just because the end of that particular practice is what it is.

II.

So far I have merely catalogued resemblances and differences between two ways in which we ascribe ends to individuals, as identified by Sokolowski. What throws further light on those resemblances and differences is consideration of a third type of ascription that he identifies, where we ascribe ends to individual human beings *qua* human beings. It is at once clear that such ascriptions raise new questions. Consider one crucial difference between nonhuman animals and humans. The members of each species of nonhuman animal achieve their determinate end within some particular type of habitat to which they are well adapted. By contrast, human animals have during their long history transformed the habitats in which they originated, adapting their environments to their purposes, while extending and also transforming those purposes. I remarked earlier that the members of each species of nonhuman animals have the purposes that they have, because their end is what it is. But, since humans do not have a limited and given set of purposes, the question arises: why should we suppose that they have a determinate end?

The same question arises when we contrast what it is to ascribe an end to someone *qua* physician or furniture-maker or musician and what it is to ascribe an end to that same someone *qua* human being. There are types of activity necessary for success in and characteristic of engagement with each type of practice. But human beings engage in such a wide and changing range of types of activity, having a similarly wide and changing range of purposes, that it is once again difficult to see how there could be a single determinate end to which these multifarious purposes and activities could be ordered. What would have to be the case for there to be such an end?

There would have to be some one distinctive type of activity characteristic of human beings and of the members of no other species, such that the end of that activity is the end of human beings *qua* human beings. As with nonhuman animals, that doubtless complex activity would have to give expression to the powers that human beings have by virtue of their distinctive human nature, both bodily and other powers that they share with nonhuman animals and those language-using powers that are exclusively human. As with those engaged in particular practices, the end of their activity would have to provide human beings with an overriding reason for having some purposes rather than others. What kind of activity might this be? What kind of end could it have? The puzzling thing about these questions is that, if there is such an activity we must all of us somehow or other be engaged in it, and, if there is such an end, we must all of us somehow or other be succeeding or failing in directing ourselves towards it. So why are we thus puzzled and how should we proceed?

III.

Perhaps what we should first do is to consider some insightful contemporary account of the practical lives of human beings, one that excludes application for anything like the concepts of a final end and of a type of activity directed towards that end, as we have understood those notions so far, so that we can ask: What, if anything has that account left out? What in human life is absent from this portrayal of it? For just such an account I turn to the writings of Harry Frankfurt.

"In my view," Frankfurt has written, "it is only in virtue of what we actually care about that anything is important to us." To the question whether there may not be a basis for regarding some things as "genuinely important in themselves, regardless of anyone's beliefs or feelings or inclinations," he replies, "In my judgment, there is not. There can be no rationally warranted criteria for establishing anything as inherently important."[2] At once the concept of a final end, as I have characterized it, has been excluded. Frankfurt's own starting point is a discussion of our relationship to our desires. We differ from animals of other species in that we are able to stand back from our desires and other motives and reflect upon whether or not we desire to be motivated as we presently are. (Hence the importance of the distinction between first and second order desires, to which Frankfurt first drew our attention in "Freedom of the Will and the Concept of a Person.")[3] We identify with some of our desires and not with others and we are free agents insofar as we are motivated by desires with which we identify and by which we therefore desire to be motivated. What we care about are the objects of those of our settled desires with which we identify. "A person who cares about something is, as it were, invested in it. He identifies himself with what he cares about in the sense that he makes himself vulnerable to losses and susceptible to benefits, depending upon whether what he cares about is diminished or enhanced. Thus he concerns himself with what concerns it."[4] What we care about is in part up to us, but in part not. "There are some things that we cannot help

[2]Harry Frankfurt, *Taking Ourselves Seriously and Getting It Right* (Stanford, CA: Stanford University Press, 2006), 20, 22.

[3]Harry Frankfurt, "Freedom of the Will and the Concept of a Person," *Journal of Philosophy* 68, no. 1 (1971), reprinted in Frankfurt, *The Importance of What We Care About* (Cambridge: Cambridge University Press, 1988), 11–25.

[4]Frankfurt, *The Importance of What We Care About*, 83.

caring about," and "[a]mong the things that we cannot help caring about are the things that we love."[5] What we *should* care about depends on what we do care about, most importantly on what we love. So, Frankfurt concludes, "our final ends are provided and legitimated by love."[6] But of course what Frankfurt means by "final end" in this passage is quite other than what Sokolowski—or for that matter Aristotle or Aquinas—means.

Frankfurt takes a final end to be some affective commitment that provides a terminus for our practical reasoning, but cannot itself be rationally justified.[7] We cannot dispense with such affective commitments. A life without them "could not provide any full satisfaction because it would provide no sense of genuine achievement."[8] But in identifying and setting such final ends, reasoning plays no part, since "the lover does not depend for his loving upon reasons of any kind." Love "creates reasons,"[9] that is, it provides reasons for acting so as to serve the object of our love.

It is not that reason has no part to play in generating actions. Frankfurt is open to the possibility that someone, by discovering through rational scrutiny that the object of their love or other desire is not what they mistakenly took it to be, might no longer love or desire that object (see footnote on p. 105). And instrumental reasoning is of course indispensable. But, should we be tempted to assimilate Frankfurt's position to Hume's, we would be mistaken. For Frankfurt, unlike Hume, reason has a further and crucial part to play. Hume notoriously held that our preferences can be neither rational nor irrational, neither according with reason nor violating its canons, so that "'tis not contrary to reason to prefer the destruction of the whole world to the scratching of my finger."[10] This thesis Frankfurt rejects. For even though "this preference involves no purely logical mistake," we would have to say of someone who chose to destroy the world rather than endure minor discomfort that he "must be *crazy*." His choice is "*lunatic*" and "*inhuman*" (Frankfurt's italics) and Frankfurt ascribes to him an irrationality that is not a cognitive deficiency, but "a defect of the will."[11] In what does such volitional irrationality consist? It consists not in the agent's preferences differing from ours, but in their being "incommensurate with ours."[12] The boundaries of formal reason are transgressed, if we believe "of some self-contradictory state of

---

[5]Frankfurt, *Taking Ourselves Seriously*, 24.

[6]Ibid., 26.

[7]Harry Frankfurt, *The Reasons of Love* (Princeton, NJ: Princeton University Press, 2004), 47.

[8]Frankfurt, *Taking Ourselves Seriously*, 26.

[9]Ibid., 25.

[10]David Hume, *A Treatise of Human Nature*, ed. L. A. Selby-Bigge (Oxford: Oxford University Press, 1888) Book II, Part 3, Section 3, p. 416).

[11]Frankfurt, *Taking Ourselves Seriously*, 29–30.

[12]Ibid., 30.

affairs that it might really be possible."[13] The boundaries of volitional rationality are transgressed, if we do not find certain choices unthinkable. Rationality consists in acknowledging constraints. Whence do the constraints of volitional rationality derive?

They are not responses to an independent normative reality. "The standards of volitional reality and of practical reason are grounded only in ourselves . . . only in what we cannot help caring about and cannot help considering important."[14] The words "cannot help" are important. Our judgments about what the norms of practical reason require conform, or fail to conform, to "an objective normative reality, which is not up to us. . . . Its objectivity consists just in the fact that it is outside the scope of our voluntary control."[15] An example of such a norm is this: "the fact that an action would protect a person's life is universally acknowledged to be a reason for that person to perform the action,"[16] even though that person may have a better reason for doing something else. Why is this so? "Our desire to live, and our readiness to invoke this desire as generating reasons for performing actions that contribute to that end, are not themselves based on reasons. . . . They derive from and express the fact that, presumably as an outcome of natural selection, we love . . . living."[17] And so it is too with other reason-generating desires such as those that derive from our love of "being intact and healthy, being satisfied, and being in touch." Frankfurt concludes that these "fundamental necessities of the will" are not the outcome of social or cultural habit or individual preferences. "They are solidly entrenched in our nature from the start."[18]

The contrast with Sokolowski's account could not be starker. For, according to Frankfurt, when we have arrived at a well-grounded account of what we do care about, there is no further question to be raised about whether we *should* care about what we do care about, while according to Sokolowski this question can always be raised by asking whether what we care about does or does not conduce to the achievement of some end, perhaps our end *qua* physician or musician, perhaps our end *qua* human being. How then are we to decide between Frankfurt and Sokolowski?

My argument will proceed in two stages. In the first, I will identify a set of concepts that are missing from Frankfurt's account, concepts without which we will be unable to distinguish between that which we have good reason to care about and that which we have every reason not to care about, and between that which we have more reason to care about and that which we have less reason

---

[13]Ibid., 31.
[14]Ibid., 33.
[15]Ibid., 34.
[16]Ibid.
[17]Ibid., 37.
[18]Ibid., 38.

to care about. In the second, I shall argue that, insofar as we find application for the concept "having good reason to care about" and kindred concepts, we presuppose that the concept of an end, understood as Sokolowski understands it and as Frankfurt excludes it, has application.

IV.

Suppose that I do indeed care about something or other and that I, as I am at present, cannot help caring about it. It always makes sense and it often is prudent to ask whether what I thus care about is worth caring about and whether I should try to change myself so that I become able no longer to care about it. Note that this is a question that I can always ask about myself. Frankfurt would have no difficulty in allowing that I may ask about someone else whether what he cares about is worth caring about, and reply "No," just because, as in Hume's example, his preferences are too different from and at odds with my own. What Frankfurt's account has no place for is the possibility of my having good reasons, and my recognizing that I have good reasons, for caring about what I do not as yet care about and for no longer caring about what I now care about, and this quite independently of my as yet being motivated to transform my caring. We can and should agree with Frankfurt, and also with Hume, that nothing can be a reason for action that is not actually or potentially motivating. Yet a reason that motivates us *qua* reason does so only insofar as it provides us not only with a motive, but also with the conclusion of a—characteristically tacit—piece of practical reasoning, one which runs, "*This* is a good reason for me to do such and such in these particular circumstances *and* there is no better reason for me to do something else; therefore, *this* is the reason to be acted on." That is, to treat some reason as a good reason for action is to judge that reason to be a better reason for acting in this particular way here and now than any reasons that we may have for acting otherwise. So to what standard do we appeal in judging between competing reasons?

In judging one reason superior to another *qua* reason we are not judging that one motivating desire is stronger than another nor giving expression to the relative strength of our desires. How much I care about or love or want something never decides what I have most reason to be, do, or have. Were it to be otherwise, there could not be the range of problems that philosophers discuss under the headings "*akrasia*" or "weakness of will." I may be thought to have a reason for doing this rather than that, I may indeed on occasion have a reason for doing this rather than that, when by so doing I can satisfy some desire, avoid some discomfort, enjoy some pleasure, while by acting otherwise I will achieve nothing that is to the point. Yet to act so as to satisfy a desire or to avoid a discomfort or to enjoy a pleasure is not necessarily to act for any reason at all.

What makes it a *reason* for me to act that by so acting I can satisfy some desire is that I judge that the good to be achieved by acting here and now to satisfy that desire is superior to the good or goods to be achieved by acting otherwise. And so it is only when, by satisfying a desire or avoiding a discomfort or engaging in pleasure, I will achieve some good, that these can furnish me with a reason for action and not just a motive or stimulus. What then is a good?

To say of something that it is a good for frogs is to say that it is the kind of thing that, if frogs achieve it, characteristically they flourish. To say of something that it is best for this particular frog here and now is to say that it is what this frog needs most to achieve here and now, if it is to flourish. So it is too with humans: a good for human beings is the kind of thing that, if they achieve it, they characteristically flourish and, if something is best for this particular human being here and now, it is what this human being *qua* rational animal needs most to achieve here and now, if she or he is to flourish. To act on a good reason then is to be directed towards some good, that is, directly or indirectly towards some end: "'*good*,'" says Aquinas, "has the *ratio* of an end," by which he means at least this, that I cannot give an account of why something is said to be good without making reference to some end.[19] Of anything towards which we are directed by our desire for it or by the prospect of pleasure from it or by our caring about it we can ask whether we have good reason to be so directed, that is, whether the ends proposed to us by our desire or by the prospect of pleasure or by what we care about are ends that provide us with adequately good reasons for pursuing them. Ends provide the measure by which desires, carings, and passions are to be evaluated. Ends provide us with the premises for sound practical reasoning.

Learning how to distinguish which kinds of desires, carings, and passions conduce to the achievement of our ends from those that instead frustrate and diminish us, and learning how to redirect and transform our own wants, tastes, and cravings so that they are of the former and not of the latter kind, must then be central to any life in which there is the possibility of achieving something that could be understood as the completion and perfection of that life. And to have a conception of a completed and perfected life, that is, of a final end for human beings, is to have a conception of a good such that it provides a measure for all other goods, so that those other goods are recognized as goods just because and insofar as they contribute to a life which is completed as a whole by the achievement of that final good. Only such a good could provide us with an overriding reason for directing our activities in one way rather than another. But, as we noted earlier, there can only be a final good for human beings if there is some type of activity that is distinctively the activity of human beings, the

---

[19]Thomas Aquinas, *Summa Theologiae* I, q. 5, a. 2, ad 2.

end of which is their final end. What then might that activity be? And, once again, we should perhaps approach an answer by asking: What would lives be like from which that activity is notably absent?

V.

Consider three examples of lives that have gone wrong. *A* cares about stamp-collecting with the passion of an obsessive. He has neglected responsibilities and alienated friends, as his mind has become devoid of other interests. Even other stamp collectors are repelled by his monomania. *B*, by contrast, lacks anything remotely like an obsession. She suffered early disappointments and responded by refusing to hope for very much and by not caring about anything very much. She is content with small achievements and never attempts anything where she foresees any possibility of failure. Consequently, her powers have never developed as they might have and she has never achieved anything worthwhile. *C*, unlike both *A* and *B*, has developed great abilities and excels in a number of areas: as winner of prizes in his profession of medicine, as marathon-runner, as philanthropist. What drives him is an intense wish to do better than others, to run faster than anyone else, to give more money than anyone else. So he devotes himself only to activities in which he is certain that he is going to be able to outstrip others. And his life therefore is both one-sided, like *A*'s, and as devoid of genuine risk taking as *B*'s, albeit in different ways.

Here are three bad ways to live and we could have listed many more. What do they have in common? For all three their failure was to evaluate goods at their true worth relative to other goods; and the cause of that failure was to have allowed their desires, their expectations of pleasure or pain, what they cared about, to prevent them from recognizing and acting on those reasons for action that would have directed them towards what it was best for them to be, to do, or to have. What was it about them that caused this to happen? It was that none of them had progressed sufficiently in a project that we can describe variously as that of becoming motivated to act only for good reasons, or as that of being able to distinguish what is genuinely desirable from what may seem desirable but in fact is not, or as that of acquiring critical self-knowledge. These are, however, not three projects, but one. Someone moved only by good reasons for acting would in so doing be exercising the power of distinguishing what is desirable for them at particular times and places from what is not, something possible only for those no longer victims of the kind of self-deception that sustains the confusion of the desired with the desirable.

How do we come to engage in this project? We begin when as children we are motivated not only to make our own the reasons for doing this rather than that which adults have given us, but also to evaluate those reasons as better or worse and to act in accordance with our evaluations. The cost of not doing so is to remain not just a child, but childish. And although some children cling to their childishness for protection, every child also wants to move beyond childishness. So children express in their development a desire directed towards the identification and achievement of goods that furnish them with good reasons. The end to which they may subsequently find themselves directed by that desire is that of being someone who has to some degree identified and aims to achieve the good and the best that it is possible for someone to achieve *qua* human being. Whether or not they do so find themselves directed depends on how far their desires have been transformed into desires only for the genuinely desirable, a transformation that failed to occur in the imaginary lives of *A*, *B*, and *C*.

What makes those lives instructive is that they exhibit only in stunted and undeveloped form the salient characteristics of the project that I have just described: the salient characteristics, that is, of that type of activity which is specific to human beings as rational agents, the end of which is our end as human beings. But, someone will object, that surely is not a type of activity. Types of activities are as various as mountain climbing, chimney cleaning, coal mining, playing the cello, and trimming one's toenails. But the project of developing and exercising the power of being moved by good reasons to achieve the genuinely desirable is not one more such type of activity, something undertaken in the time left over from mountain climbing, chimney cleaning, coal mining, playing the cello, and trimming one's toenails. It is a project less or more successfully implemented in all those different types of activity, indeed in every type of activity. To which, the reply must be, "Indeed, that is among the distinguishing marks of this type of activity."

To what final end then is this type of activity directed? It can only be that end, that good, which is presupposed by our evaluation of and motivation by all other goods. It can only be that good which provides an overriding reason for acting so that we are directed towards its achievement, so making it the case that it is only because and insofar as other goods are means to it or parts of it that they are goods. It can only be that good which completes and perfects our flourishing by providing our desire with an object whose desirability is incomparable with any other. But is there such a final end? This is a theoretical question that I shall not pursue here. It has an answer only if each of us is able to ask and answer the questions "What is *my* final end?" and "What subordinate ends should I pursue here and now?" as practical questions, ones whose answers gives expression to an awareness of a directedness towards that end in our choices and actions. Such practical questions and answers will necessarily be framed in terms of the particularities of each agent's situation, in terms of the contingencies of her or his social and historical context, of her or his responses to the accidental and the unpredictable.

An accurate account of what it would be for one or more particular individuals to be more or less coherently directed towards their final end would, just because of its concern with particularities, have to be a narrative account, whether a true history of real individuals or a novelist's or dramatist's account of imaginary characters. This is why the brief stories that I told about *A*, *B*, and *C* are not to be regarded as mere illustrations of theoretical generalizations. These were fictional narratives of individual failures, narratives of the particularities of failure, of the failure of each of those individuals to be directed towards her or his final end. And such failures can only be understood in and through such narratives.

Theoretical generalizations and narratives complement one another, indeed each requires the other if it is to be fully intelligible. One interesting consequence is that it is not possible either to engage in the enquiries of moral philosophy or teach it as an academic subject except in part by making use of histories, novels, biographies, short stories, and plays. For it is only through such works that we can understand how the concepts of a final end and of subordinate ends have application. But there is even more than this to the relationship between the concept of an end and narrative form.

What the structure of a story is, what kind of story it is, depends upon the kind of ending that it has. And what kind of ending it has depends upon the relationship of one or more of the central characters to some end, generally and characteristically some important, but far from final, end. Yet if, as I have suggested, our relationship to our subordinate ends is always also a relationship to our final end, then even small successes or failures in respect of subordinate ends have a larger significance. So without the concept of an end, we would, it seems, lack the concept of a story. Yet things are a little more complicated than that.

VI.

In what I have to say next I am strongly indebted to the work of Francis Slade, who has argued that "the narrative arts presuppose the ontological priority of ends to purposes because without that priority there is nothing to be revealed about the adequacy or inadequacy of human purposes to the completeness of human life."[20] It is on Slade's view, as on Sokolowski's and mine, the ends of our activities that provide the measure of our purposes—and also of our desires, choices, and intentions—and therefore without reference to ends we would not be able to understand each of our lives as a whole or each of our particular projects either as completed and perfected or as in various ways and from various

[20]Francis Slade, "On the Ontological Priority of Ends and its Relevance to the Narrative Arts,'" in *Beauty, Art, and the Polis*, ed. Alice Ramos (Washington, DC: American Maritain Association/Catholic University of America Press, 2004), 58–69, at 67.

causes frustrated and imperfect. But that we have this kind of understanding and share it with others is presupposed both in our telling of stories and in our listening to and responding to them.

Slade's thesis must seem not just compelling, but unproblematic, when we consider the vast majority of stories from Homer through authors as various as Euripides, Ovid, Dante, Shakespeare, Sterne, Flaubert, and Henry James: stories in which the qualities of mind, heart, and character of the protagonists are revealed through struggles and conflicts to achieve some end that issue in success or failure and sometimes in the discovery that success and failure are quite other than they were originally taken to be. But with the twentieth century, new kinds of storyteller and new kinds of story emerge, some of them storytellers who take the concept of an end to be a metaphysical illusion and some of them stories of characters who inhabit imaginary worlds constructed so as to put that concept in question . Slade considers two contrasting examples: the screenplays of Quentin Tarantino and the novels and short stories of Kafka.

Tarantino's characters, so Slade points out, inhabit a fictional world in which ends, whether ultimate or subordinate, have been erased, so that there are only rival and conflicting desires and purposes directed towards achieving the satisfaction of those desires, among them the desires and purposes of some characters to give aesthetic form and grace to the exercise of their skills and to the violence of their encounters. The outcomes of those encounters are artfully imposed by Tarantino, so that we are presented with an aesthetically disturbing world which is not our world. Kafka by contrast shows us—in an even more aesthetically disturbing way—our world as we sometimes fear it to be, a world in which the possibility that we have ends and not just desires and desire-serving purposes, the possibility that there is a point and purpose to our lives, is never quite foreclosed, but in which we cannot but continue in a protracted state of suspicion that at most "There is a goal, but no way; what we call way is only wavering."[21] So there is characteristically no ending to Kafka's stories, but simply a breaking off, sometimes a work left unfinished, sometimes a work artfully incomplete at the moment of its ending. Once again, although in a very different way, author and characters are at one.

Both Tarantino and Kafka illustrate and confirm Slade's thesis that narrative art, as it has been traditionally understood , presupposes the ontological priority of ends to purposes, even if they do so by showing what the absence of ends amounts to; but they at least open our minds to the possibility that there is still a further step to be taken, one in which the exercise of narrative art finally succeeds in portraying a human world that is compellingly recognizable as the real

---

[21]Franz Kafka, *The Great Wall of China*, trans. W. Muir and E. Muir (London: Schocken Books, 1946), 145.

world and yet is wholly devoid of ends. This would have to be an exercise of art that communicated both a sense of reality lacking in Tarantino's fictions and an absence of hope more radical than Kafka's. Were there such a narrative, it might seem to offer a decisive counterexample to Slade's thesis and so also to mine.

What characteristics would characters in such a story have to possess? If my earlier argument in this paper is sound, they would be motivated by desires, by passions, by their caring for this or that, but they could not treat these as reason-affording, since, lacking application for the concept of an end, they would lack the resources to evaluate them as better or worse reasons. Each of them would be unable to ask concerning themselves whether what she or he cared about was worth caring about, although they might judge concerning others that what they cared about was not worth caring about. Of them, that is to say, something like Frankfurt's account would hold good. There would in such a story be no such thing as success or failure *qua* human being or movement towards such success or failure, although there might be the burden of caring, the loss of desire, the frustration of hope, the disappointment of expectation. Above all there could in such a narrative be no finality, for there would always be more to come, more of the same, except for, we might suppose, that accidental termination afforded by death.

It might seem that no novelist could find in such material a novel, that the great art that would be required to give narrative form to the thought that there is nothing more to human beings than this would be just too disproportionate to its subject-matter. But in fact there is such a novel, one of the great European novels of the twentieth century, *Cré na Cille*, by Máirtín Ó'Cadhain (1906–1970), published in 1949.[22] Not just its greatness but its existence have gone largely unrecognized, perhaps because it is written in Irish, a wonderfully impressive and expressive Irish whose translation presents unusual difficulties. (There is a splendid film with English subtitles made from it, which gives the title as *Graveyard Clay*.) It is a novel of many voices, the voices of the dead in a graveyard on Ireland's Western seaboard, speaking sometimes to each other, sometimes to themselves, expressing feelings and cares that they brought with them to the grave, enmities, resentments, anxieties, pleasure in the misfortunes of others, obsessions, pretensions, wishes to puncture the pretensions of others. Those now dead are forever, endlessly, what they were when alive.

The central character , Caitriona Phaidin, is not only angrily resentful that her son buried her in the fifteen shilling plot in the graveyard, rather than in the pound (twenty shillings) plot, but nurses a longstanding grievance against her still-living sister, while also filled with malice towards her son's mother-in-law, Nora Sheainin, another inhabitant of the graveyard. From time to time the

---

[22]Máirtín Ó'Cadhain, *Cré na Cille*, 2nd ed. (Dublin: Caoimhin O'Marcaigh Ltd., 2007).

newly dead and buried bring news of what has happened above ground among the living and to each of them Caitriona anxiously enquires whether her son has as yet arranged for the green basalt headstone on which her heart is set.

Like the dreadful Caitriona, the large cast of other characters are moved by what they care about, by what they cannot help caring about. Sometimes one of them will judge that what someone else cares about is not worth caring about and mock them or chide them. So Nora Sheainin complains bitterly that the school master is too preoccupied with the gossip that his widow had immediately after his death taken up with Bileachaian Posta (Bileachai, the mailman) when, as an educated man, he should be cultivating his mind. So Caitriona Phaidin in turn mocks Nora's pretentions to culture. But none of them are able to ask about themselves, "'Is what I care about worth caring about?'" The possibility of an appeal to something other than and beyond their own cares has been excluded. So in this respect at least they are what Frankfurt takes all of us to be. In Ó'Cadhain's imagined world there are no reason-affording ends of human activity as such and the only such activity left open to the dead, the activity of conversations and monologues, has become unending.

It is not that nothing happens. There is even an election with rival candidates from the one-pound plot, the fifteen-shilling plot, and the half-guinea (ten shillings and sixpence) plot, during which the half-guinea candidate gives a Marxist analysis of the class structure of the graveyard. (Ó'Cadhain here is parodying views close to his own.) But his, like all the rhetoric, is nothing more than self-serving self-expression, talk leading to nothing but more talk, so that on the novel's last page there are still voices competing with other voices, and no finality and no prospect of finality.

Ó'Cadhain succeeded brilliantly in showing us both what human life would be if it were deprived of ends, and how, if so deprived, it would be unending. But in so doing he also showed us that and how we, the living, are unlike the dead of *Cré na Cille*, how and that their world lacks crucial features of ours, how and that we are able to engage in rational self-questioning as they are not. More than this, *Cré na Cille* is a work of great linguistic art, not only giving expression to the purposes of Ó'Cadhain as artist, but vindicating those purposes just because it is a novel in which its author achieves the end of the novelist's art in exemplary fashion. The voices in the novel speak only through Ó'Cadhain's book, but he, in making those voices heard, speaks as they cannot speak, acts as they cannot act, achieving a finality in completing and perfecting the art of his novel which is wholly absent from his characters' afterlives. The author is what is left out of his book.

So Slade's thesis, and Sokolowski's distinctions and arguments, and my own arguments directed to justifying further Slade's and Sokolowski's conclusions, are confirmed rather than undermined by Ó'Cadhain's masterpiece. What I have tried to achieve is twofold: first, to establish that the underlying unity in our ascriptions of ends derives from a basic conception of an end as the end of some type of activity, as that which completes and perfects such activity, and that beings of different kinds have different ends because and insofar as each has a specific nature, which is expressed in its specific activity or range of activities; and secondly, to show that it is not just that without ends there are no endings, but also that concerning any individuals to whose activity an end is to be ascribed there is always a story to be told, a story that has an ending. So it is also true that there are no ends without corresponding endings.

University of Notre Dame
Notre Dame, Indiana

CONTENTS OF VOLUME 88 (2014)

Articles

©2014, *American Catholic Philosophical Quarterly*, Vol. 88, No. 4   pp. 823–826
doi: 10.5840/acpq201488433

Discussion: Lonergan and Hegel

Review Essay

Book Reviews

PHILOSOPHY THEOLOGY

MARQUETTE UNIVERSITY JOURNAL

This peer-reviewed biannual journal addresses all areas of interest to these two ancient disciplines and explores the common ground that joins them. One issue each year includes articles dedicated to critical contact with the thought and legacy of the theologian Karl Rahner. Rahner's creative appropriation of diverse theological and philosophical sources provided an innovative conceptual framework that established his reputation as one of the most influential systematic theologians in the Vatican II era. *Philosophy and Theology* is published for Marquette University by the Philosophy Documentation Center.

Individuals
Print $40
Online $40

Members of the Karl Rahner Society
Print subscription included with membership

Institutions
Print $40
Online $120
Print + online $144

Online access includes all issues

ISSN 0890-2461 (print)   ISSN 2153-828X (online)

Philosophy Documentation Center
P.O. Box 7147, Charlottesville VA 22906-7147
Tel: 1.800.444.2419 (US & Canada) or 434.220.3300

order@pdcnet.org

www.pdcnet.org/philtheol

Choose the Titles You Need!

PHILOSOPHY DOCUMENTATION CENTER'S E-COLLECTION contains essential journals, book series, and other publications in **applied ethics**, **philosophy**, **religious studies**, and related fields. The collection continues to expand and coverage of most titles is complete.

Online Content and Features:

- Over 130 titles
- FREE search & page preview
- Online First pre-publication
- Single document access
- Discovery via Google Scholar, EBSCO, ProQuest, OCLC
- DOIs, CrossMark identification
- OpenURL linking
- Metasearch of all PDC resources
- COUNTER-compliant statistics
- Preservation via Portico and CLOCKSS

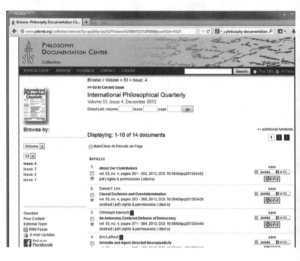

American Catholic Philosophical Quarterly
The American Journal of Semiotics
The American Philosophical Association
  Centennial Series
Ancient Philosophy
Augustinian Studies
Augustinianum
Business and Professional Ethics Journal
The Chesterton Review
Environmental Ethics
Environmental Philosophy
Epoché: Journal for the History of Philosophy
Faith and Philosophy
Forum Philosophicum
Graduate Faculty Philosophy Journal
Idealistic Studies
International Journal of Applied Philosophy
International Philosophical Quarterly
Journal for Peace and Justice Studies
Journal of Business Ethics Education
Journal of Philosophical Research

The Leibniz Review
The Owl of Minerva
Philosophia Africana
Philosophical Topics
Philosophy and Theology
Philosophy in the Contemporary World
Philosophy Today
Proceedings of the International
  Association for Business and Society
Process Studies
Radical Philosophy Review
Renascence: Essays on Values in Literature
Res Philosophica
The Ruffin Series in Business Ethics
Semiotics
Social Philosophy Today
Social Theory and Practice
Teaching Ethics
Teaching Philosophy
Techné: Research in Philosophy & Technology

and dozens of other titles . . .

Philosophy Documentation Center
P.O. Box 7147, Charlottesville, Virginia 22906-7147
Tel: 434.220.3300   order@pdcnet.org
www.pdcnet.org/ecollection